Classical Music Radio in the United Kingdom, 1945–1995

Tony Stoller

Classical Music Radio in the United Kingdom, 1945–1995

palgrave
macmillan

Tony Stoller
Bournemouth University
Poole, UK

ISBN 978-3-319-87852-2   ISBN 978-3-319-64710-4 (eBook)
https://doi.org/10.1007/978-3-319-64710-4

© The Editor(s) (if applicable) and The Author(s) 2018
Softcover reprint of the hardcover 1st edition 2017
This work is subject to copyright. All rights are solely and exclusively licensed by the Publisher, whether the whole or part of the material is concerned, specifically the rights of translation, reprinting, reuse of illustrations, recitation, broadcasting, reproduction on microfilms or in any other physical way, and transmission or information storage and retrieval, electronic adaptation, computer software, or by similar or dissimilar methodology now known or hereafter developed.
The use of general descriptive names, registered names, trademarks, service marks, etc. in this publication does not imply, even in the absence of a specific statement, that such names are exempt from the relevant protective laws and regulations and therefore free for general use.
The publisher, the authors and the editors are safe to assume that the advice and information in this book are believed to be true and accurate at the date of publication. Neither the publisher nor the authors or the editors give a warranty, express or implied, with respect to the material contained herein or for any errors or omissions that may have been made. The publisher remains neutral with regard to jurisdictional claims in published maps and institutional affiliations.

Cover credit: © VolodymyrV/Getty Images Plus

Printed on acid-free paper

This Palgrave Macmillan imprint is published by Springer Nature
The registered company is Springer International Publishing AG
The registered company address is: Gewerbestrasse 11, 6330 Cham, Switzerland

For Andy

Preface

I was born in May 1947. Along with the million baby-boomers born in the UK that year, I have been offered throughout my life access to the most audacious provision of high culture as entertainment that had ever been attempted, and accepted it as a normal state of affairs; as—if you like—my birthright as a citizen of post-war Britain. The transcendent significance of the fusion of radio broadcasting and classical music—confirmed in September 1946 by the establishment of the BBC's three radio services, each carrying classical music—was something I really only came to understand when I undertook my Ph.D. research more than 60 years later.

My career has brought me into contact repeatedly with that aspect of radio broadcasting. As a junior official at the Independent Broadcasting Authority (IBA) between 1974 and 1979, when it was responsible for establishing and then overseeing Independent Radio, I watched and listened as the fledgling commercial radio stations embraced their new almost-obligations to this genre of output. Then, from 1981 to 1985 as the Managing Director of Radio 210 in Reading, the smallest of that first tranche of Independent Local Radio (ILR) stations, I produced, presented and found the funds for classical music broadcasts and concerts of our own. In later years, as Chief Executive of the Radio Authority from 1995 until 2003, I was responsible for the regulation of Classic FM, the pre-eminent example of commercially funded, national classical music radio. Thus, it was probably inevitable—and certainly enjoyable—that I would come to complete though Bournemouth University a Ph.D. into classical music on UK radio, from which this book has been derived.

The first proper history book I ever read was E.H. Carr's *What is history?*, given to me in the Sixth Form. Ever since, I have been influenced by Carr's observation that everyone is born into a society, and is moulded by that society. He cites as an example Robinson Crusoe, who is not to be regarded as an abstract individual but an Englishman from York, who carries his Bible with him and praises his tribal God. For my part, I am an English grammar school boy, university-educated in the late Sixties, who has spent much his working career in the commercial, managerial, editorial and regulatory aspects of media, especially radio.

From that experience, I have come to espouse a series of opinions about this genre of radio—and its place within the ecology of UK broadcasting—which inform this history. I share the approach of those in radio with whom I worked for many years, that to deploy sound broadcasting both to entertain and to enlighten a large number of people who may not naturally seek such enlightenment is an activity to be approved of; that to restrict access only to those who meet some set of self-referential elite qualifications is to be disapproved of; and that the use of the limited public resource of the airwaves solely for commercial ends is deeply regrettable.

Can you write history of a period which represents your lived experience? The five decades in question are certainly 'my half-century', which introduces a particular subjective bias. Yet it would not be possible for anyone to write broadcasting history without being at least partly in the same circumstance: broadcasting—and perhaps radio in particular—has been all-pervasive and ever-present through the second half of the twentieth century.

The educative potential of radio appears in the pages of this history mainly in the form of specific programmes intended to improve the knowledge or awareness of listeners. However, there is another, arguably stronger influence at work in classical music radio. If awareness of classical music had to depend only upon attending concerts, or on the—alas, sadly diminishing—provision of music through the school system, it would have been a poor lookout. However, for millions of listeners, the availability of classical music simply to be listened to without let or hindrance, enabled them to absorb an outstanding musical education. These auto-didacts—such as my father, who left school well before the then official age of 14, but became a self-taught classical music buff, not least through his radio listening—give the lie to those who argue that a pre-existing level of musical education is essential for a 'proper' listening experience. Their prejudices appear frequently in the following pages; my own predisposition in their presence will be clear.

I believe that there is a natural affinity, even a symbiosis, between classical music and radio broadcasting. That is not to diminish the value of live performances heard in the concert hall or recital chamber (or even in the open air alongside Kenwood House, where much of my early musical education took place). However, radio is ideally suited to the dissemination, explanation and advancement of classical music. Theodor Adorno and Walter Benjamin would have disagreed: the former considered that a classical symphony in particular was somehow diminished in scale by being heard only through the distorting box of a radio set; the latter decried the mechanisation of culture. But neither of them had the opportunity to enjoy radio through modern transmission and reception technology. In any event, just as Robinson Crusoe's culture distorted his 'pure' perception of society, so our ears, our cultural predispositions, those we are with and those who are unwrapping sweets in the row behind us, all distort the experience of hearing live music. Radio provision of classical music is both personal and potentially sociable, and offers infinite range and scope. This history has been written in admiration and not a little awe at the potential of this medium, and at all that those working in it—and listening to it—have achieved.

Winchester, UK
November 2017

Tony Stoller

Acknowledgements

When I began my doctoral research, which underpins this history, I was warned that it would be a solitary task. On the contrary, I have been helped along the way at all stages. I owe particular thanks to my academic colleagues and supervisors at Bournemouth University, especially Sean Street, Hugh Chignell, Kristin Skoog and Kate Murphy, and to both Kathryn McDonald and Emma Wray as we walked parallel paths in our research into the endlessly fascinating medium of radio. Jean Seaton graciously allowed me early access to her draft and notes for her recent history of the BBC after 1974. Emily Russell and Carmel Kennedy and Aishwarya Balachandar at Palgrave Macmillan agreeably encouraged and guided the book to completion and publication. Trish Hayes and her fellow archivists at the BBC Written Archive Centre in Caversham have once again been endlessly helpful; how could broadcasting history ever be written without them?

I am grateful to all those who agreed to be interviewed for my research, and for their openness, generosity and encouragement: Kevin Appleby, Ralph Bernard, Leo Black, Tim Blackmore, Michael Checkland, Paul Gambaccini, Peter James, Nicholas Kenyon, Rodney Livingstone, David Owen Norris, Gillian Reynolds, Susannah Simons, Fiona Talkington, John Thompson and Roger Wright, together with others who prefer not to be named. I had talked previously on this topic with Michael Bukht and Gerard Mansell, before their deaths, and all too briefly with the late Ian McIntyre. The death of John Thompson—'JT'— as this book was being finished is a huge loss to all his colleagues and friends, and truly the end of an era.

Many of those I have worked with in radio and elsewhere over the years have offered advice and encouragement. Friends and colleagues have read earlier drafts of this book and I am grateful for their detailed and constructive criticism. The final result is so much better for their efforts, but the flaws which remain are my responsibility alone.

My wife Andy has been my most faithful reader of endless redrafts, and has put up with my preoccupation with this task with unfailing support and encouragement. In this, as in everything else she does and has done for me, even after 50 years I still cannot believe my luck.

Contents

1 Introduction: The Music we are accustomed to call Classical — 1

2 The Forties: A Pyramid of Taste — 31

3 The Fifties: Defending the Elite — 67

4 The Sixties: Simple and Conservative Tastes — 95

5 The Seventies: Breaking the Monopoly — 127

6 The Eighties: Keeping the Philistines at Bay — 155

7 The Nineties: Saga Louts and Dumbing Down — 187

8 Conclusions: Engaging on Equal Terms? — 227

Appendix A: Content Database — 247

Appendix B: Audience Database — 255

Appendix C: Timeline — 261

Appendix D: Senior Personnel in Classical Music
Radio 1945–1995   275

Appendix E: Glossary of Terms, Acronyms and Abbreviations   281

Bibliography   283

Index   293

List of Figures

Fig. 8.1   Highpoints for inclusive classical music radio   229
Fig. 8.2   Total hours of classical music radio in sample weeks 1945–1995   233

List of Tables

Table 2.1	Classical music as a percentage of total BBC radio output before 1945	37
Table 4.1	Audience comparison between Music Programme and Radio 3	122
Table 7.1	Radio 3 classical music content 1990–1995 in sample weeks	195
Table 7.2	Radio 3 classical music composers featured 1990–1995 in sample weeks	195
Table 7.3	Key attributes of Radio 3 and Classic FM	215
Table 7.4	Weekly audiences for Classic FM and Radio 3, 1991–1996	216
Table 7.5	Weekly audiences for Classic FM and Radio 3 from 1995 onwards	220
Table A.1	Total classical music programmes broadcast 1945–1995	249
Table A.2	Summary of each station's output 1945–1995	250
Table A.3	Composers selected as either *This Week's Composer* or *Composer of the Week* in each sample week 1945–1995	252
Table A.4	Most played composers in BBC output in each sample week 1945–1995	253
Table B.1	Maximum and median audiences ('000s) for individual classical music programmes in each sample week	256
Table B.2	Weekly reach for classical music radio stations 1977–1995	259

List of Tables

CHAPTER 1

Introduction: The Music we are accustomed to call Classical

Shape of this history—themes and variations—'the music we are accustomed to call classical': the emergence of a classical music canonic repertoire; terminology and taxonomy; a working definition of 'classical music radio'—sources and metrics: programme content database; audience database; written archives; interviews.

This book tells the history of classical music on UK radio between 1945 and 1995. It begins therefore before the launch of the Third Programme on Sunday 26 September 1946, and continues beyond the launch of Classic FM on Monday 7 September 1992. These events were not just bookends for the period; they are often regarded as totemic encapsulations of the two approaches of classical music radio—sometimes complementary, sometimes warring—of high art *vis-à-vis* popular culture. The BBC's classical music output was broadcast on a variety of channels, and was rarely as rarified as it is often regarded, or as some of its proponents wished it to appear. Commercial radio's provision of classical music was never as slight and meretricious as its critics wished to paint it. Nor was either sector immune from some of the supposed characteristics of the other. It has been the fusion of the two which has been so potent for cultural entertainment provision in its own right, and as a signifier for how culture and its consumption has developed in modern UK society.

History is built upon the foundations of previous scholarship. For this study, two five-volume works dominate their own general fields: Richard Taruskin's *Oxford History of Western Music*, from the sixteenth century to the present day; and Asa Briggs' *History of British Broadcasting* from the early Twenties to 1974 (effectively, for radio, just the BBC). Specific to this study is Alex Ross' survey of twentieth-century music, *The Rest Is Noise*; Humphrey Carpenter's history of the Third Programme and Radio 3, *The Envy of the World*; Nicholas Kenyon's study of the *BBC Symphony Orchestra* up to 1980; and my own history of Independent Radio, *Sounds of Your Life*. The full bibliography at the end of the book lists some of the many other relevant works.

The importance of this new study is that, unlike existing scholarship in this field, it reviews the whole range of radio output, not just the relatively contained provision on the Third Programme and later on Radio 3. Since most of the previous discourse has addressed classical music on UK radio as comprising merely the output of the Third Programme, and subsequently of Radio 3, this has tended to perpetuate the fallacy that this aspect of radio broadcasting was merely the preserve of the well-educated, higher class elite. On the contrary, for most of this period there was a richer, multi-channel offering of surprisingly broad appeal. In the years before 1970, the Third Programme was never the major provider of this type of radio; the Home Service, the Light Programme and then the Music Programme were much more significant in terms of quantity of output and audiences. In the last quarter of the twentieth century, the Radio 3 offering was accompanied by a demotic classical music provision on Independent Local Radio (ILR); and eventually radically augmented—even overtaken, in some respects—by the success of Classic FM from 1992 onwards.

Further, this history is informed by an original analysis of the actual output across 50 years—albeit on a sample basis—and of the audiences for this genre of radio. It cannot escape some institutional history, but that is not its focus. It seeks rather to broaden the previous narrow preconception of what this genre of broadcasting comprised, which itself reflected educational and class assumptions, by addressing the programmes and their listeners more than the institutional and political infrastructure. As such, the book represents the first comprehensive, longitudinal narrative of classical music broadcast on UK radio in the second half of the twentieth century, relating to the changing political, social and economic circumstances of those decades. It describes and analyses the wide range of services which offered this style of music, describing a far broader spectrum than previous discourse had addressed.

The wide relevance and appeal of this topic is demonstrated by quantitative audience data. Across the whole of the period between 1945 and 1995, there has existed a consistent potential audience for classical music radio of between 5 and 6 million adults, for whom the happy conjunction of an easy, cheap reception technology and an aspirational production resource meant that in varying degrees they were consistently able to indulge their taste for the greatest of all art forms without cost or restriction.

Popular music on the radio was one of the defining features of the second half of the twentieth century, whether splashing in the early shallows with Perry Como or the *Billy Cotton Band Show*, saluting the arrival of pop culture with skiffle and rock 'n' roll, encapsulating the cultural revolution of the Sixties and Seventies, stumbling into the punk counter-revolution of the Eighties or falling for the sleight of hand of Cool Britannia as the century ended. Other more substantial musical art forms found their welcome on and onto the radio more constrained, with jazz, folk, country and world music held outside the British broadcasting mainstream and steered apart from the cultural tides.

But *classical* music in these years flourished as never before, thanks almost entirely to its prominence on the UK radio wavelengths, and that is hugely informative too of the social and cultural history of the long post-war half-century.

Shape of This History

The period 1945 to 1995 was a telling historical one for Britain, with a nation forged in the wars of the Empire eventually coming to terms with a post-imperial existence; working through a complete change of economic status, from memories of being the world's manufacturer to becoming eventually merely its banker; and by way of a post-war renaissance, and then the cultural ferment of the Sixties, achieving a position of considerable cultural eminence. For UK broadcasting, this is when television became dominant, when radio reinvented itself in both the public and private sectors, and when old and new electronic media pointed towards the obsolescence of the printed page (It is an open question, and not yet one for the historian, whether broadcasting is now contemplating its own potential obsolescence, in the digital age of the twenty-first century). In music, successive technological innovation through the LP, audio cassette and CD, and latterly—too recent to be treated as 'history'—on to MP3, streaming and music file sharing, expanded geometrically the opportunities for listeners to hear in their own time and place what had once been available only by public or personal performance, or latterly the broadcasting of that performance.

For classical music on UK radio, those 50 years were characterised by a series of high points, when classical music services were broadcast across a number of different channels, offered highbrow and middlebrow content, provided links between elite and popular output, and were accessible to a broad range of potential listeners. Each of those then provoked a reaction from the self-appointed intellectual elite, concerned at the diminishing of what they regarded as 'high art' in the interest of mass appeal, and reflecting the class-based assumptions of British society during these years.

The history of post-war classical music radio in the UK falls remarkably neatly into individual calendar decades. This narrative will follow that pattern. This initial **Introduction** takes as its title Theodor Adorno's reference to 'the music we are accustomed to call classical',[1] and looks at the main themes which run through the 50 years, and the emergence of the concept of 'classical music' in the nineteenth century and the taxonomy. It continues by examining that the taxonomy and then establishing a definition for 'classical music', extending that to the 'classical music radio', and concludes by reviewing the sources and metrics for this study.

The first narrative chapter, Chap. 2, sketches a brief prologue of classical music radio in the Twenties and Thirties, before looking in more detail at classical music in wartime Britain and at the key twentieth century inflection points for a modern approach to this genre of radio. It then considers how matters developed after the war was over, examining classical music on the Home Service and the Light Programme in the immediate interwar years, the start of the Third Programme and then the combined output in the remaining years of the decade.

Chapter 3 looks at the efforts made by the elite to defend their view of classical music as high art. It considers the extent to which a 'new Britain' had emerged at this time, the pattern of classical music radio in the early years and rising conservatism and high-brow retrenchment. The reorganisation of classical music radio in the mid-Fifties, a subject of

---

[1] See below, p. 10.

intense debate among the intelligentsia if little among the general listening public, then leads into a report of the changing senior personnel taking responsibility for this output.

The Sixties are the subject of Chap. 4. Beginning with a review of the state of classical music radio in 1960, the narrative goes on to assess the impact of William Glock as Controller of Music at the BBC, the developing output in the first years of the Sixties and then the institution of the Music Programme, a daytime service of classical music radio which seems largely to have vanished from historical consciousness. The chapter continues with an examination of the later years of the decade, before considering the report, *Broadcasting in the Seventies*, which changed the whole BBC approach to the provision of radio, including a move to a genre-specific Radio 3 for classical music alone.

The Seventies are covered in Chap. 5, a decade that saw the end of the BBC's monopoly over radio which had existed since 1922. This examines the arrival of Radio 3 and the White Paper *An Alternative Service of Radio Broadcasting* which paved the way for the arrival of competition in the form of ILR. It describes how ILR progressed in its early years, and considers ILR's programming approach. It concludes by sketching the clouds which began to gather over BBC radio's attitude towards its in-house orchestras.

Chapter 6 continues the narrative of the BBC musicians' strike and its impact. It analyses BBC classical music output in the years up to 1984 and the apex of ILR classical music output over the same brief period, including consideration of audiences, secondary rental and programme sharing. Just as the musicians' strike was a pivotal time for BBC radio, so the so-called 'Heathrow Conference'—related in this chapter—was a seminal event for all independent radio. The effect of both can be seen in the output in the second half of the decade.

The historical narrative is completed in Chap. 7 which sets out the story of the near-accidental arrival of Classic FM, and the background to the recasting of Radio 3. The chapter compares in detail the respective output of Radio 3 and Classic FM in the years up to 1995, when this detailed history ends, before offering a coda containing some reflections on more recent times.

Chapter 8 draws conclusions from the 50-year history. It summarises the pattern of classical music radio provision between 1945 and 1995 in terms of programme content and audiences, and then how the interplay between elite and mass culture, mediated through the influence of class, is relevant to any overall social and political history of the UK during this period. The chapter offers observations on the nature of listening to classical music radio and the impact of approaches to its presentation, the relevance of biography and finally the changing nature of public service radio broadcasting.

The book includes a range of support material as **Appendices**: a content database; an audience database; a list of the key senior personnel involved in classical music radio; an outline chronology; and a glossary of acronyms and abbreviations, followed by a **Bibliography**.

THEMES AND VARIATIONS

The history of classical music radio through these 50 years was not a straightforward progression. It was characterised by a series of high-water marks—the late Forties; the late Sixties; the late Seventies and the early Eighties (but then only in particular localities); and the mid-Nineties. At those times, multi-channel provision of classical music on UK radio, in an accessible and approachable manner, attracted to the genre a wide range of listeners. Conversely, each of those provoked a reaction, an ebbing of the tide, in which that very accessibility was retreated from, and the concept of classical music as high culture rather than widely available broadcast content became dominant. That pattern of peaks and troughs dominates this narrative.

In this way and in others, the story of classical music radio is a powerful analogue of the nature and development of the UK in the second half of the twentieth century. It has a different significance from the pop music radio revolution, being at once more subtle and less linear. While popular music was about the impact of an invasive and classless youth culture, the varied lines of development of classical music radio speak to the shifting nature of tradition and institutions in Britain—mediated by the influence of class—and how that culture was only periodically opened up to a broader audience. But it is not just an academic signifier; it is primarily a compelling new story, adding to the understanding of broadcasting history in the UK, and of post-war British society as a whole.

Running through the entire history, as an *idee fixe*, are continuing tensions between serving elite and mass audiences. The elite could be very rarefied; in some formulations it was defined as 'Fellows of Balliol and All Souls'.² As for mass audiences, it was by no means only the middlebrow and middle class, though it was frequently perceived that way. There is an element of self-referencing here too, by those involved at the time and by subsequent scholars. Although a study in the first year of the Third Programme showed that around one third of its listeners were working class, that was counter-intuitive for the programme producers and any positive response was roughly set aside.³

To validate the discourse about mass culture, there must be some quantitative understanding of what a 'mass audience' comprises, especially given that much of that debate elides 'mass' with 'popular' culture. Television was the obvious post-war 'mass' medium, with audiences for individual programmes routinely approaching or exceeding 10 million viewers. Between 1962 and 1972, *Coronation Street* on ITV achieved top ratings of between 8,300,000 and 9,710,000.ⁱ It was received wisdom within BBC senior management in 1969 that there was a constituency of 'serious music lovers' numbering '5 million people'.ⁱⁱ Arguably that would justify the 'mass' epithet, as it does for Classic FM reaching a weekly audience of 4.7 million adults in 1995.ⁱⁱⁱ ILR services probably attracted some 1 million listeners each week to their classical music programmes.

It is not necessary to have a quantitative cut-off for a 'mass' patronage, although a million or more is a handy rule of thumb. However, in writing about 'mass' or 'elite' audiences, key considerations for this history must take into account that any qualitative assertions must necessarily be suspect without some quantitative underpinning. Take two examples. The CD recording of Gorecki's *Symphony of Sorrows*, promoted by Classic FM in 1993, sold over 1 million copies.ⁱᵛ While a more tonal work than much contemporary composition, it is not obviously a mass-market offering. Yet it serves to illustrate how an 'escalator effect' between high and mass taste can operate, just as BBC Director General William Haley foresaw with the early years of the post-war settlement for radio, which included the Third Programme.⁴ Searching for that escalator, and noticing when it is not there, is one of the features of this history.

---

²See Chap. 2, p. 59.
³See Chap. 2, p. 53.
⁴See Chap. 7, p. 188.

By contrast, the capacity of the Royal Albert Hall for a Promenade concert is around 6,000.[v] The history of the Proms has—correctly—been a matter of significant interest for radio historians, and plays a prominent part in existing literature; but in the context of a general narrative and evaluative history of classical music radio, such a small patronage figure means that the Proms themselves—as distinct from broadcast relays of the concerts—are significant more as indicators of producer thinking than of mass listener response.

The bias of the producers, especially in the high-altitude thin air of the Third Programme, has at times drawn an echo in historical scholarship. It is remarkable how much of the—admittedly scanty—academic attention to classical music radio in this period regards the Third Programme/Radio 3 as the only show in town. As this history demonstrates, it was in truth only one part—and usually not the major part—of the total offering.

Running through the story also, as a 'ground bass' in musical terms, is the nature of class in British society. Its influence was all-pervading and at times pernicious. D.L. LeMahieu (1988: 144) has observed that:

> It was in its policy towards music that the BBC most self-consciously constructed a flattering image of bourgeois cultural traditions and social identity. Music occupied a large share of BBC programming and best exemplified the Corporation's sense of its own mission. Although programmers recognised their obligation to satisfy the diverse tastes of all segments of British society, the BBC defined 'music' in a way which marginalised and sometimes excluded matter which the majority, including many within the middle classes, considered acceptable forms of entertainment.

Pierre Bourdieu (1984: 10) avers a specific place for classical music in the discourse about class, culture and taste, arguing that 'nothing more clearly affirms one's "class", nothing more infallibly classifies, than tastes in music ... there is no more "classificatory" practice than concert-going or playing a "noble" instrument'. Yet he is writing in a European context about a Continental bourgeoisie, and this approach does not stand up entirely for classical music radio in the UK. Although the origins of the classical canonic repertoire lie unequivocally in the correctly named 'bourgeoisie' of nineteenth-century Europe, it is, as Arthur Marwick asserts, an unhelpful term when applied to twentieth-century Britain. Marwick (1991: 7) takes the view that the British middle class is the most variegated in composition, background, education and outlook, so that the term 'bourgeois' lacks relevant analytical meaning in a UK context.

It is probably more accurate to say with Ross McKibbin that 'there were three musical publics, though the relationship between them was always fluid. There was a very small public for "serious" music; a considerably larger one for "middlebrow" music; and a much larger one for "popular" music' (2000: 418). Such an approach resembles that of Bourdieu, but avoids an over-close correlation with class. The most convincing generalisation about the relevance of class remains Marwick's (1990: 48):

> The social effects of post-war Britain cannot be *explained* solely by reference to class. But they certainly cannot be fully *understood* without reference to class [original emphasis].

This history will follow—through the 50 years under consideration—the *idee fixe* of elitism and the ground base of class, along with other themes about the nature of listening, the effect of different approaches to presentation, the role of biography and the changing nature of public service radio, returning to them in the final chapter. Yet most of all, this is a story worth the telling. It has only ever before been approached in a partial way, looking at shorter time periods or considering only some of the services offered. Drawn together, it is the history of a continuing inter-relationship between culture and society in the UK during a time of intense change and reappraisal.

'The Music We Are Accustomed to Call Classical'

There is no commonly accepted definition of 'classical music' in scholarship, even though it is in common usage and is therefore widely if imprecisely understood. Percy Scholes' classic *Oxford Companion to Music* reflected the uncertainty by offering three usages for the term 'classical music':

> 1. The large class of music (roughly from the end of the sixteenth century to the end of the eighteenth century) in which a more or less consciously accepted formalistic scheme of design is evident, with an emphasis on elements of proportion and of beauty as such … The antithesis here is Romantic …

2. A label to distinguish what is obviously or more or less established and of permanent value from what is ephemeral … The antithesis here is Modern …
3. Among less educated people 'Classical' is used in antithesis to 'Popular' ('Do you like classical music?' 'No, I like something with a *tune* to it!'). (1955: 192–193)

The phrase 'less educated' is revealing of the attitude of the music establishment to wider dissemination of classical music. Similarly, Pierre Bourdieu (1984: xx) chose to write about 'legitimate culture', in which he intends to include the canon of serious music for which we seek a working definition. More neutral—and therefore more helpful—is Theodor Adorno (1933/2002: xiii) who was content to use the term as shorthand: 'the music that we are accustomed to call classical'.[vi]

The Emergence of a Classical Music Canonic Repertoire

There is general agreement that a discrete body of largely but not exclusively orchestral music came into being early in the nineteenth century in Western Europe, distinct from 'concert music'. Scholes (1965: 193) makes clear that public concerts, 'organized as such and *open to the general public for a payment at the door*' [original emphasis], date back at least to John Bannister in London's Whitefriars in 1672. David Owen Norris dates the invention of 'public opera' to Venice in 1635.[vii] As Norman Lebrecht notes, 'J.S. Bach first took "serious" music out of the church and into the Leipzig coffee houses at the end of the eighteenth century, and in doing so began to build a commercial audience for concerts' (1997: 29). However, in these and similar instances, virtually all the repertoire for music performance had been contemporary.

By around 1830, that repertoire had expanded to include works composed in the past as well as contemporary material. Concerts newly patronised by the emerging middle classes in Western Europe now included works by 'revered, usually deceased composers, and music being thought to elevate taste' (Weber 2012: 57). As the nineteenth century progressed, compositions by members of what we now call the First Viennese School—Haydn, Mozart and Beethoven in particular, whose names recur so often together—began to be offered in series of concerts. William Weber (1984: 175) notes that 'essayists began calling this music "classical", conservatories made it into a curriculum and critics defined it as a highest musical authority'. By the 1870s, it became the norm for public concerts to include these works above all others, giving birth to modern classical music taste. There is even a sense among some commentators that performing these now-revered works was a way of stopping the growing degeneracy in musical culture.

The notion that the 'Viennese Classics' composed by Haydn, Mozart and Beethoven constituted a 'classical period' 'arose among German writers in the nineteenth century by analogy with the *Weimarer Klassik* created by Goethe, and, to a lesser extent, Schiller' (Heartz 1980: 450). Comparison with the literature is significant, as it shows music to be part of broader cultural trends in the classical period, just as it was to be in the romantic, modernist and post-modern eras. Owen Norris also argues that 'classical music is German music; and it's the sort of German music that was established during the classical period ... what we're talking about really is Haydn, Mozart and Beethoven'.[viii] Edward Said (2008: 278) is equally forthright, noting not only the dominance of the small number of German and Austrian composers over the classical canon but also the commonalities of form, melody, harmony and rhythmic consistency that was simply not repeated in contemporary painting or literature.

The concept of 'classical music' was centrally affected by the emergence of a distinction between 'serious' and 'light' music in the 1850s, reflecting the influence of a new Europe-wide bourgeoisie for whom 'the old framework of concert life could not maintain order'. As a consequence, 'musical life began to break apart into separate regions of repertory and taste' in which 'a dichotomy between music deemed more serious and that deemed less serious became established' (Weber 2008: 2). This division was heightened by what Weber (1984: 57) has called 'a dichotomy between commercial and idealistic notions of musical activity', and is consistently present in any consideration of how radio channels compile and present classical music output.

The rise of concert-going among the middle-classes increasingly included rituals which are commonplace today: when to applaud, what to wear, maintaining silence during performances. It is widely argued that music became 'like a religious service, and the religion it served was music' (Eisenberg 2005: 22). Such ritualisation extended also to private recitals, as the celebrity musician became sought after, and 'soirées and their etiquette revolved around the piano'. That still pertains, although it is more common now to refer to this as 'sacralisation'—which is not quite the same thing, but in effect makes an equivalent point. Small

(1977: 25) notes 'the small rituals of the concert hall and opera house—the purchase of tickets, the reserving of seats, the conventions of dress and behaviour for both performers and audience'.

This has been a factor in conditioning the production and consumption of classical music programming. The BBC had adopted this approach for its classical music broadcasts between the wars, instructing listeners in 1930 to:

> listen as carefully at home as you do in the theatre or concert hall. You can't get the best out of a programme if your mind is wandering, or if you are playing bridge or reading. Give it your full attention. Try turning out the lights so that your eye is not caught by familiar objects in the room. Your imagination will be twice as vivid.[ix]

David Goodman writes of the remarkable amount of classical music on pre-Second World War commercial radio in the USA. Recent work has generally acknowledged what he calls the '"sacralisation" of art music in the later nineteenth century', whereby concert audiences were brought 'to sit in reverential silence before great performers of great works'. However, as he also observes:

> the subsequent complexities of maintaining sacralization in the era of broadcasting and mechanical reproduction, when classical music was available to all for the first time in history, and hence when audiences became able to listen to canonical classical music in the mundane surroundings of their homes, have been surprisingly little explored. (2011: 127)

It is a feature of this history that the development of classical music radio between 1945 and 1995 included the de-sacralisation of classical music to a considerable degree, although that was not a smooth or uninterrupted process. On the one hand, this challenged and potentially diminished the position of classical music as high art; on the other, it significantly advanced the cause of the democratisation of this genre of radio output.

In Britain, a distinction between classical and popular music had begun to emerge alongside the efforts of Prince Albert from 1840, who was 'consciously on a mission to civilise the British', although his influence, along with that of Handel and Mendelssohn (completing the German trio), was probably 'merely the concrete manifestation of something that was happening anyway'.[x] In Britain also, as in Germany, the impact of municipal and amateur music-making was significant in the evolution and acceptance of a canonic repertoire (Pieper 2008). However, this process was by no means definitive. The boundaries between 'serious' and 'popular' music remained highly porous until the arrival of broadcasting. Before the BBC 'took over' the Henry Wood Proms in 1927, each concert had been in two parts: the first 'more serious, often focusing on the work of a featured composer', while the second comprised ballads and light material: '"platitunes" about June and little cottages'.[xi]

The existence of a canonic repertoire became increasingly important as classical music moved from the concert hall onto the broadcasting airwaves. The notion of a 'canon' is well known from the field of literature, where F.R. Leavis wrote about 'The Great Tradition' (1965), promoting the notion that only selected works and authors had the necessary 'total significance of a profoundly serious kind' (1965: 19). In some ways, the history of developing canons in serious literature and classical music are similar up to around the middle of the twentieth century. Queenie Leavis (1932: 158) noted the change in the consumption of literature in the nineteenth century, where 'because of new commercial conditions the beginnings of a split between popular and cultivated taste infection is apparent. [In *David Copperfield* and *Great Expectations*] ... the production of cheap editions ... drove a wedge between the educated and the general public', which is analogous with the split between serious and popular music over that period.

In the later twentieth century, however, there has been a divergence between literature and classical music. For written culture, the primacy of a canon of works has been substantially challenged and revised by among others Raymond Williams (1967), Jonathan Rose (2010) and John Carey (1992). For music, however, the existence and importance of such a canon has generally remained undisputed, and the concept and its actual deployment in performance and broadcasting remained throughout this period at the heart of a proper understanding of 'classical music'.

The most notable challenge to this view comes from Eric Hobsbawm (1983), who asserts that present interests construct a cohesive past to establish or legitimise present-day institutions or social relations, and that classical music is such an 'invented tradition'. In this interpretation, the music classical canon—in his view aristocratic and bourgeois music; academic, sacred and secular; music for public concerts, private soirées and dancing—achieves its coherence through its function as the most prestigious musical culture of the twentieth century.

That is surely an incorrect reading. Richard Taruskin's contrary claim is much more credible, that 'the literate tradition of western music is coherent at least insofar as it has a completed shape. Its beginnings are known and explicable, and its end is now foreseeable (and also explicable)' (2010: xi). It could be argued that even to write simply of a 'canon' is potentially misleading for this art form. It is more appropriate to talk about the 'canonic repertoire' of classical music, which distinguishes it from the literary canon where the element of performance is largely absent. The situation for music changed only with the arrival of the gramophone record, by which time the canonic repertoire was well established and formed the basis for the subsequent reification of classical music for individual listening.

Terminology and Taxonomy

When broadcasting arrived in the UK, the BBC did not use the term 'classical music'. Even as late as 1955, successive *BBC Handbook*s offer output statistics separated into 'serious music' and 'light music',[xii] but never 'classical music'. The text of that year's BBC Annual Report speaks of 'the Classics and Romantics' in the BBC's music output.[xiii] The Home Service is said to broadcast 'the great standard works of music'.[xiv] The Music Programme in 1964 was heralded as offering 'a continuous sequence of serious music',[xv] or 'of good music'.[xvi] The term 'classical music' does not even gain much currency with the arrival of the fully-fledged Radio 3 in 1970. *BBC Handbook*s still avoid the term, preferring 'serious music' or, as the decade progresses, no genre-specific term at all. In a rather archly stage-managed 'conversation' in the *Radio Times* in 1970, to launch the completed Radio 3, Peter Maxwell Davies, Edward Greenfield, Howard Newby and William Glock talk of 'serious', 'mainstream' and 'contemporary' music, but never once of 'classical' music.[xvii]

Media historians have tended to follow suit. Briggs usually but not invariably writes of 'serious music', for instance, when analysing the BBC's wartime music output (1970: 538). Doctor uses the term 'art music' when discussing 'the unique contributions of the early music programme builders' (1999: 14). It seems to be a particularly British approach to terminology, betraying cultural preconceptions which are absent, for example, across the Atlantic. Writing about the USA in the middle years of the twentieth century, Goodman (2011) can readily refer to 'classical music' throughout his study of American commercial radio.

The taxonomy of classical music's many sub-genres is complex. For output between 1939 and 1944, Briggs (1970: 35) lists the BBC's sub-genres within 'classical music' [*sic*] as:

> Opera (whole or part, not excerpts); Orchestral (with soloists); Chamber music; Instrumental recitals; Song recitals; Cantatas, oratorios, church music

whereas 'light music' comprised:

> Orchestral, band, small combination (with soloists); Operetta, comic opera, musical comedy; Ballad or chorus; Café, restaurant, cinema organs.

Briggs also identifies a separate main genre of 'Gramophone records', and a sub-genre within 'Light entertainment' of 'Music hall' and 'Revue'.

The BBC's administrative approach right up until the establishment of generic radio services from 1967 onwards, which also reveals the approach and perhaps prejudice of its programmers, was for the Music Department to handle all 'serious music', while the Gramophone Department was mostly responsible for what was initially described as 'dance music' but later 'popular music', with 'light music' involving also the Variety Department.[xviii]

Actually, all radio stations broadcasting classical music are reflexive in their definition of what falls within their acceptable playlists: that is to say, when the work is identified by the programme planner as classical music, and then accepted as such by the listeners, it enters the canonic repertoire. Classic FM came on air in 1992 with an audience-based approach, with consultant Robin Ray listing all the tracks likely to be played as either 'essential repertoire', 'standard repertoire', 'widely popular' or 'universally popular' with each item placed in only one category. Thus, Bruch's G Minor Violin Concerto was programmed by the station as 'widely popular', but not 'essential' or 'standard repertoire'; with the second movement 'universally popular'.[xix]

Similarly, although reticence over use of the term 'classical music' seems to have been peculiarly British, what to include or exclude within it should not be regarded as only a domestic UK issue. Lüthje's study of Klassik Radio in Germany (2008) and Goggin's of Lyric FM in Ireland (2006) both address similar issues. Lüthje (2008: 281) deploys a tripartite taxonomy for that station of 'Klassik, New Classics and Filmmusik'. Her examples for orchestral music classify John Williams' *Give Me Your Name* as Film; the adagio from Haydn's Symphony No. 26 as Klassik; and the *Elizabethan Serenade* by Ronald Binge as New Classic. All are part of Klassik Radio's standard repertoire, rather as they would be for Classic FM in the UK. However, Lyric FM in Ireland—avoiding a specific 'classic' label—ranges far more widely. Goggin shows how that station includes substantial amounts of folk music and jazz in addition to 'medieval, renaissance, baroque, classical, romantic, twentieth century and film music' (2006: 25).

There is no need to agonise over the margins of any such taxonomy. It has been common for the canonic repertoire to come in time to encompass works which might previously have been frowned upon, and also to embrace what at the time had been uncomfortably modern works into the mainstream. Owen Norris observes that serious composers can produce popular works which still fit centrally into the canon for definitional purposes:

> Poulenc writes one of his piano improvisations as a homage to Édith Piaf. Debussy is writing cakewalks, Ravel a piece called *Boléro*. These guys were across the whole board.[xx]

A reflexive approach can also be used for individual sub-genres. That involves fairly straightforwardly rejecting the notion of 'concert music' as a sub-genre of classical music, as it is consciously popular (but not 'pop') music. Equally, both jazz and world/cross-over music are by definition almost entirely outside the Western tradition of classical music. Four potential sub-genres of classical music pose greater challenges for a working taxonomy: film music, church music, light music and modern music.

A number of twentieth-century composers whose work falls firmly within the classical canon have composed music for films. American exiles such as Korngold—who won an Oscar for his score for *The Adventures of Robin Hood* in 1938—and Soviet era composers such as Shostakovich—whose music for the film *Meeting on the Elbe* won a Stalin State Prize in 1952 for the politically anguished composer—relied on it to make a living. Classical music is often used as film music: for example, the second movement of Mozart's Piano Concerto No. 21 in the film *Elvira Madigan*.

However, even where it is clearly orchestral, and meets other of the nominal criteria for classical music, film music as such is distinguished from classical music by being composed for a specific purpose which sidelines the altruistic creative impulse. It is in effect a pastiche of classical music, using the stylistic mannerisms of that genre. Owen Norris argues that:

> film music ... isn't classical music. [Many film composers are] trying to be classical musicians, but what they are actually doing is ... choosing the bit of classical music that makes the right noise for that, so that's a cynical process, and one that we regard as being artistically less worthy.[xxi]

On that basis, this book will treat film music as a separate genre, and not a sub-genre of classical music, except for compositions for films which have subsequently entered the classical canonic repertoire as orchestral suites or similar in their own right. An obvious example is Walton's music for Olivier's film of *Henry V*. Adopting a reflexive taxonomy allows such marginal works to enter the main sub-genre without negating the broader conclusion.

Church music is a further substantial challenge. Much classical music is either directly composed for liturgical or related purposes—Bach's motets, the oratorios so characteristic of English composers, and much more—or inspired by (mostly Christian) religiosity, yet can be central to the classical canon. The distinction here is the context in which it is being performed (and broadcast), rather than the purpose of the composition. Direct broadcasts of church services, notably the regular programme *Choral Evensong*, have been a staple part of the output of the Third Programme, the Home Service and Radio 3. This book will treat those broadcasts as liturgical rather than classical music output, unless specific instances require otherwise. Broadcasts of 'sacred' works in concert circumstance will be classified as choral or orchestral sub-genres within classical music.

The 'early music' movement had been stimulated by Third Programme broadcasts in the Fifties, and given a whole new lease of life by the work of David Munrow in the Seventies.[5] However, it has almost always consciously stood outside the main classical canonic repertoire, regarding itself as a separate genre rather than as part of the classical continuum. This book will respect that approach.

---

[5] See Chap. 5, p. 133.

Light music was seen by the BBC from the outset as wholly separate from serious music; indeed, as described above, that was the fundamental taxonomic distinction. At the outset, 'light' and 'popular' were effectively synonyms for the purposes of classification. The Performing Right Society separated classical music from all other compositions until 1987; for example, paying the composer of *Prolation*, Peter Maxwell Davies, double the rate of the writer of *Nicola*, Steve Race, on the grounds that classical music reflected extra work per minute of score (Towse 1997: 147–151).

So-called 'light classical' works are less problematic. There is no adequate reason why, for example, Gustav Holst's *Brook Green Suite* should be considered mainstream classical music while the contemporaneous *London Suite* by Eric Coates is 'merely' light classical. Such light classical works so readily enter the mainstream classical canonic repertoire that it seems self-defeating to exclude them. This book will therefore regard 'light classical' as a sub-genre of 'classical' music.

What is variously described as modern, contemporary and/or avant-garde music has been and remains in many ways the touchstone for the BBC's seriousness in classical music. These terms are not strictly interchangeable, but they may fairly be treated as such for this taxonomy. Haley, the begetter of the Third Programme, was unsympathetic to some of this new music:

> there was a natural tendency to find things which nobody had ever heard of and, quite frankly, once they'd been broadcast nobody wanted to hear again.[xxii]

Timing is crucial. A work initially categorised as stridently 'modern' or unapproachably 'avant-garde' when composed may easily enter the mainstream repertoire if it stands the test of (quite a short period of) time. It is obvious that a reflexive approach is required for this taxonomy also. For example, radio output such as works included in *Hear and Now* on the Third Programme occupy an evolving sub-genre of contemporary works not initially part of the mainstream canonic repertoire, but steadily entering into what is regarded reflexively as 'classical music'.

A Working Definition of 'Classical Music Radio'

'Classical music radio' can be defined along these same lines. The readiness of producers to accept an inclusive rather than an exclusive canonic repertoire varied during this period, but was always central in shifting degrees to the programmers' approach. From the start of broadcasting, they initiated a reflexive process whereby broadcasting adopted the concert canonic repertoire, and added to it or subtracted from it as the needs and opportunities of radio dictated (and concert programmes then adapted accordingly). Although the works broadcast on the Third Programme in, say, 1954 would differ a little from those offered by Radio 3 in 1974 and more markedly from the playlist of Classic FM in 1994, almost all would be generally accepted by consumers/listeners as being 'classical music radio'.

Might the nature of listening modify this approach? David Hendy (2010) writes about his perception of a 'hierarchy' of listening in the context of late-night radio. Kate Lacey (2013) treats listening as a 'cultural practice' which can change over time. For classical music, there are ever-present contradictory and value judgements about the respective worth of 'foreground' or 'background' listening, and related controversies around the rearrangement of radio services in 1957, and the introduction of the Music Programme in 1964 and Classic FM in 1992.

The reality is that any one person will deploy different modes of listening at different times. If somebody is listening attentively, and consciously excluding other activities in favour of this 'primary listening', then one might assert that they are listening in a 'highbrow' way, whether or not they would apply that label to themselves. If the programme is simply on in the background, then it is typical of the 'secondary listening' which is the default mode for the great majority of radio listening and listeners, and even for classical music is probably by far the most common. This practical approach is persuasive. It resembles Hendy's hierarchy of listening, referenced to individuals—or groups enjoying 'collective listening and intersubjective experience' (Lacey 2011: 19)—rather than to a *class* of listener.

There remains one other necessary element in any definition. The quality that other terminologies try to encapsulate—'art', 'serious', 'educated' music, etc.—is that this genre offers to involve more than just the emotions, thus providing Benjamin's (1936/2008) 'auratic' quality. It *may* be merely sensual, but at all times it offers the *prospect* of engaging the intellect with the music itself. That concept was at the heart of the BBC's initial experiment with the Third Programme and characterises debates which run on to this day: Why may it be wrong to play just one movement of a symphony? Why might it be necessary to introduce listeners to 'hard' as well as 'easy' music?

This is music radio's counterpart to Lacey's (2013) consideration of the evolving discourse over 'passive audiences' and 'active audiences', where the spoken word is deployed in broadcasting to open up political understanding and experience among the listening publics. In her view, there has been an 'ongoing association … of radio as the paradigmatic medium of the age of "mass" communications' (2013: 116). She asserts that 'listening is not just an acoustic, embodied experience, it is also a cognitive activity'. Her concept of 'listening out' implies by analogy that *some* classical music radio should have *some* intellectual content, and consequently any definition must provide for that possibility.

Add this element, and the working definition for 'classical music radio' used in this book becomes:

> a radio service which broadcasts the corpus of works which at any given time comprise the acknowledged classical, light classical and contemporary canonic orchestral, vocal and chamber repertoire, including works entering from other genres, sustained on a reflexive basis, offering the opportunity for intellectual engagement with the music as well as sensory enjoyment.

Or, to echo Adorno succinctly, we might say that classical music radio comprises *the radio programmes that we are accustomed to call classical music radio.*

Sources and Metrics

The data for this study, and broadly for all broadcasting media history, are both qualitative and quantitative, but they are invariably proxies of the actual output. The prime challenge for any historian of radio is that posed by Jean Seaton, that 'writing broadcasting history is ultimately about programmes … But how should one deal with the programmes?' (Seaton in Cannadine 2004: 141). For this history also, the programmes broadcast and the listeners who tuned into them are the key subjects. However, it is not practicable to listen to more than a tiny percentage of the output even where that survives, which it does only in an unrepresentative sample of 'stand-out' programmes (although those are fascinating in their own way, and as a subject for separate scholarship). Even if listening were a practicable option, that would only add to subjective qualitative data—available anyway in other forms—whereas this story needs also quantitative metrics.

Thus the radio historian needs to be a listener in a time machine, an eavesdropper of the past but also to carry with them the tools of an audio surveyor. There is a limit to what can be achieved by listening to such programmes as have survived. The BBC is steadily but selectively making available historic recordings such as those of *Desert Island Discs*, but they represent no more than the merest fraction of the output, and a highly selective one at that. The British Library Sound Archive collection is extensive, but it is largely concerned with special rather than routine output. For the private radio sector, there is very little audio material apart from some selected programming sharing tapes in the Felicity Wells Memorial Archive at Bournemouth University. And anyway, the radio time traveller cannot listen with the perception of the audience at the time the programme was broadcast.

The BBC's Audience Appreciation Indices (AIs), available at the BBC's Written Archives Centre (BBC WAC) up to 1979, only patchily address classical music programmes, and suffer from undue subjectivity and the self-selection of respondents. The most valuable proxies for actual listening with contemporary awareness are therefore the observations of those who were involved in the broadcasting process at the time as either producer or consumer, and those of critics and others in the secondary sources of published journalism. Josie Dolan (2003) has observed that recovering radio's 'voice' is not a task for a sound archive alone, but rather is achieved through a relationship between the researcher, their methodology, and various written and aural archives. That is convincing so far as it goes, but it misses the need for contemporary observation, which this book derives from both its databases and from secondary, mostly journalistic sources.

This history draws upon the memories of key players in the story: some from interviews conducted for this history; others drawn from the BBC's Oral History project (discussed below); some expressed in autobiography; and some revealed by existing scholarship. Yet almost all of that is qualitative too, and is qualified by the unreliability of matters recalled often long after the event, and adjusted by the at least subconscious wish to explain past events favourably, and to justify them. Much existing scholarship is content to leave it at that. This history seeks to contextualise the qualitative date with quantitative material where that is available.

Programme Content Database

This narrative account therefore deploys an original database of programme content on a sample week basis derived from *Radio Times* listings. The sample used is of the listing of a complete week of output each year, with the second week of May selected as the most appropriate. The rationale behind that approach, the way that the data have been compiled, and a longitudinal summary of the content database, are set out in Appendix A, which also includes summary aggregates of the findings.[6] Those data provide an invaluable snapshot of the daily output across each week of the 50 years covered by this narrative; how else can a history hope to encapsulate the half a million hours of classical music output across the period?

This is not to argue that quantitative data can replace qualitative assessment. They cannot and should not, but they are a complement and a sense-check, illustrative rather than definitive. Neither the hours of output nor the audience levels changed with any rapidity, so the sample analysis enables qualitative assertions to be tested against objective data. As the narrative chapters demonstrate, some received assertions in existing scholarship are shown to be valid, others less so. This narrative history has the unprecedented advantage of being able to base its own qualitative value judgements on quantitative material. Such data are referred to in the text as being derived from the sampled week in each year, and allow the reader to access a sense of the output as it would have been heard at that time; to become that auditory time-traveller.

There are obvious caveats to be entered: a sample week cannot be entirely representative of an entire year; programme highlights in the other 51 weeks of the year need to be identified separately, as they are in the narrative chapters; and the research must be careful not to assign undue significance to small fluctuations which are not in themselves statistically significant in a technical sense. Nevertheless, the consistency of longitudinal data summarised in Appendix A is remarkable, and that series shows very clearly the key points of inflection in the changing narrative.

The *Radio Times* is less useful for non-BBC radio broadcasts. It prints listings for Classic FM from 1992 onwards—and these are analysed in the database in the same way as the BBC national channels—but gives

---

[6] See Appendix A, pp. 249ff.

no indication of the works actually broadcast in sequence programmes,[7] which comprised the great majority of Classic FM's output. Fortunately, there still exist detailed analyses of Classic FM's content produced by BBC research.[8] This history is also informed by two catalogues prepared by Robin Ray for Classic FM, which go into exhaustive detail about the music tracks broadcast.[xxiii] In addition, there are two published catalogues of classical music played on Radio 3 and Radio 4 for 1974 (Grimley et al. 1977) and 1975 (Wiegold et al. 1976). Successive *BBC Handbooks* (1955–1973) provide some very limited output statistics.

For ILR station output between 1975 and 1990, the main source is descriptive: the programmes identified each year in the Independent Broadcasting Authority's *Television and Radio Handbook*, and in its *Annual Reports*. This means that ILR content data are less detailed and robust than for the BBC or even Classic FM, and that no quantitative check can be done. This gap is partly filled by interviews with those involved in making the programmes and contemporary descriptive written material, but any reporting on programme content in the independent sector is necessarily qualitative.

Audience Database

Alongside the programme content database, this history deploys two original databases of audience figures: a year-by-year analysis of maximum and median audiences[xxiv] for the sample weeks; and annual patronage/reach data showing the trends in audience support for each of the stations, reconciling conflicting data sources. These provide, for the first time, comprehensive longitudinal data on audience levels for classical music radio. Actual audience levels—like actual programme content data—should underpin qualitative observations wherever available. The processes for compiling the audience database and the audience figures, and a summary of the results, are set out in Appendix B.

Quantitative data about audience size involve two separate, sequential sets of figures. From 1946 until around 1977, they comprise chiefly audience averages for individual programmes gathered by the BBC's

---

[7] Programmes featuring as a series of works, or parts of works, without any conscious link between them and not within a concert setting.
[8] See Chap. 7, pp. 213ff.

own Audience Research Department and reported in what was called the Daily Listening Barometer. From 1977 onwards, and in particular from 1992, there are broader quantitative data sets, produced by independent research initially for the commercial radio companies, agencies and advertisers—the Joint Industry Committee for Radio Audience Research (JICRAR)—and then from 1992 jointly for the BBC and the private sector under the Radio Joint Audience Research (RAJAR) banner.

There is a further difficulty for the earlier period, in that BBC audience research analysis and special reports are very largely concerned with the Third Programme, which as this history will show was never the majority provider of classical music. Thus many of the reports start from an assumption that the classical music audience is somehow 'higher brow' than the radio audience as a whole, examine those who are attracted to the Third Programme with its highbrow target, and then demonstrate that classical music—as defined by what is provided by the Third Programme—is essentially a highbrow matter. Yet the size of audiences for classical music programmes on the Home Service and the Light Programme suggest that it is inconceivable these could be as predominantly upper class as those for the Third Programme, and that is borne out *inter alia* in a 1963 study about the other stations listened to by those who patronised the Third Programme.[xxv]

There are some quantitative data also about audience composition. These are much scantier, but are included where available in individual narrative chapters. Qualitative references to 'height of brow' or 'class' abound in the literature of this period; they have to be deployed in this book, but are used merely as subjective value-judgements. The terms 'high-brow', 'middle-brow, 'mass' and 'popular are used here in their casual, everyday, meanings. Class terms—'upper class', 'middle class', 'working class'—are also simply colloquial, except where specific demographic segmentation data are being quoted.

Written Archives

There are challenges for any document-based historical approach, to get the right balance between the written words that have survived and 'reality'. Although written material is essential in compiling this history, there is a peculiar paradox between the relative permanence of what is kept on paper, on the one hand, and the ephemera of radio programmes and the evanescence of listening, on the other.

The extensive paper and microfilm files held at the BBC Written Archives Centre at Caversham are the essential source for broadcasting history research in Britain. These contain contemporary reports, memoranda and related material covering most aspects of the BBC's classical music output, and are a major source for this book. Items from these archives are identified as 'BBC WAC' with the relevant file number and date. I am most appreciative that certain files dated 1980 and after, which I knew of from the published works of the BBC's 'official historians', were specially cleared for this history.

However, the BBC only routinely makes available to researchers material up to 1979. Bizarrely, therefore, while the UK Government is moving toward a 20-year rule for state papers under the Constitutional Reform and Governance Act 2010, the BBC currently operates something close to a 40-year rule, which is surely neither defensible nor sustainable. Even when some files are released, as they generously were for this history, it is not possible to know what other material exists which the researcher does not know to ask to see. This places particular emphasis on contemporary journalism and original interviews for this period.

As already discussed, the *Radio Times* has been a prime source of listings information, from which indicative quantitative data can be compiled. Some of the *Radio Times* has been digitised, and is available as part of the BBC Genome project.[xxvi]

The full paper archives of the regulator of independent television and radio, the Independent Broadcasting Authority (IBA) are held at Bournemouth University and are a valuable original source. The files of the Radio Authority, which was the radio-only regulator from 1991 until 2003, are still kept by the Office of Communications (Ofcom), since 2003 the regulator for the whole communications sector, but they are available through Freedom of Information requests and are used in this book. These contain formal reports and related correspondence about the classical music programmes broadcast by ILR stations, and about the system for sharing exceptional programmes across the network. In addition, this history has been informed by the private papers of key players, referenced as relevant in the text.

Interviews

This history draws also upon material from a range of original interviews, listed in the Acknowledgements section above and referenced as they occur in the text. They are valuable in understanding the genesis and production of output in the areas where those interviewees were directly responsible for it, and the subjects have been notably generous with their time and open recollection. Even so, what they say has to be approached with caution. In most instances, they are speaking about events many years in the past, sometimes from notes but often just from memory. That may well introduce inaccuracies, and their own part in events recalled so many years later will inevitably be coloured by the subjective remembrance of things past.

There is further such material from the BBC Oral History Research Project. This comprises a series of interviews with major BBC luminaries, conducted by other senior figures such as the distinguished former Managing Director of BBC Radio, Frank Gillard—once also a notable war correspondent—or by 'official' BBC historians such as Humphrey Carpenter. The transcripts of some of these interviews are available, and they are notable for a considerable level of frankness, only slightly moderated by the transcripts having been subsequently corrected by the interviewees. However, the BBC does not release any Oral History interviews with living people, not least to encourage such frankness. As a result, for example, the interview with John Manduell—the overseer of the Music Programme—has been withheld, although that is compensated for to a degree by his recent memoir (Manduell 2016).

Notes

i. Source: Joint Industry Committee for Television Advertising Research (JICTAR).
ii. Presentation slides for the Final Report of the Policy Study Group, 12 May 1969. BBC WAC R34/1583.
iii. RAJAR/RSL Q4 1995.
iv. Nicholas Williams. The symphony … latterly won widespread success, fuelled by a single recording which during the nineties sold more than a million copies. BBC Proms Programme Notes, 4 September 2013.
v. http://www.bbc.co.uk/proms/features/royal-albert-hall
vi. In *Gesammelte Schriften* (collected writings) 1933, vol. 17, pp. 303–306.
vii. Interview with David Owen Norris, 24 July 2012.
viii. Ibid.
ix. *BBC Handbook* 1930, p. 61.
x. Ibid.

xi. *The Times*, 20 August 1927, also quoted in Doctor and Wright, eds., 2007, p. 98n.
xii. *BBC Handbook* 1955, p. 163.
xiii. *BBC Handbook* 1955, p. 75.
xiv. *BBC Handbook* 1962, p. 58; 1963, p. 31.
xv. 1959 Area and Local Broadcasting Final Report. BBC WAC R34/1585/1.
xvi. Ibid.
xvii. *Radio Times*, 2 April 1970, pp. 11–14.
xviii. *BBC Handbook* 1955, p. 163 onwards.
xix. Ray, 31 January 1992 in Bernard, private papers.
xx. Interview with David Owen Norris, 24 July 2012.
xxi. Ibid.
xxii. Haley interviewed by Gillard p. 60, 6 July 1976. BBC WAC R143/60/1.
xxiii. From the private papers of Ralph Bernard.
xxiv. The median figure for the individual programme average audiences during the period under review.
xxv. The Home Service Listening of 'Third Programme Listeners'. Audience Research Report, January 1963. BBC WAC R9/9/27.
xxvi. http://genome.ch.bbc.co.uk/.

Bibliographic Sources

Adorno, T.W. and R. Leppert. 1933 [2002]. *Essays on music: Theodor W. Adorno*. London: University of California Press.
Benjamin, W. and J.A. Underwood. 1936 [2008]. *The work of art in the age of mechanical reproduction*. London: Penguin.
Bourdieu, P. 1984. *Distinction: A social critique of the judgement of taste*. London: Routledge.
Briggs, A. 1970. *The history of broadcasting in the United Kingdom. vol. 3, the war of words*. Oxford: Oxford University Press.
Cannadine, D. 2004. *History and the media*. Houndmills: Palgrave Macmillan.
Carey, J. 1992. *The intellectuals and the masses: Pride and prejudice among the literary intelligentsia 1880–1939*. London: Faber.
Doctor, J.R. 1999. *The BBC and ultra-modern music, 1922–1936: Shaping a nation's tastes*. Cambridge: Cambridge University Press.
Dolan, J. 2003. The voice that cannot be heard. *Radio Journal: International Studies in Broadcast & Audio Media* 1 (1): 63.
Eisenberg, E. 2005. *The recording angel: Music, records and culture from Aristotle to Zappa*. New Haven: Yale University Press.
Goggin, C. 2006. Radio 3 or classic FM. (BMus) thesis, University of Wales, Bangor.

Goodman, D. 2011. *Radio's civic ambition: American broadcasting and democracy in the 1930s.* Oxford: Oxford University Press.
Grimley, M., and M. Wiegold. 1977. *Catalogue of music broadcast on radio 3 and radio 4 in 1974.* London: British Broadcasting Corporation.
Heartz, D. 1980. Classical. In *The new Grove dictionary of music and musicians*, ed. S. Sadie. London: Macmillan.
Hendy, D. 2010. Listening in the dark. *Media History* 16 (2): 215–232.
Hobsbawm, E.J. and T.O. Ranger. 1983. *The invention of tradition, past and present publications.* Cambridge: Cambridge University Press.
Lacey, K. 2011. Listening Overlooked. *Javnost—The public?* 18 (4): 5–20.
Lacey, K. 2013. *Listening publics: The politics and experience of listening in the media age.* Cambridge: Polity.
Leavis, Q.D. 1932. *Fiction and the reading public.* London: Chatto & Windus.
Leavis, F.R. 1965. *The common pursuit.* London: Chatto & Windus.
Lebrecht, N. 1997. *When the music stops: Managers, maestros and the corporate murder of classical music.* London: Pocket.
LeMahieu, D.L. 1988. *A culture for democracy: Mass communication and the cultivated mind in Britain between the wars.* Oxford: Clarendon.
Lüthje, C. 2008. *Das Medium als symbolische Macht: Untersuchung zur soziokulturellen Wirkung von Medien am Beispiel von Klassik Radio.* Norderstedt: Books on Demand.
Manduell, J. 2016. *No Bartok before breakfast.* Todmorden: Arc Publications.
Marwick, A. 1990. *British society since 1945*, 2nd ed. London: Penguin.
Marwick, A. 1991. *Culture in Britain since 1945: Making contemporary Britain.* Oxford: Basil Blackwell.
McKibbin, R. 2000. *Classes and cultures: England, 1918–1951.* Oxford: Oxford University Press.
Pieper, A. 2008. *Music and the making of middle-class culture: A comparative history of nineteenth-century Leipzig and Birmingham.* Basingstoke: Palgrave Macmillan.
Rose, J. 2010. *The intellectual life of the British working classes.* New Haven: Yale University Press.
Said, E.W., 2008. *Music at the limits: three decades of essays and articles on music.* London: Bloomsbury
Scholes, P.A. (ed.). 1965. *The Oxford companion to music*, 9th ed. Oxford: Oxford University Press.
Small, C. 1977. *Music, society, education.* London: Calder.
Taruskin, R. 2010. *Music in the late 20th century.* Oxford: Oxford University Press.
Towse, R. 1997. *Cultural economics: The arts, the heritage, and the media industries.* Cheltenham: E. Elgar.

Weber, W., 1984. The contemporaneity of eighteenth-century musical taste. *The Musical Quarterly* 70 (2): 175–194.

Weber, W. 2008. *The great transformation of musical taste: Concert programming from Haydn to Brahms.* Cambridge: Cambridge University Press.

Weber, W. 2012. Political process, social structure and musical performance in Europe since 1450. In *Cambridge history of musical performance*, eds. C. Lawson and R. Stowell. Cambridge: Cambridge University Press.

Wiegold, M., C. Wilkinson, and P. Plaistow. 1976. *British Broadcasting Corporation catalogue of music broadcast on radio 3 in 1975.* London: British Broadcasting Corporation.

Williams, R. 1967. *Culture and society 1780–1950.* London: Chatto & Windus.

CHAPTER 2

The Forties: A Pyramid of Taste

Prologue, the Twenties and Thirties—classical music radio in wartime Britain—after the war was over—classical music on the Home Service and the Light Programme 1945–1946—start of the Third Programme—Classical music radio 1947–1949—assessing the Forties output.

This history is primarily concerned with classical music broadcasts on the radio during the years after the end of the Second World War, from 1945 onwards. Those did not come out of the void, and this chapter will begin with a brief sketch of the pre-war years as relevant to the later period. However, the relevance is limited. Although attitudes and indeed orchestras founded in the Twenties and Thirties carried over into the second half of the century, the break represented by the war years was perhaps as substantial as any in modern British history. More attention will therefore be given to wartime, its implications for classical music radio and its legacy. The chapter will then move on to examine the state of such radio output before the arrival of the Third Programme on 26 September 1946; and then recount the years of multi-channel and wide-appeal radio over the final years of the decade. Central to those later years was the notion of a 'pyramid of taste', an image coined by the BBC's wartime Director General, William Haley, to reflect an aspiration to move listeners from the entry level to the peak of cultural awareness, considered in detail later in the chapter.

Prologue: The Twenties and Thirties

Classical music had featured on BBC radio services from the very beginning, even before the earliest radio companies had come together in the new British Broadcasting Company in 1922. Opera diva Dame Nellie Melba famously broadcast a recital on Marconi's Chelmsford radio station on 15 June 1920 (Street 2005: 11), before performing it for King George V two weeks later.[i] In the very first edition of the *Radio Times*, a year after the formation of the Company, its Music Director, Lionel Stanton-Jefferies, wrote of the 'astounding progress' that the broadcasting of concerts had made in that short time, despite early teething problems:

> We had that enthusiastic soprano who 'blasted' – technically speaking, of course – on every note and shook both the valves and the engineers' patience to their utmost endurance by singing *ffffffff* throughout her performance, in order that her friends in Scotland might hear her more distinctly.[ii]

The first outside opera broadcast was a relay of the *Magic Flute* from Covent Garden in January 1923, and classical music comprised between a fifth and a quarter of all BBC radio programmes between 1927 and 1930 (Briggs 1965: 35). Interwoven with the total output, 'serious music'—as John Reith's BBC insistently described it—was a consistent feature. In these very early years, large-scale concerts, operas, smaller chamber ensembles and individual recitals all featured. Lighter music, typically dance band material, attracted listeners but seems to have occupied less of the attention of those creating a distinctive sound for the BBC (Briggs 1961: 277).

The BBC's approach towards 'serious music' was consistently high minded. Guided initially by Percy Pitt, its first Director of Music, and from 1930 by his successor, the conductor Adrian Boult, it offered what Pitt described as a 'panorama of music', covering the entire canon of classical music and not shying away from more avant-garde works (Briggs 1965: 170). This fitted well with the aspiration to lift the cultural level of audiences. However, all this belonged firmly to the pre-war world, its attitudes, technology and insularity. As this chapter will discuss substantively, there was a paradigmatic shift in British culture, attitudes and broadcasting once the Second World War had ended, already starting to become evident as the conflict progressed and the existential threat diminished.

A key manifestation of its initial aspirational approach was the BBC's creation and support of its own in-house orchestras. Pre-eminent among those was the BBC Symphony Orchestra (BBCSO) which gave its first performance in London's Queen's Hall on 22 October 1930, after almost a decade of wrangling with the classical music establishment (Kenyon 1981: 49). Its first Chief Conductor, Adrian Boult, was in charge of the BBCSO from 1931 until 1950, and was also the BBC's first Director of Music, serving from 1930 to 1942, when he was succeeded by composer Arthur Bliss. This emphasises the extent to which the BBC in the Twenties and Thirties gave primacy to concerts and live performances of classical music. This is a significant distinction with the post-war years, when commercial recordings steadily assumed ever-greater importance in classical music output as well as for popular music.

The British Broadcasting Company, formed in 1922, had quickly established a range of provincial orchestras (Briggs 1965: 306) in Manchester, Glasgow, Cardiff, Belfast, Newcastle, Bournemouth and Aberdeen, reflecting the nature of the semi-independent regional stations which comprised the Company, but they were reduced in the centralisation which followed the establishment of the Corporation at the start of 1927. The Northern and Midland Orchestras were formed in 1934, followed in 1935 by the BBC Scottish Orchestra and the BBC Welsh Orchestra.[1]

Conductor Henry Wood and music administrator Robert Newman had begun the Promenade Concerts—the Proms—in 1895, the same year that Marconi had carried out the first wireless telegraph transmissions (Langley in Doctor, ed. 2007: 32). In 1927, the Proms were failing, and the BBC stepped into save them from disappearing, with the first 'BBC Prom' broadcast across all the Corporation's stations on 13 August 1927 (Doctor in Doctor, ed. 2007: 94). The BBC's relationship with the Proms continues to the present, with a break in the early war years.

Generally, Britain in the Thirties had been a troubled place. Just as across the rest of Europe, the bleak twins of communism and fascism threatened the democratic state. Economic dislocation had joined with political uncertainty to produce a bifurcated culture, where the elite were

---

[1] The BBC orchestras are a research topic in their own right. At one time or another, there were 18 orchestras under the BBC banner and three choral ensembles.

diverted by the avant-garde, such as the British premiere on BBC radio of Schoenberg's *Gurrelieder* on 14 April 1927, while the contemporary mass culture of Hollywood and Tin Pan Alley was mostly ordinary and unambitious, certainly compared with the post-war years. That finds an echo in the music policy adopted by Reith's BBC. The Company and then the Corporation were increasingly willing to offer ultra-modern 'serious' works, defending this approach with spirit (Doctor 1999: 118). On the other hand, 'popular music was low in the musical hierarchy and bore the taint of commercialism while serious music existed for its own sake' (Baade 2012: 18).

Pre-war radio had been broadcast by the BBC on one National Service, supplemented by separate regional output, and from 1932 the Empire Service (renamed the Overseas Service in 1939). Classical music, largely concerts or recitals, was woven into the general programming. From its earliest years, the BBC was the dominant provider of UK classical music radio, although European state broadcasts could be heard in parts of the UK at times. In the mid-Thirties, the BBC had become obsessed by the challenge from English-language commercial radio stations, such as Radio Luxembourg and Radio Normandy, broadcasting popular programming into Britain from the near continent (Street 2006). These stations included a little accessible classical music. Schedules published in *Radio Pictorial* and *World Radio* list some light classical works from these commercial stations, and more formal concerts from other European state broadcasters. The *Radio Times* continued to list major music broadcasts by European state broadcasters right up until 1970, but by the Thirties certainly it was the BBC which defined the acknowledged canon by what it broadcast.

CLASSICAL MUSIC RADIO IN WARTIME BRITAIN

BBC radio regained its domestic monopoly of broadcasting when the Panzer divisions rolled across Belgium and Northern France in 1940, silencing Radio Luxembourg (for a while), Radio Normandy and the rest. For better or worse, the BBC was the dominant voice of Britain and in Britain throughout the Second World War. The pre-1940 National Service/Regional Services/Overseas Service structure was soon changed into a Home Service and something variously named the Forces Service or the General Forces Service. In all of those, classical music played an important part.

Classical music was very much a soundtrack to the Second World War: Hitler ordering that the overture of Wagner's *Die Meistersinger* should introduce each of the Nuremberg rallies; Stalin arranging the broadcasting of Shostakovich's Seventh Symphony across the front line of the siege of Leningrad, by flying in the orchestral parts to the beleaguered city; Messiaen composing modernism's seminal *Quartet for the End of Time*, while imprisoned in the Stalag Luft VIIIa prisoner of war camp; and Laurence Olivier commissioning Walton's *Agincourt* music for his wartime propagandist film of Shakespeare's *Henry V*.

In wartime Britain also, classical music radio acquired a particular resonance, as the BBC orchestras played concerts in cities around the nation (Kenyon 1981). These events, and especially the BBC's rescuing of the Proms from the ashes of the Queen's Hall in 1941 described below, were among many symbols of the British 'wartime spirit' expressed through classical music, as Arthur Marwick encapsulates:

> Wars quicken the pulse ... Myra Hess, the distinguished concert pianist, put on her favourite lunch-time recitals in the National Gallery in London; the Sadler's Wells Opera company, driven out of that same London by the bombing of its theatre, carried opera around the provinces. (Marwick 1991: 14)

For the BBC's classical music radio broadcasts—and much other programming—there were challenges and issues to confront, good and bad solutions adopted, and both creditable and discreditable results. As discussed below, such music raised issues about the playing of works by 'enemy composers'; the position of 'new' music; the significance of émigré refugees in British musical life; and the impact of de-nazification on British radio broadcasts after the war.

The significance of classical music on UK radio was enhanced by the role which such music played within a society at war, symbolised by Myra Hess and Sadler's Wells Opera. The wartime government created the Council for the Encouragement of Music and the Arts (CEMA) in 1940 to promote musical activity on the 'Home Front', while the Entertainments National Service Association (ENSA) was not just about comedians and variety, but brought a good range of concerts and live music to the troops at home and overseas. Many people speak about a 'cultural renaissance' during the later years of the war, which carried forward into peacetime. Among its fruits was the Arts Council, the successor to CEMA, and in broadcasting the introduction of the Third Programme in September 1946.

During the war, BBC radio included many more 'gramophone record' programmes (in the terminology of the times) than would have been permitted before the war. Nevertheless, the main source of programmes was the BBC orchestras, variously reorganising as wartime pressures permitted. The BBC Symphony Orchestra itself was evacuated first to Bristol, on the assumption that it would be safer there than in London. The bombing of the Bristol docks from June 1940 onwards put paid to that idea. Kenyon (1981: 166) has written about how 'as the raids increased, it became progressively more difficult to justify moving about at night. Concerts began to be recorded in the afternoons and broadcast by the engineers at night'. Its next home was Bedford, where the Orchestra (but not its administration) was to remain from June 1941 until the end of the war.

Despite all the upheavals, the Sunday of the sampled week in May 1942 included on the Home Service three live orchestral concerts, two live chamber music recitals and one on gramophone records, plus a talk by BBC critic Ralph Hill on 'the essence of Brahms'. The rest of this sample week indicates a similar pattern and volume, a level of output which was sustained almost until the end of the war, when scarcity of both resources and manpower shifted the emphasis more towards commercial recordings. From 1940 until the end of 1943, classical music accounted for around 15% of the Home Service output and nearly 4% of the Forces Programme, with Home Service output slipping to 10% only in the last year of the war (when the General Forces percentage actually rose). The audiences for classical music programmes reached levels which were rarely to be achieved in peacetime. For example, on just one Friday in May 1945, a lunchtime performance of Beethoven's Fifth Symphony was listened to by 1.25 million adults, while an evening concert of Gilbert and Sullivan operettas reached a remarkable 3.5 million (Table 2.1).

Malcolm Sargent, who was to take over as the chief conductor of the Henry Wood Promenade Concerts in 1947, at least partly made his popular reputation as provincial orchestral tours became a feature of wartime. Alison Garnham et al. (in Doctor, ed. 2007: 149) recounts that 'his "Blitz Tour" with the London Philharmonic Orchestra, bringing orchestral music to the music halls and variety theatres of major provincial cities, then suffering heavily under the bombings, had been a tremendously popular contribution to the war effort'.

Table 2.1 Classical music as a percentage of total BBC radio output before 1945

Classical music as % of total programme output	National programme	Regional programmes	Home service	Forces/overseas/general forces programme
1936	19.96	15.03		
1938	17.83	16.84		
1939	15.97			
1940			17.80	2.54
1941			13.51	1.28
1942			12.27	6.00
1943			15.88	4.75
1944			9.62	5.31

Source Analysis of *Radio Times* listing for sample weeks

The Proms themselves were dealt a shattering blow when their traditional home, the Queen's Hall in Langham Place, was destroyed by firebombing during the night of 10–11 May 1941. The photograph of Henry Wood standing amid the ruins of the hall became, in Jenny Doctor's words, 'a powerful symbol of defiant survival in Britain during the Blitz' (in Doctor, ed. 2007: 122). The Proms were relocated to the Royal Albert Hall. Once the BBC resumed running them in 1942 after a short gap in the hands of the Royal Philharmonic Society, these concerts—along with the recitals of Myra Hess—gave London some cultural continuity in a time of change and horror. The Proms had to be suspended late in June 1944, after a near miss with a V1 flying bomb, but resumed in time for the dying Henry Wood to conduct his final performance 'with a forceful and memorable broadcast of Beethoven's Seventh Symphony' on 28 July 1944 (Doctor 2007: 128).

Beethoven's music was everywhere, notably in the audio symbol of wartime resistance, the opening notes from his Fifth Symphony (the Morse Code rhythm for the letter V, for 'victory'). That happened despite debates about the playing of 'enemy music'. The BBC was reluctant to broadcast the works of living German, Italian or Finnish composers on the proffered grounds that their royalty payments would be destined for hostile nations (or could at least be collected once the war had ended).[iii] Robert Mackay (2000) has suggested that the BBC operated a much more jingoistic process of exclusion, especially of German composers: that in a phrase taken from the words of a Noel Coward popular song—itself banned by the BBC—it was 'being beastly to the Germans'.[iv] However, the dominating presence of Beethoven and Bach confounds any suggestion of a policy of 'racial' exclusion. The composers for the sampled week in 1942 were overwhelmingly the late masters of the nineteenth-century classical canon, with the March from Wagner's *Tannhauser* in the Forces Programme striking a German, martial note.

From a modern perspective, we might assume that Wagner's work would be at the centre of any such exclusion, given his authorship in 1850 of the article *Das Judenthum in der Musik*, one of the seminal texts of modern German anti-Semitism (Wagner and Evans 1850), and the fondness of the Nazi leadership for his music. In the event, many of his works were played regularly. The first concert in the BBC Symphony Orchestra's 1940 series 'boldly devoted its entire second part, which was broadcast, to extracts from Wagner's operas' (Kenyon 1981: 163). In response to a letter of complaint, the *Bristol Evening Post*'s music critic expressed the majority and the BBC view that 'by their unstinted applause, the audience gave the lie to the fantastic myth that the music of Wagner cannot or should not be appreciated by civilised people at war with Germany'.[v]

Much more difficulty surrounded the work of Richard Strauss, as a consequence of his willingness to accept musical posts in the Third Reich; and, for a while, broadcasts of Sibelius' *Finlandia*, because of its nationalistic tone relating to a country at war with Britain's 'ally', the Soviet Union. Bizarrely, Max Bruch, banned by the Nazis for his presumed Jewish ancestry, was put by the BBC on the list where 'the Corporation wishes to limit the performance of [their] works ... to a minimum far below their appearance in peace time, because the royalties payable for performances of his works would mean less available for "British, Allied and friendly composers"'.[vi] The BBC 'ban' was a dubious distinction Bruch shared with Verdi, Puccini and others; but he was surely alone in being excluded by both sides.

Analysis of the *Radio Times* listings largely exonerates the BBC from any claims that it was excluding musical works of value on a jingoistic basis. However, the British Government is much less easily defended over the internment of so-called 'enemy aliens', many of whom were actually refugees from those countries with which Britain was at war. Foremost among them was Hans Keller, a Viennese Jew who was to become one of the dominant forces in British music radio after the war, but he is simply the best known of dozens of musicians detained in camps on the Isle of Man and elsewhere. It might be said with a little exaggeration that during these years the Ramsay Internment Camp was the centre of European musical life: with Norbert Brainin, Martin Lovett, Peter Schidlof and Siegmund Nissel, who met in Ramsay and were to form the Amadeus Quartet, not least among its distinguished residents. There is more than a slight echo here of Oliver Messiaen's composition in Stalag Luft VIIIa.

Senior BBC figures—notably Boult and Bliss—were active in agitating for the internees' release, often but not always with some success. Keller himself was released from internment on 23 March 1941, having made friends with a number of notable musicians, such as Peter Gellhorn, who would play a major part in British musical life after the war as a distinguished conductor, composer, pianist and teacher (Kenyon 1981: 183). The role of BBC figures in challenging government in this respect was especially creditable given what is now acknowledged as the endemic anti-Semitism within the BBC generally at the time. Jean Seaton, who was for a time the Corporation's official historian, has written that 'the BBC displayed, both before and during the war, views and decisions that were quite simply anti-Semitic' (1987: 71), although there were clear exceptions as the efforts of Boult and Bliss on behalf of internees illustrate. Before the full reality of the death camps was known—or at least truly comprehended—there was an evident wish to stay out of what was thought to be simply a 'domestic issue' for Germany; even, on occasion, to avoid addressing any issues relating to the Jews in that country for fear of making their situation worse.

The real impact was felt on 'new' music (which represented, then, before and since, only a small proportion of radio broadcasts, albeit one which attracts perhaps disproportionate critical attention). Bliss had succeeded Boult as the BBC's Director of Music in 1942, a post the latter had held since 1930. Bliss took the view 'that in wartime, the BBC ought to give special support and encouragement to British Empire composers'.[vii] As a result, from 1942 until after the end of the war, almost all the new music heard broadcast by the BBC originated from countries allied to, or sympathetic with, the cause of Britain in the war (Kenyon 1981: 175). In the sampled week of 1942, there was no non-British 'new music' broadcast at all.

In Germany itself after the war, classical music became a tool of reconstruction and denazification, an effective if ironic riposte to the use which the Nazi regime made of the Austro/German music canon.

Under the influence of American musicologists, the annual *Ferienkurse* (summer school) at Darmstadt from 1946 became the central event of modernist music, featuring composers such as Schoenberg, Berg and Webern, and their successors including Milhaud, Varese and Honneger. This approach was to dominate musical scholarship—though not usually radio output—for much of the rest of the century.

After the War Was Over

The war marked the end of Britain as a major imperial power. After the existential struggle of the early wartime years, the nation, its broadcasters and its musicians began a rebuilding process which was to produce a post-war state substantially different from that before 1939. This was surely deliberate. Peter Hennessy entitled his study of the Forties *Never Again* because:

> the phrase captures the motivating impulse of the first half-dozen years after the war – never again would there be war; never again would the British people be housed in slums, living off a meagre diet thanks to low wages or no wages at all; never again would mass unemployment blight the lives of millions; never again would natural abilities remain dormant in the absence of educational stimulus. (1992: 2)

He observed that the UK emerged from Hitler, Stalin and Hirohito's wars impoverished, but infused by a consciousness of what had been its finest hour. 'We were, in short, morally magnificent but economically bankrupt' (1992: 95).

Christopher Logue accurately recalls Britain in the mid-Forties as 'sad ... a place of war-damaged, unpainted houses'.[viii] Alan Taylor (1965: 600), who was 33 and an established historian when war broke out, strikes a more resilient and aspirational note. He saw it as the time when 'the British people came of age'. Britain had been—along with Germany—the only nation to fight both the First and the Second World War from beginning to end, 'yet they remained a peaceful and civilised people, tolerant, patient and generous'. In place of some of the traditional values such as Imperial greatness came a new welfare state. 'The British Empire declined; the condition of the people improved. Few now sang "Land of Hope and Glory". Few even sang "England Arise". England had risen all the same'.

This dichotomy informs any assessment of the cultural response to those years, despite growing austerity which saw the nation far worse off in the years immediately after the war than it had been even in 1945. Paul Addison (1985: 114) notes that 'leisure has to compensate for many other things'.[ix] Central among those 'other things' was encouragement for the arts as a whole. Secretary of State John Anderson told the House of Commons on 12 June 1945 that the wartime Council for the Encouragement of Music and the Arts was to be succeeded by the Arts Council in 1946, because wartime experience had demonstrated that 'there will be a lasting need after the war for a body of this kind to encourage knowledge, understanding and practice of the arts in the broad sense of that term'.[x]

It was in the same spirit, and against this background of aspirational austerity, that the Third Programme was authorised by the Cabinet in January 1946 and began broadcasting on Sunday 26 September of the same year. This new service was to become 'almost notorious' as an icon of high culture (Kynaston 2008: 176). But it is important to note—and most academic and critical discourse does not—that the Third Programme was just one part of the post-war broadcasting settlement, and not necessarily the most important one even for classical music radio broadcasting. More substantially, the resumption of television services in June 1946, contemporaneous with the establishment of the BBC's new radio structure, soon began to have a significant impact on the resources and audiences available for sound broadcasting.[2]

There were three different international aspects to the way in which classical music developed from 1945. The major block was led by the United States, which 'unquestionably inherited musical leadership during this period from Europe' (Taruskin 2010: xix–xx). It was American sponsorship of the annual modernist *festschrift* at Darmstadt which set the tone for classical music composition in Europe and America. Through this, classical music in Western Europe experienced what amounted to a cultural insurrection, represented by modernist music.

The chief exception in mainland Europe was the Soviet Union, where serial and open-form music were developed in 'a direct correlation with contemporary political events' (Fox 2007: 5).

---

[2] Lacey (2013: 38) points out the paradox in using the term 'audience' indiscriminately for radio *listening* and for television *viewing*. For classical music, however, it is appropriate since television has rarely managed to find a satisfactory way of matching the sound with pictures which add to the auditory experience.

The post-war response in British classical music was the other dissenting voice. Wartime broadcasting of classical music in Britain had taken a notably isolationist approach, and that set the tone for the post-war radio pattern. The two works by British composers which rank with the compositions of Shostakovich as great signifiers of that war—Britten's *War Requiem* and Tippett's *A Child of Our Time*—are unmistakably British works, in a style and idiom which is different from that dominating the rest of the musical world. Both composers were to have a close relationship with the BBC in the succeeding decades.

Beginning in the middle years of the war, but of particular significance after its end, Britain enjoyed a remarkable resurgence of cultural activity. The prevailing ambition is reflected in the Dartington Arts Enquiries conducted between 1941 and 1947, which considered first the literary and performing arts, and then music in post-war England. Despite the harshness of the wartime years and afterwards, British cultural identity as a whole—in painting, sculpture, architecture as well as music—took a different route from the European continent, embracing modernism—even pastoralism—but mostly rejecting brutalism. The ambition of classical music radio in the UK in the late Forties owed almost everything to this cultural renaissance which began in the darkest years of the war.

Benjamin Britten and Peter Pears, who willingly returned to Britain in the spring of 1942 after having followed Auden to America in 1939, were not alone in feeling that Britain in wartime was undergoing such a renaissance (Kennedy 1991: 37, 43). That was especially marked for classical music, where both the Royal Liverpool Philharmonic (in 1942) and the Hallé (in 1943) became full-time orchestras during the war, with notable implications for the post-war classical music revival. The later war years, during which both radio and classical music had played significant parts in sustaining the Home Front, saw the confirmation in popular taste of the English pastoral composers. Championed by Bliss at the BBC from 1942, their works were to characterise British music after 1945. That modernist critics dubbed this the 'cow-pat' school of music, mattered not a whit to concert audiences or listeners.[3]

---

[3] Elizabeth Lutyens in a lecture at the Dartington Summer School in the Fifties, where she spoke also of 'folky-wolky melodies on the cor anglais' (*Oxford Dictionary of Music*, Rutherford-Johnson, T. and Kennedy, M, eds., 2013: 202).

For consumers of classical music, whether on gramophone record, in concerts or on the radio, there was a distinction between British culture as it was asserted by critics and academics, and what the British consumed. And what was true from the mid-Forties in this respect continued right through the rest of the century, and is key to understanding what classical music radio has to say about the relationship between elite and popular culture in the UK during these years. The Forties provided the canvas on which radio began to picture its post-war output. The arrival of the Third Programme in September 1946 in the form which it took owed much to the democratisation of taste in these brief years before the musical elite reasserted itself in the Fifties.

Yet while accepting that, in 1945, British classical music as a whole 'was basking in the warmth which the work of CEMA and ENSA and thousands of wartime concerts had kindled' (Kenyon 1981: 198), that does not mean the quality was all that good. The years of isolation from continental European music meant that 'musical chauvinism had by now reached a pitch of unreality in England' (Pirie 1979: 181). The younger progressive composers in Britain saw themselves as opposed and hamstrung by the older conservative musicians, including conductor and Hallé Orchestra boss John Barbirolli, whom the BBC had tried and failed to recruit as Chief Conductor for the BBCSO, as discussed further below. Only by the end of the decade was the standard of playing much improved, and the number of genuinely accomplished composers active in the country began to increase: notably including Alan Rawsthorne, Lennox Berkeley and Peter Maxwell Davies, and women composers such as Elisabeth Lutyens, Thea Musgrave, Priaulx Rainier and Elizabeth Maconchy.[4]

As far as UK radio broadcasting was concerned, three particular considerations affected classical music after the war. The first was a keen awareness, especially among BBC staff either returning from war service or through involvement with the BBC German Service, of the significance of classical music in the reconstruction of post-war Germany and Austria. It was deliberate Allied policy to use classical music, including in radio broadcasts, as part of the process of re-establishing civil society (Thacker 2007: 3). That fitted in with the sense among many

---

[4] The phrase 'women composers' is uncomfortable to modern reading, but it reflects the context of the UK classical music scene in these years.

Germans—as they struggled with the privations of the immediate post-war years—that among the things which could be rescued from the wreckage of the Third Reich was their great classical music tradition. One result of that was that these became 'golden years', as German orchestras and performers returned to their former prominence, at least as far as the programme of denazification would permit, and this in turn influenced the UK classical canon and the broadcast repertoire.

Second, the war changed classical music itself. As discussed above, in both the West (Europe and the USA) and the East (essentially the Soviet bloc), the end of the war and its aftermath released a second wave of modernism which was to last as a dominant feature in self-regarding musical circles until the fall of the Berlin Wall in 1989. That challenged radio programmers accordingly, if only to provoke a conscious negative reaction.

The third issue was the treatment of those composers who were considered to have collaborated in the enemy war effort, or whose music was integral to the Nazi project. In the immediate aftermath of the war, it was straightforward to exclude certain works, and music with militarist themes. The Nazi 'anthem' of the *Horst Wessel Lied* was banned outright.[xi] But what about Beethoven, Brucker, Wagner and above all Richard Strauss, who was—along with Hans Pritzner—the most frequently performed twentieth-century composer in the Third Reich?[xii] Wagner remained a staple part of the BBC's musical output, with the BBC going out of its way to broadcast his operas. Two complete 1946 performances of *Tristan und Isolde*, with Thomas Beecham conducting the BBCSO, and then of *Die Walkure* in December, were singled out for positive mention in the 1947 *BBC Handbook*.[xiii]

Otherwise, the BBC's post-war response was equivocal, especially about Richard Strauss. A list 'of those [alien] composers most in demand' whose works might now be broadcast was prepared in 1946, but with the warning to 'guard against a flooding with foreign works as a result of this clearance ... the actual choice of works also should be made more discreetly: for example, apart from its use in an appropriate feature programme, we should not yet perform Strauss' "Ein Heldenleben"'.[xiv]

Similarly, in 1947 a BBC producer was warned that:

> you will have to watch your step about the Strauss Festival, in view of the Board ruling that ex-Nazis can be employed ad hoc but not glorified by a festival or anything equivalent.[xv]

Yet a photograph of Richard Strauss adorns the *BBC Handbook* of 1949,[xvi] in resolution perhaps of the shattering discord of the image of the firebombed Queen's Hall in 1941.

The BBC had been planning with government the pattern of post-war sound broadcasting since 1943, proceeding on the basis of three national services: two on medium wave and long wave, respectively, as soon as the General Forces programme became otiose, and a further service on medium wave 'to be introduced at a later stage'.[xvii] Plans were well advanced by March 1945,[xviii] and once victory in Europe was confirmed the first part of the new pattern was implemented from Sunday 29 July 1945 on the basis of a Home Service and a Light Programme, with a 'programme C' to follow later; which was to be the Third Programme.[xix]

As discussed further below, BBC Director General Haley envisaged a 'pyramid of taste' for classical music radio: the mass audiences, listening to the Light Programme, would form the base of the pyramid; the middle block would comprise those giving more serious attention through the Home Service; the pinnacle would be the Third Programme. Crucially, listeners could rise from one level to the next (and presumably descend as well), in that way making possible the entire range of cultural appreciation to each potential listener, irrespective of their class or education.

Nevertheless, many of the BBC's instincts were at odds with the democratisation of cultural interest during the wartime cultural renaissance. It was as if many of the elite within the BBC (and elsewhere) wished to return to the pre-war class division of culture. The themes of 'height of brow', and the extent to which listeners were 'entitled' to engage with programme output outside their 'designated' class, run throughout this history, not least in the establishment of the aspirational pyramid of music radio in 1946 and its all-too-swift abandonment by the early Fifties.

From the outset, many at the BBC approached the new pattern of radio broadcasting according to an assumed hierarchy of class and taste:

> The new Home Service, it is hoped, will contain something for all tastes in radio and some of the best of everything in each field ... By its side will be the Light Programme, intended as the name suggests to provide the civilian listener with first-rate light entertainment. At a later date – on May 8 next year – it is planned to add to those a third programme so far unnamed, which will be frankly 'serious' in subject-matter and treatment. It can thus be seen that broadcast programme structure in this country will

soon be nicely balanced if the horrid but convenient terms can be permitted. *High-brows, low-brows, and middle-brows will each have a programme to themselves* [my emphasis] – thereby, one hopes, decreasing mutual jealousies and increasing the general stock of happiness. Personal taste of course cuts across frontiers. There will be nothing to prevent the lover of serious music listening, say, to a broadcast of a sporting event on the Light Programme, nor is the thriller 'fan' debarred from tuning into a talk on foreign affairs or astronomy on another wavelength.[xx]

It is significant that at this point the BBC had no intention of restricting classical music to any sort of cultural ghetto on the Third Programme. Quite the reverse. Not until the arrival of genre-defined national radio services at the end of the Sixties did the idea arise that such music should not be heard right across the BBC's output. BBC Senior Controller Basil Nicholls and composer/conductor Bliss, who was soon to become the BBC's Director of Music, had debated in 1941 what the latter called 'coaxing Caliban'—getting a maximum audience for classical music radio—in the light of Nicholls' view that 'it was the size of audience that was primarily important, not what in a later decade was to be called the "quality of listening"' (Kenyon 1981: 174–175).

CLASSICAL MUSIC ON THE HOME SERVICE AND THE LIGHT PROGRAMME 1945–1946

Food rationing became steadily tighter in the later years of the war and beyond, as shortages of credit exacerbated supply issues. By May 1945 each person was allowed only 2 oz of cheese and 2 oz of butter per week. It might be thought that classical music radio was similarly rationed. In the sample week in May 1945, fewer than 20 hours programming was listed, with only 39 composers featured. The dominant musical offering was light music, with occasional classical items sprinkled within dance band programmes. Yet popular appetite for classical music remained. In the 1945 sample week, the highest audience for a scheduled classical programme on the Home Service was nearly 2 million adults, and that on the General Forces Programme getting on for 1.5 million. On VE Day itself, Tuesday 8 May 1945, a half-hour of the BBCSO and Chorus was listened to by 3.3 million people across the two networks.

Analysis of the first week of peace in 1945 provides a valuable picture of the *status quo ante*. There were 13 hours of classical music broadcast on the Home Service, and 6 hours on the General Forces network. The median audience for such Home Service output was over 1 million adults, with the highest nearly 2 million; while the Forces Programme had a median audience of just over 500,000 and an audience high of 1.3 million.

Of the scheduled programmes on the Home Service, the most popular was the fortnightly *Music Magazine* on Sunday morning of the sample week, and there was a substantial evening audience for a Tchaikovsky *Serenade* on Monday evening of 1.5 million listeners. Daytime audiences of around 700,000 adults heard music very much centred on the conventional canonic repertoire, with hardly any current composers apart from a scattering of British music. Contemporary perception was that there was 'a constant demand for more programmes of good music', not least from servicemen overseas:

> We want music. Thank you for the records, they have been invaluable: but please send us more live music and musicians, and instruments and copies to that we can make our own music as well as enjoy more fully what is made for us by others.[xxi]

As discussed above, classical music was changing across the Western world. After the cataclysm of the atomic bombs dropped on Hiroshima and Nagasaki in August 1945, new compositions for a nuclear age were substantially different from those of the pre-war canon. Meanwhile, the American occupying forces in Germany, in the form of the Office of Military Government, United States (OMGUS), were helping to inaugurate in Darmstadt the principal show-place for the avant-garde from 1946 onwards. How would BBC radio respond to the new world? And how would it blend that with the very different nature of the British cultural renaissance, now firmly underway. For classical music that included the premiere of Britten's *Peter Grimes* at Sadler's Wells in June to mark the reopening of that theatre in London.

The imminent arrival of Programme C, now designated the 'Third Programme', was therefore not merely an internal BBC concern. Wittingly or not, it was part of a world-wide response to post-war realities and opportunities, albeit modified by British musical and cultural isolation which had arisen as a consequence of wartime conditions and decisions.

By May 1946, the Home Service and the Light Programme were firmly established. Director General Haley, writing at the time of the launch of the Third Programme, asserted that:

the range of the BBC Home Service and the Light Programme is admitted by all who have studied broadcasting programmes throughout the world to be outstanding.[xxii]

While not accepting such puffery uncritically, BBC radio classical music output before the arrival of the Third Programme in 1946 certainly indicated a broad appeal, aimed at meeting the expectations of a relatively wide audience. On both networks, the majority of the output fell firmly into the centre of the canonic repertoire, and as such may be thought to have been generally accessible, not least to an audience which had been quite extensively exposed to this type of music during the war. The largest audience of the 1946 sample week on the Home Service was for Mendelssohn's *Elijah*, broadcast on Wednesday evening. For the Light Programme, it was *Music in Miniature*—billed in the *Radio Times* as 'a musical entertainment'—of works by Françaix, Liszt, Beethoven and Mozart. Each programme was listened to by almost 3 million adults, an audience well beyond any supposed elite.

The importance of the Light Programme in the totality of classical music radio in these years—and later—deserves to be stressed. It illustrates the broad availability of the genre in those early post-war years, and how in this period—and others later in this history—it escaped from its elitist preserve. *Music in Miniature* was picked out by a 1949 report on BBC music output as 'one of the best things' on the Light Programme. This exemplar brought together a wish to open classical music to a wide audience with a continuing concern not to make it seem too 'serious', and frighten listeners off:

> As far as the Light Programme is out to catch the wandering ear and teach it to be musical this feature shows the best method. The title is no more forbidding than 'album of familiar music', 'time for music', 'musical memories' and other enticements; and for a beginning the listener is given some fairly tuneful and go-ahead piece without being put off by the words 'chamber music' or 'string quartet'. The songs and singing are the kind to catch the fancy; and other items are in keeping. A half-hour of pretty good entertainment-value music that handed out good stuff without giving the game away.[xxiii]

Worrying about 'giving the game away' is just as patronising to modern ears as Bliss' characterising the mass audience as a collection of Calibans, but in the context of the Forties the total approach reached for genuine democratisation, at least to begin with.

Among other programmes attracting substantial audiences in the sample week on the Home Service were a piano recital late on Tuesday evening of Beethoven, Weber and C.P.E. Bach, a Hallé orchestral concert under Barbirolli of Weber, Delius, Ravel and Berlioz, and the Light Programme's weekday *Concert Hour* which—although never lasting for a full hour—featured Schubert, Tchaikovsky, Holst, Borodin, Haydn, Tchaikovsky, Beethoven and Rimsky-Korsakov, and regularly attracted an audience of around 1.5 million adults. Taking the Home Service and the Light Programme together, the BBC was doing an excellent job of demonstrating the existence of a popular audience for classical music radio well before the Third Programme arrived.

The total output of around 26 hours across the 1946 sample week was modest by later standards, and there were still very few contemporary composers included, apart from a few living British composers. There was no early music, and little baroque. In the year of the first Darmstadt *Ferienspiele*, the BBC's *Composers of the Week* in May 1946 were Bax and Vaughan Williams. When the Home Service ventured to broadcast Wagner's *Tristan und Isolde* in June, it was in the form of four excerpts rather than the entire opera. When the Home Service broadcast from the Festival of Contemporary Music in July 1946, it did so in the knowledge that 'contemporary' music was thought by most 'to stand for every kind of nerve-wracking cacophony or deliberate experimentation'.[xxiv]

START OF THE THIRD PROGRAMME

1946 was a year of new institutions in the UK. The Bank of England was nationalised in March, the Arts Council was established in August and the National Health Service Act was passed in November. Modern broadcasting also arrived. BBC television transmissions resumed on 7 June 1946, though there had been test transmissions from February, and the BBC ran trials of new-fangled frequency modulation (FM) transmissions for sound broadcasting.[xxv]

The Third Programme began broadcasting at 6 pm on Sunday 29 September 1946, and was to continue as an evening-only offering until the channel was succeeded by Radio 3 in 1970. Broadcasts were initially planned to be for 6 hours daily, although that was soon reduced for a while, as the impact of the 1947 fuel crisis was felt, leading to a reduction in hours for all BBC radio and its suspension for two weeks in early

February. The hours of the Third Programme continued to vary thereafter, according to prevailing economic stringencies within the BBC.

This history is more concerned with the programmes and who listened to them than with the internal politics of the BBC, the latter having been covered exhaustively already by Humphrey Carpenter (1996) and Asa Briggs (1979), among others. They trace the BBC's wish to have a cultural programme back to an idea for a 'Minerva' programme, suggested in 1930 by J.C. Stobart, the Head of the BBC's Education Department, and relate the progress made from 1943 onwards up to Cabinet approval in January 1946. In Carpenter's view, 'the Third was born at an exciting time' (Carpenter and Doctor 1996: 14), although it encountered immediate and continuing reception difficulties. Its initial leadership, Controller George Barnes, along with Assistants Etienne Amyot and Leslie Stokes, faced the prospect at a late stage of having to postpone the new service in the light of the transmission challenge from a Latvian/Soviet station at Riga which threatened—and actually caused—extensive interference to the intended wavelength of the Third Programme.

The BBC expected that its audience 'would doubtless widen as the years went by' but intended that 'no effort should be made to force the process', explicitly rejecting 'an identifiable educational dimension' (Briggs 1979: 69). Arguably, this was to misunderstand the opportunity presented by an unprecedented British public interest in and appetite for classical music. Briggs understood that there was a real risk that the apparent objectives and the actual achievement of the Third Programme might well not match. This arose, as he observed, 'from the tendency of some producers and planners to go beyond Haley's initial rubric and to select avant-garde items which at times reduced the minority audience to a series of coteries' (Briggs 1979: 75). That risk crystallised early on, and continued to exist for much of the period covered by this book.

Haley perceptively saw the Third Programme as 'a cultural reinforcement and not a replacement' for the output on the Home Service or the Light Programme.[xxvi] Briggs notes—and analysis for 1947 confirms—that the arrival of the Third Programme increased the total cultural and 'serious' music offering by the BBC (1979: 80), although it was not exclusively or even primarily about 'serious' music. Yet scholarship has had almost nothing to say about the classical music output on either the Home Service or the Light Programme, which distorts understanding of a central part of British radio history, and suggests that historians too are seduced by the concept of the Third Programme as new, unique to Britain, and almost validated by that alone. That ignores the key dimension that, while the Third Programme flared briefly and then faded in the minds of much of its potential audience, classical music radio continued and flourished on the Home Service and the Light Programme. It was the wide provision and consumption of classical music radio across *all* the BBC channels which was the notable occurrence, and indicative of the relationship between culture and society in those years.

The agreed terms of reference for the Third Programme noted that:

> this programme is designed to be of artistic and cultural importance. The audience is one already aware of artistic experience and will include *persons of taste, of intelligence, and of education* [my italics]; it is, therefore, selected not casual, and both attentive and critical. The programme need not cultivate any other audience.[xxvii]

Thus in the view of some, perhaps most, of its begetters, class distinction was built into the new service from the very start, although they disagreed on what that should mean. George Barnes, the first Head of the Third Programme, told the Board of Governors in June 1947 that:

> the programme is for the serious, attentive listener, and not as a background to work, to reading or to washing-up. It can be assumed, therefore, that the audience would include the most intelligent and receptive listeners – persons who have a thirst for knowledge, and who wish to hear ideas discussed even if their own education is limited.[xxviii]

He went on to insist in September 1947 that the Third Programme would set out to serve:

> those who dislike being 'talked at', who demand 'performance' and nothing else, who find popular exposition often condescending and often irritating – highbrows is the name given to them by their opponents ... We shall provide the programme and not the notes. There will be few 'hearing aids' for listeners to the Third Programme. We hope that our approach will be at once sensitive and adult: that our audience will enjoy itself without crutches and will satisfy its desire for knowledge without a primer.[xxix]

However, Haley was telling the Governors in July 1947 that:

> we do not intend that the three programmes shall be rigidly stratified. Rather will they shade into each other, their differences being in approach and treatment rather than in range of content. Music, plays, and talks, for

instance, will be found in each … care will be taken consistently to ensure that the general aim of the BBC to raise public taste is not weakened. We feel, however, that it cannot be achieved simply by plunging the unsuspecting listener from Ivy Benson to Bach. We shall seek to do it more subtly; the classical music in the Light Programme will, we hope, be attractive enough to lead listeners onto the Home Service; the Home Service should lead onto the Third Programme. Items will, of course, be interchangeable. The Home Service and the Third Programme will repeat some of each other's broadcasts. So will the Home and Light programmes. Light and Third Programme exchanges will be rarer.[xxx]

Haley was to argue 30 years later that he had envisaged an active 'pyramid of taste' up which even the most ill-educated working-class listeners might ascend:

> I designed these three programmes with the idea that we would have a Light Programme which would cover the lower third of the pyramid. We would have a Home Service which would take more than the middle third, take everything up to the tip. Then we'd have a Third Programme … It was not meant to be a static pyramid … my conception was of a BBC through the years, many years, which would slowly move listeners from one strata of this pyramid to the next … I would want the Light Programme to play the waltz from *Der Rosenkavalier*. Then about a week or 10 days later I would hope the Home Service would play one act – the most tuneful act – of the opera. And within the month the Third Programme would do the whole work from beginning to end, dialogue and all.[xxxi]

Listeners—especially the potential wider audience available in 1946—were exposed to the contradictions in the BBC's approach, and the implicit (often explicit) class-based assumptions. Hennessy encapsulates the ambition shared by the founders of the Third Programme:

> Haley … would have wanted to be remembered for the pioneering, unique Third Programme, the kind of cultural gem that could only have been produced in early post-war Britain under conditions of broadcasting monopoly. In their way, Haley and George Barnes, the first Controller of the Third, were licence-funded Medicis. (1992: 312)

It was not likely, therefore, that the Third Programme would seize the opportunity presented by a newly hungry popular audience, although for a while that seemed a genuine possibility. Promotion of what was in store for the early weeks cited performances of new works by home-grown composers Britten, Tippett, Bax, Berkeley and Rubbra, but nothing from contemporary composers playing and being talked about at the annual festival of modern music in Darmstadt—Hindemith, Schoenberg, Messiaen, Leibowitz, or Cage. The Third Programme was envisaged as being part of the distinctively British cultural renaissance, notably separate from the American leadership of the classical music world and from the continental European composers.

An early research study of the Third Programme noted in November 1947 that the audience initially averaged 3.1% of the civilian adult population (or a little over 1 million), but had steadily declined to below 2% by the end of the year, when the 'patronage' of the Third Programme was (probably ambitiously) claimed to be 2,350,000 adults.[xxxii]

From the first, BBC research was built around stereotypical assumptions of the nature of the audience for the Third Programme. That early study found that:

> the section of the population which holds the Third Programme in real affection did not grow between October and June, despite the fact that during these months many people tried this programme for the first time [and that] the Third Programme's public – those who are in sympathy with its aims and to whom its broadcasts frequently appeal – is about eight percent of the listening public, or roughly 2,600,000.

As to who they were, the class-based assumptions of the Forties could not be escaped even when the data challenged them:

> as might be expected, the Third Programme appealed far more to middle class than to working class listeners (30 per cent of upper-middle-class as compared with 4 per cent of working class gave a warm welcome to the Third Programme). Nevertheless, the numerical preponderance of the working class in the population is so great, that among the 2,600,000 Third Programme enthusiasts ... about one in three are working class listeners.[xxxiii]

The Third Programme never made the progress in appeal which some of its designers had hoped for; rather, it quickly found its audiences falling fast, and had to seek justification in that very elitism which evidently was a factor in the decline. It may be argued that this was because class-based preconceptions were built into its approach from the start, or that they surfaced all too quickly once it was broadcasting. That one third of Third Programme listeners initially were working class was counter-intuitive for the station's designers, and they mostly failed to act upon that finding.

CLASSICAL MUSIC RADIO 1947–1949

Nevertheless, 1947 showed what could be achieved even in the most challenging of circumstances, by bringing together the elite and the popular in the three radio networks, and by extension in respect of British culture as a whole. The winter of 1946/1947 had been a brutal test of the realism of the UK's post-war optimism, 'as the big freeze started to tighten its grip' (Kynaston 2008: 190), and even broadcasting hours were curtailed. Yet across the country, the cultural renaissance was sustained despite privations. Covent Garden Opera gave its first post-war performance in January 1947, of *Carmen*, and the first Edinburgh Festival took place in the autumn. As the unusually harsh weather began to retreat, with the arrival of May 1947, the sample week provides an opportunity to look in detail at how BBC radio output of classical music compared with the initial ambition and rhetoric which had accompanied the launch of the Third Programme the previous autumn, and how far audience response to the products of the cultural renaissance continued after the initial relief and bloom of victory.

In line with Haley's expectations, there was interplay between the Home Service and the Third Programme. The Home Service broadcast on Wednesday evening a BBCSO concert of Bach, Mozart and van Dieren; the Third Programme repeated that the following evening, adding the second half of Schoenberg's Piano Concerto and a Dvořák overture. Van Dieren's overture, *Anjou*, was exactly the sort of curiosity which the Third Programme had been expected to provide, but hearing it first on the Home Service indicated a wish to make it more popularly available—though it had disappeared from the BBC repertoire 30 years later (Grimley and Wiegold 1977). Notably, the Home Service was the major provider, offering over 16 hours of classical music programmes compared with 13 hours for the Third Programme. Add in the Light Programme's 6½ hours and the Third Programme represented just 37% of this genre in the sample week.

In terms of the works selected for broadcast, the Home Service majored on works by Mozart, Haydn, Bach and Schubert, giving space also to Elgar as *This Week's Composer* and to British composer Lennox Berkeley. The repertoire on the Third Programme ranged more widely, featuring British composers such as Walton, Vaughan Williams and Bax, but finding space also for Schoenberg and Hindemith. The Light Programme maintained a consistent level of mainstream classical music, including works by Rossini, Mozart, Massenet, Tchaikovsky and Weber. The *Friday Concert* exemplified the genuinely popular but still unashamedly major works offered by the Light Programme: Schubert's 'Unfinished' Symphony, Bruch's Violin Concerto No. 1, Ravel's *Pavanne* and Kodály's *Dances of Galanta*.

A listener of whatever class or level of education could spend the weekend of 4/5 May 1947 listening on the Home Service to two concerts by the BBCSO, one of Mendelssohn, Rousel, Rimsky-Korsakov and Lennox Berkeley, the other of Schumann, Carl Nielsen, Dvořák and Hindemith; plus the BBC Scottish Orchestra offering Rossini, Elgar and Tchaikovsky. He or she could also take in scenes from *Tosca*, and a Haydn string quartet, be educated, informed and diverted by the fortnightly *Music Magazine*, or even hear 'gramophone records' of short works by Elgar, Dvořák, Wagner and Debussy on Saturday morning. On the Third Programme, there was string quartet music from Purcell and Walton, a Vaughan Williams mass and Schubert lieder. Not to be outdone (although more of its classical music output was available during the week than at weekends), the Light Programme chipped in with a concert of works by Rossini, Pierné and Vaughan Williams.

The significance of the Home Service was evident also on weekdays. For example, on the Tuesday of the sample week, there were five separate classical music programmes: a song recital; a Berlioz overture on records; a Schubert symphony; a concert by the BBC Northern Orchestra of works by Mozart and Harty; and a piano recital given by Clifford Curzon. For the 'ordinary' listener, this was surely the BBC's main classical music radio channel. The BBC's audience research shows audiences of over 2 million adults for a concert. Over on the Light Programme, the weekday *Concert Hour* consistently attracted between 1 million and 1.5 million listeners. *Music in Miniature* on Thursday evening—a 'musical entertainment' of works by an ensemble supporting contralto Kathleen Ferrier—was heard by a remarkable 11% of the adult population, nearly 4 million people, while the *Friday Concert* on the Light Programme the following evening attracted over 3 million listeners to hear Schubert, Bruch, Ravel and Kodály. On the Third Programme, the

Berlioz *Requiem* played to an audience of 700,000 on Friday evening, despite being up against the Light Programme's popular concert.

Taking the week as a whole, this was a cornucopia of classical music radio. Genuinely accessible music across all three networks was supplemented by enough high-brow ambition to produce a rounded whole. The late Forties were one of those spells of benign balance, replicated in the late Sixties and early Nineties. The output was multi-channel, ambitious but accessible. It was relatively heedless of 'brow' or of class, driven rather by the reflexively related taste of producer and consumer, of broadcaster and listener.

The musical purist might argue that what was missing was significant reflection of the new modernism in classical music, pioneered by American-based composers and finding continued expression at Darmstadt, but British culture still ran along very different lines from that of the continent in terms of art, theatre and literature as well. Aware of this isolation, Barnes sent music critic William Glock on a fact-finding trip around Europe in May 1947, a trip which was to yield unexpected fruit in the Sixties when Glock was a radical Controller of Music for the BBC.[5]

1947 marked the apogee of the post-war settlement for radio. There were renewed ambitions for the BBCSO, specifically stimulated by the arrival of the Third Programme, with 'two series of public concerts … most impressive in terms of repertoire' (Kenyon 1981: 198). Within the 1946–1947 season, Kodály conducted his own *Concerto for Orchestra*, Walton directed his *First Symphony*, and there were performances of symphonies by Balakirev, Goossens and Martinů.

Already, things were changing in British musical life. The use of outside orchestras in the Proms from 1947 onwards was, in Alison Garnham's words, 'a decisive step away from the past', reflecting a growing awareness of a changed musical world beyond the BBC and indeed beyond Britain (in Doctor, ed. 2007: 144). London's cultural life enjoyed a surge, as a result of both the recovery from the war and the wider English cultural renaissance. There was an increasing number of concerts, and sales of gramophone records increased as they became more affordable.

---

[5] See Chap. 4, p. 100.

Even at this moment of excellence, radio was about to lose its dominance. The televising of part of the 1947 *Last Night of the Proms* was very much an experiment, being the first television broadcast of an orchestral concert ever attempted in the UK, but it opened a window onto the new media landscape. The BBC's multi-channel approach to the broadcasting of classical music had already meant that the post-war Proms might appear on any one of the three national radio channels; now television was entering the field as well, 'bringing with it a host of new technical demands and yet another audience to stake its claim to the series' (Garnham et al. 2007: 156–157).

Change was on the march by the late Forties, arguably stimulated by the needs and inventiveness of the war years. In technology, the transistor had been devised in 1947 by Bardeen, Brattain and Shockley, and was to revolutionise radio receivers along with much more in the emerging field of electronics. In 1948, Norbert Wiener published *Cybernetics* and the first long-playing record was produced. Socially, in April the *Empire Windrush* arrived at Tilbury, bringing the first group of postwar Caribbean immigrants. Yet academically, 1948 was a year for codifying the old certainties in literature: T.S. Eliot published *Notes Towards the Definition of Culture*, F.R. Leavis completed *The Great Tradition*. In classical music, 1948 saw the institution of the Aldeburgh and Bath Festivals, confirming British attention on largely British music.

In 1948 also, BBC music was beset by shifts in its leadership, and started to lose the impetus of the previous years. The BBC Music Department was hit by a series of agonising changes among its directors. Victor Hely-Hutchinson, who had taken over the Music Department in 1944, died suddenly in 1947. He was succeeded briefly by Kenneth Wright and then by operatic tenor and musical administrator Steuart Wilson at the beginning of 1948. Wilson lasted only until 1950, before heading off to the Royal Opera House. He was succeeded by his deputy, Herbert Murrill, who in turn fell ill after only a few months in post and also died in office, leaving Kenneth Warr as Acting Head in 1952. Richard Howgill, who as Controller of Entertainment had overseen the Music Department through this period, was then appointed as its Head. He at last provided stability and continuity until Glock arrived in 1959.

Wilson's tenure in particular was not a happy one. He was a divisive figure, who had successfully sued the BBC for libel in the Thirties over a report about the quality of his singing.[xxxiv] He took the decision to remove Boult (to whom Wilson's first wife was then married) from his role as Chief Conductor of the BBCSO, but without telling him in advance what he had in mind. Wilson then proceeded to fluff the appointment of Boult's successor, approaching and then alienating John Barbirolli with a suggestion of a shared role, while 'disgracefully ignoring' Boult's own impossible position (Kenyon 1981: 214). Raphael Kubelik was eventually offered the post, in due course declined, leaving Malcolm Sargent as Hobson's Choice for this key role in the BBC and in the UK's musical life.

The pattern of programmes did not greatly change in 1948, but what stands out from the sample week analysis is a dramatic falling away in the audiences for the Third Programme classical output. Listening had shaded down a little on the other networks too—and in daytime, so not as a result of competition from television—but on the Third Programme it seems little short of catastrophic. There was no measurable audience at all for the Third Programme classical music output on Sunday, Tuesday, Thursday, Friday or Saturday. The highest audience of the week was just 360,000. When the Third Programme repeated Tchaikovsky's opera *Eugene Onegin* on Friday evening, which had been broadcast on the Home Service the previous Wednesday evening to the second largest classical music audience of the week, 2,160,000, no one could be measured as listening.[6] The sample week analysis shows no previous example of an audience blank for an entire evening, and only rarely for a single programme.

Despite BBC Research Department assertions of a potential audience for the Third Programme in 1946 of around 2.5 million, it was becoming clear outside the BBC that no equivalent audience was being reached.[xxxv] Carpenter (1996: 84) notes that 'by the summer of 1948 the press was beginning to get wind of the drastic drop in audiences'. It is likely that some of this was due to worsening reception, and there was no early solution to this until the revised frequency allocations under the Copenhagen Frequency Plan came into effect from 1950 onwards.[xxxvi] However, what seemed to be alienating listeners was the concept of the

---

[6] Where the research findings reported in the Daily Listening Barometer (see Appendix B) failed to identify an audience of at least 0.1% of all adults for a programme, it was marked as being 'below measurable levels'. The audience might have been zero, or it might have been, say, 49,999 (subject to caveats about sample sizes and their extrapolation to 'actual' audience levels).

network as an 'intellectual and aesthetic experiment'. This phrase, from that quintessential member of the Bloomsbury set, diarist and diplomat Harold Nicolson, was part of a restatement of the high-brow purpose and target which the elite had intended for the Third Programme. Nicolson went on to address what he described as 'the problem of audience' against a background that:

> the Fellows of Balliol and All Souls, the editors of the weeklies, are very busy people; they rarely listen to the wireless.[xxxvii]

Harman Grisewood had succeeded Barnes as Controller of the Third Programme, in 1948. His response to Nicolson was that some light music should be seeded into the Third Programme output (Carpenter 1996: 85–87). However, that was seeing the BBC's classical music output only in narrow institutional terms. Such lighter classical music was already available—and widely listened to—on the Home Service and on the Light Programme. Arguably, the problem confronting the Third Programme was that as the decade progressed it became less one part of the whole of the BBC's output, and more something which would be regarded in its own right according to the elite aspirations of those responsible for it. The initial inclusiveness of the BBC radio offer in 1947 was starting to fray at the edges.

That continued as the decade drew to its close. There was a further reduction in the amount of classical music on the Home Service in 1949, in the ambition of its programmes and in the audiences for them too. Only a few classical music programmes on the Home or the Light now attracted as many as a million listeners, with the median audience on both much lower than in previous years. The median audience for the Third Programme, which had been 750,000 in 1947,[xxxviii] was down to a median of barely more than 100,000 in 1949.

Assessing the Forties Output

Programme output broadened significantly in the years after 1945. The number of composers in the weeks sampled rose steadily from 39 to 62, as the multi-channel output found its feet. The effect of the introduction of the Third Programme was to increase by around a third the amount of classical music programming broadcast. These years established the pattern which was to continue throughout the period, whereby the most played composers were from the centre of the canonic repertoire, with Beethoven and Mozart consistently dominant. The Light Programme was a significant source of classical music, sustaining mass audiences often in excess of the other channels. Overall, however, audience levels were declining partly as television got into its stride, partly in the face of the returning normality of post-war distractions and partly in response to the loss of popular ambition among the producers, among whom the wartime democratisation of cultural tastes was beginning to wear rather thin.

Haley evidently felt enough concern to commission three reports into the BBC's music output in November 1948.[xxxix] Those reports—by Julius Harrison on the Home Service, William McNaught on the Light Programme and Dyneley Hussey on the Third Programme—concerned themselves firmly with 'serious music', and provide a view from the music establishment of the position as the Forties were ending and the impetus of the post-war reorganisation had dissipated. Harrison was a distinguished composer and conductor in the tradition of Elgar, and had recently given up conducting through deafness. McNaught was editor of the *Musical Times*, while Hussey was a music critic and a regular contributor to *The Listener*.

Harrison's report shows a high regard for the Home Service music output. He saw no grounds for believing that any particular group of composers were neglected, including British composers, and judged the great majority of performances to be a satisfactory level. He observed that:

> the problems which confront programme planners in the compilation and arrangement of programmes designed to satisfy both a majority and minority of listeners are nowhere more apparent than in the Home Service. Here the programmes must, like Janus, face both ways; music as an Art and as Entertainment must be provided in something like equal proportions and in contra-distinction to the more esoteric nature of what is heard in the Third Programme, or to the more frankly popular appeal defining the Light Programme.[xl]

His conclusion serves to highlight further the significance of the Home Service's role as a classical music provider:

> there was so much that was worthy of high praise both in the standard of performance, the choice of items and the general presentation of the

programmes that the conclusion is reached that the Home Service programmes are providing the listening public with little short of as good and varied a selection of music as is possible in the existing circumstances within the framework of the Corporation and general policy.

In respect of the most popular network, on the other hand, McNaught felt that there was a prevailing notion that 'as it is only the Light Programme there is no need to try hard' in terms of its serious music output.[xli] He argued that there should be a particular repertoire for the Light Programme within a self-contained allocation of music, praising the approach of *Music in Miniature* in offering a wide and inclusive repertoire (including the programme's use of single movements), distinct from the canon of the other two radio channels.

His views drew particular criticism from Head of Music Wilson, never one to shirk a disagreement. Wilson saw the Home Service and Light Programme as to a degree interchangeable in their deployment of the music from his department:

> In respect of the lunch-time concerts, which form the bulk of the Light Programme's output of serious music, the Light Programme label is irrelevant and largely fortuitous. At lunch-time, as on Saturday nights, the Light Programme and Home Service roles are reversed and the Home Service carries variety programmes. The sensible thing is, therefore, for the Light Programme to carry popular classical music ... the audience that listens to these concerts is, I imagine, the same as listened to the Proms and the studio concerts.[xlii]

Hussey wrote a report on the Third Programme very much from the perspective of those who ran it. He was concerned with the detail of programming far more than with its appropriateness or appeal to audiences. Thus, while feeling that:

> the programme has admirably fulfilled its purpose and, no doubt, as time goes on such gaps as there are will gradually be filled.

He went on to note the comparative neglect of the operas of Gluck, the failure to explore thoroughly Haydn's symphonies and the absence of the performance of Richard Strauss' less well-known operas.[xliii] Arguably, the increasing isolation and rapidly fading relevance of the Third Programme was shown all too well by this narrow understanding of the wider potential for the channel, which had been so apparent just three years previously.

Taken together, these reports illustrate well the approach of the three networks—one trying to look both ways, one popular and one elite. They do so without reference to the declining audiences for all of such output on whichever station. They each offer specific recommendations regarding content, presentation and scheduling, but none takes a broader look at the pattern and structure of output, or its likely appeal to listeners. These 'outsiders' actually confirm the BBC at its most self-referential. With a diminishing amount of output and dwindling audiences, they presage and do little to prevent the Fifties becoming a disappointing decade for classical music radio.

From an historical perspective, the Forties contain many of the issues which were to dog the rest of the century: a spasmodic wish to democratise the services, then qualified and limited by an unwillingness among the elite to keep open the doors to a potential mass audience; concern about balancing the demands of the high-brow while addressing the middle-brow listener; and institutional uncertainties about the use of multiple channels. The assumptions of class were ever-present, and they undermined the perception of who might listen to classical music on the radio. Yet these years also featured one of the high points in the provision of classical music radio, the years around 1947 when the BBC got the balance right between these conflicts and therefore provided inclusive programmes which ranged across the spectrum of classical music, achieving popular appeal and intellectual approval. That this lasted only a short time is an outcome which would recur in later decades.

Notes

i. Melba's Concert. *The Times*, 29 June 1920, p. 14.
ii. *Radio Times*, 28 September 1923, p. 18.
iii. See *inter alia* R.S. Thatcher, BBC Deputy Director Music. Memorandum, 11 September 1939. WAC R27/3/1. Also R.S. Thatcher. Copyright music by alien composers, undated, probably July 1940. BBC WAC R27/3/1.
iv. Noel Coward recorded the song in July 1943. 'Don't let's be beastly to the Germans/When our victory is ultimately won,/It was just those nasty Nazis who persuaded them to fight/And their Beethoven and Bach are really far worse than their bite …' *The Guardian* claims that it was banned by the BBC 'by public demand': www.theguardian.com/culture/2002/apr/12/artsfeatures.popandrock.
v. Quoted in Kenyon (1981: 163).

vi. R.S. Thatcher, Deputy Director Music. Copyright music by alien composers, undated, probably July 1940. BBC WAC R/27/3/1.
vii. Arthur Bliss. BBC policy with regard to copyright music by composers of enemy nationality, 21 October 1942. BBC WAC R27/3/3. A later draft dated 23 November allows latitude to producers where particular music is needed to meet 'special dramatic needs'.
viii. Quoted in Leese (2006: 114).
ix. Quoted in Hennessy (1992: 309).
x. *Hansard* (1945) House of Commons, 12 June 1945. Col. 1482 W.
xi. Anderton (2012: 46).
xii. Anderton (2012: 46) quoting Levi, *Music in the Third Reich* (1994: 217–219).
xiii. *BBC Handbook* 1947, p. 43.
xiv. K.A. Wright, Deputy Director of Music. Copyright music by alien composers, undated, probably February 1946. BBC WAC R/27/3/6.
xv. Basil Nicholls, Senior Controller. Memo to A/C Ent, 26 June 1947. BBC WAC R27/3/7.
xvi. *BBC Handbook* 1949 pp. 16 and 17. Strauss died on 8 September 1949.
xvii. Sir William Haley. Memorandum from WJH to BBC senior managers, 13 September 1944. BBC WAC R 34/580.
xviii. File note: Tory Reform Group Broadcasting Sub-committee, 8 March 1945. BBC WAC R 34/580.
xix. Memorandum from Director General to BBC heads and others, 24 July 1945. BBC WAC R 34/420.
xx. *The Listener*, 26 July 1945, p. 92.
xxi. Music in the Forces. *The Times*, 23 March 1945, p. 6.
xxii. Sir William Haley. Breaking new ground in radio. *The Listener*, 26 September 1946, p. i.
xxiii. William McNaught. Music on the Light Programme, August 1949. BBC WAC R27/495/2.
xxiv. Edward Clark. A Festival of Contemporary Music. *The Listener*, 4 July 1946, p. 29.
xxv. Next Steps in Broadcasting. *The Times*, 29 June 1920, p. 14.
xxvi. Address to the General Advisory Council, 20 October 1947, quoted in Briggs (1979: 80).
xxvii. Programme C terms of reference (approved by Director General) for Coordinating Committee, 22 January 1946. BBC WAC R34/890/1.
xxviii. George Barnes, Head Third Network. The Third Programme: draft for board, 18 June 1946. BBC WAC R34/420.
xxix. George R. Barnes. The aims of the programme. *The Listener*, 26 September 1946, p. i.

xxx. Sir William Haley. The Home Programme policy of the BBC 4 July 1946. BBC WAC R39/420.
xxxi. Haley interviewed by Gillard for the BBC Oral History project, 6 July 1976. BBC WAC R143/60/1. Haley was interviewed by Gillard for the BBC Oral History project. Carpenter (1996: 9) dates this as 4 April 1978, since this was when Haley corrected the manuscript of the transcript. This quote is from the original transcript.
xxxii. A year of the Third Programme. BBC Audience Research Special Report, 6 November 1947. BBC WAC R9/9/11.
xxxiii. Undated, but reporting on a study into audience and appreciation data for October to December 1946. BBC WAC R9/9/11.
xxxiv. Singer's libel action against the BBC. *The Times* Law Report, 20 June 1934, p. 4.
xxxv. A year of the Third Programme. BBC Audience Research Special Report, 6 November 1947. BBC WAC R9/9/11.
xxxvi. Changes in BBC wave-lengths *The Times*, 29 September 1948, p. 2.
xxxvii. Harold Nicolson. Birthday of the Third Programme. *The Listener*, 7 October 1948, p. 526.
xxxviii. A year of the Third Programme. BBC Audience Research Special Report, 6 November 1947. BBC WAC R9/9/11.
xxxix. Memorandum from Director General (Haley) to DHB (Nicholls), 18 November 1948. BBC WAC R27/495/2.
xl. Steuart Wilson, Head Music. Music in the Light Programme, undated but probably August 1949. BBC WAC R27/495/2.
xli. William McNaught. Music on the Light Programme, August 1949. BBC WAC R27/495/2.
xlii. Steuart Wilson, Head Music. Music in the Light Programme, undated but probably August 1949. BBC WAC R27/495/2.
xliii. Dyneley Hussey. Report on Music in the Third Programme, probably summer 1949. BBC WAC R27/495/2.

Bibliographic Sources

Addison, P. 1985. *Now the war is over: A social history of Britain 1945–51*. London: British Broadcasting Corporation.
Baade, C.L. 2012. *Victory through harmony: The BBC and popular music in World War II*. Oxford: Oxford University Press.
Briggs, A. 1961. *The history of broadcasting in the United Kingdom, vol. 1, the birth of broadcasting*. Oxford: Oxford University Press.
Briggs, A. 1965. *The history of broadcasting in the United Kingdom, vol. 2, the golden age of wireless*. Oxford: Oxford University Press.

Briggs, A. 1979. *The history of broadcasting in the United Kingdom, vol. 4, sound and vision*. Oxford: Oxford University Press.
Carpenter, H., and J.R. Doctor. 1996. *The envy of the world: Fifty years of the BBC Third Programme and Radio 3, 1946–1996*. London: Weidenfeld & Nicolson.
Doctor, J.R. 1999. *The BBC and ultra-modern music, 1922–1936: Shaping a nation's tastes*. Cambridge: Cambridge University Press.
Doctor, J.R., A. Garnham, D.A. Wright, and N. Kenyon. 2007. *The Proms: A new history*. London: Thames & Hudson.
Fox, C. 2007. Music after zero hour. *Contemporary Music Review* 26 (1): 5–24.
Grimley, M., and M. Wiegold. 1977. *Catalogue of music broadcast on Radio 3 and Radio 4 in 1974*. London: British Broadcasting Corporation.
Hennessy, P. 1992. *Never again: Britain, 1945–51*. London: Cape.
Kennedy, M. 1991. *Britten*. London: J.M. Dent.
Kenyon, N. 1981. *The BBC Symphony Orchestra: the first fifty years 1930–1989*. London: British Broadcasting Corporation.
Kynaston, D. 2008. *Austerity Britain, 1945–1951*. London: Bloomsbury.
MacKay, R. 2000. Being Beastly to the Germans: Music, censorship and the BBC in World War II. *Historical Journal of Film, Radio and Television* 20 (4): 513–525.
Pirie, P.J. 1979. *The English musical renaissance*. London: Gollancz.
Seaton, J. 1987. The BBC and the Holocaust. *European Journal of Communication* 2 (1): 53–80.
Street, S. 2005. *A concise historical dictionary of British radio*, 2nd ed. Tiverton: Kelly Publications.
Taruskin, R. 2010. *Music in the late 20th century*. Oxford: Oxford University Press.
Taylor, A.J.P. 1965. *English history: 1914–1945*. Oxford: Oxford University Press.
Thacker, T. 2007. *Music after Hitler, 1945–1955*. Aldershot: Ashgate.
Wagner, R., and E. Evans. 1850 and 1869/1910. *Das Judenthum in der Musik (Judaism in Music)*. London: William Reeves.

CHAPTER 3

The Fifties: Defending the Elite

A new Britain?—classical music radio 1950–1953—conservatism and retrenchment 1954–1955—reorganisation of classical music radio 1956–1958—changing the guard.

When the Fifties started, food was still rationed; before they ended, Harold Macmillan would be re-elected on the slogan 'you've never had it so good'. At the start of the decade, radio could still claim to be the senior broadcast medium in the UK; by its end, there were two mass television channels, and radio risked becoming merely an historical curiosity.

Classical music radio on the BBC entered the Fifties with every opportunity to flourish, both in itself and in its societal impact. The legacy from the Forties' innovation was extensive output, both popular and high brow, and an aspirational social purpose, even if the BBC's performance and appeal had fallen away quite sharply from a high point of achievement towards the end of the previous decade. The dislike of the Frankfurt School theorists for the effect of radio broadcasting on the auratic quality of classical music in performance had been asserted by Theodor Adorno in 1941:

> [the symphony's] qualities are radically affected by radio. The sound is no longer 'larger' than the individual. In the private room, that magnitude of sound causes disproportions which the listener mutes down. The 'surrounding' function of music also disappears, partly because of the

diminution of absolute dimensions, partly because of the monaural conditions of radio broadcasting. What is left of the symphony even in the ideal case of adequate reproduction of sound colours, is a mere chamber symphony. (1941/2002: 257)

Ten years later that seemed an incorrect reading. Writing in the *BBC Handbook* in 1951, in defiance of Adorno and Walter Benjamin's concerns about the mechanisation of music inherent in broadcasting technology (Benjamin and Underwood 1936/2008), Ernest Newman, the doyen of British music critics, went out of his way to stress:

the generally beneficial influence of broadcasting on the listener's range of musical experience ... I would say that broadcasting is potentially the most vital factor in the broadening and the subtilization [*sic*] of musical taste that the world has ever known.[i]

Few now disagreed that sound broadcasting and classical music were made for each other. Despite this, the decade was notable for the witting abandonment by the BBC of the role it had so long embraced to elevate listener taste. Further, just as the decade nationally saw a weakening in the radicalism of post-war ambitions, so in classical music radio the BBC's response to the mass-audience challenge posed by television was a withdrawal into conservative programming, responding chiefly to the demands of the elite. This chapter examines the output and audiences for classical music radio in the years between 1950 and 1953; growing conservatism and retrenchment from the experimental achievements of the Forties in mid-decade; the establishment of a new pattern of output in 1956–1957; and the general changing of the guard in British classical music—and radio too—at the end of the decade.

Politically, these were the years of centrist conservatism, when the administrations of Churchill, Eden and Macmillan adapted but maintained the social reforms of the Attlee Governments—which themselves were apotheosised in the 1951 Festival of Britain—but largely eschewed cultural change. Popular music began to take off in a new guise as the long post-war boom got into its stride. The arrival in the UK of skiffle, and then the first rock and pop music, looked forward to a Sixties society in which youth taste and economic clout would be prominent as never before, while the explosive growth of television changed the face of society as well as that of broadcasting.

A New Britain?

The very make-up of the UK was changing. British pretensions to great power status had to be abandoned: a decade which began with intervention in Korea in 1950 ended with the 'winds of change' blowing away the final shreds of Empire. The Fifties saw the Notting Hill race riots in August 1958, after which, in Peter Hennessey's words, 'things were never the same again. The comfortable shared notion [of] a nation that prided itself on tolerance and civility ... was gone for ever' (2006: 501).

Classical music in the UK was painfully slow to respond to the harbingers of cultural and social change, and BBC radio's approach to such broadcasting was a key factor in this. The chief tensions were between the generality of performance and listening, on the one hand, and modernist composition on the other, but without regard for the opportunity to influence popular tastes and consumption. The influence of the anti-modernist Malcolm Sargent, Chief Conductor of the BBCSO from 1950 to 1957, whose appointment was one of Steuart Wilson's parting gifts to the BBC from his short spell as Head of Music at the end of the Forties, contrasted strikingly with the first performance of Stockhausen's *Gesange der Jünglinge* in 1956. Yet both in their own ways contracted rather than expanded the classical music patronage base.

From 1955 onwards, when ITV brought competitive energy to that medium, the exponential growth in television set ownership, licences and viewing seemed to most commentators to be leaving radio in the doldrums or worse. The shift of the BBC's ever-pressed resources away from radio was hastened because the BBC was being 'humiliated' by the overwhelming public preference for ITV services over the BBC's (Kynaston 2009: 607). In December 1955, 57% of viewers told Gallup that ITV was better than the BBC, while only 16% expressed a preference for BBC.

The question of an alternative service of radio remained dormant throughout the Fifties. Radio Luxembourg continued to be a surprising force, despite its rotten frequency. It was in these years that radio advertisements (never heard on UK domestic radio until 1973) for Bulova watches or for Horace Batchelor's football pools tips, 'defined the station in the memory as did the Ovalteenies for listeners up to 1939' (Street 2006: 199).

However, Radio Luxembourg was undermined by the impact of commercial television, which among other things adopted its sponsored quiz shows such as *Take Your Pick*, *Double Your Money* and *Opportunity Knocks*, all of which had found large family audiences on the radio station, and became a niche record-based station. BBC radio therefore had to stand on its own, dominated by just that lack of financial, technical and political attention which was leading the medium towards seeming anachronism.

CLASSICAL MUSIC RADIO 1950–1953

The Third Programme moved onto more suitable medium wave frequencies on 15 March 1950. With substantial output on the Home Service and the Third Programme, and the Light Programme still making a considerable impact, BBC classical music radio had the potential to recover quickly after slipping from the high plateau of a couple of years earlier. The reports of Harrison, McNaught and Hussey, considered in the previous chapter, described a robust and wide range of output across the three national radio channels, largely borne out by analysis of output and audiences in 1950 and 1951.

The programming during the 1950 sample week in May showed a good balance between high-brow and accessibly popular, with a solid middle ground. Verdi operas seemed to epitomise that middle ground, whether in the Home Service's *Sunday Afternoon Concert* or in the Light Programme's *Come to the Opera* on Tuesday evening. A full hour of excerpts on the Light Programme from *La Traviata*, not that different in content from the Home Service offering two days earlier, attracted an audience of as many as 15% of all adults, over 5 million. It neatly encapsulated Haley's 'pyramid' aspirations considered in Chap. 2 (although the example he had chosen was *Der Rosenkavalier*).[1] The Wednesday evening *Orchestral Concert* on the Home Service was a dominant feature, with Yehudi Menuhin featuring as a soloist in the Brahms Violin Concerto which, together with the Bach's sixth *Brandenburg Concerto*, represented the channel's largest classical music audiences of the week of 1.5 million.

There were two high-brow milestone broadcasts on the Third Programme. On Friday, the revival of Vaughan Williams' opera *Hugh the Drover* was relayed from Sadler's Wells to a creditable audience for

---

[1] See Chap. 2, p. 52.

such a difficult work of around 70,000. The previous evening, a broadcast of *Jephtha* by Handel hit much the same mark. There were two or three hours of classical music broadcast almost every night on the Third Programme, many of which were not lacking in ambition—works by Rubbra and Yrjö Kilpinen on Monday evening, for example—but even here it was the mainstays of the classical music canonic repertoire who dominated. In total, 62 separate composers were broadcast on the three BBC channels during the sample week, with Beethoven and Bach the most often played, closely followed by Wagner and Haydn. One feature of the following week was a broadcast of Richard Strauss's tone poem *Ein Heldenleben* on the Third Programme on Sunday evening. This work had been at the centre of the BBC's distaste for the alleged Nazi-collaborating composer, and had been among the relatively few works specifically banned from broadcast during the war. The rehabilitation of Strauss was evidently complete by 1950.

There were yet more institutional changes afoot and internal politics dominated. Wilson's replacement as BBC Head of Music came from the music establishment; Herbert Murrill joined the BBC from the Royal Academy of Music. Although described in the *Radio Times* as 'the BBC's new music chief',[ii] the novelty was in the administrative appointment and not the music that he was to champion.

Conservatism was to rule at the BBCSO as well. As discussed in the previous chapter, Adrian Boult retired from his position as its permanent conductor on 17 June 1950, after 20 years at the helm.[iii] In a mixture of muddle and insensitivity, he was succeeded by Sargent 'who could not have been more different from the self-effacing Boult' (Carpenter and Doctor 1996: 102). Personalities and institutional politics aside, in that change also there was a shift from dynamism to caution in terms of what was to be broadcast and performed.

The Music Department became a Music Division, and if you were 'Sargent's man' like the new Head of Music Programmes, Maurice Johnstone, you were well set (Kenyon 1981: 237). Johnstone, a composer and classical music expert, had been brought down from the BBC in Manchester at his friend Sargent's insistence, although he was to be one of the first to become alarmed at Sargent's failure to get on with the Music Division and to press for his replacement. On the other hand, 'adventurous newcomers were scarcely recognised', so that while 'backwaters were explored; risks were rarely taken' (Kenyon 1981: 238).

There was nobody at the top level of the Music Division who understood or felt brave enough to champion new music, let alone address the key question of the declining popular audience. Live music, or music recorded for broadcast purposes, dominated the schedules. In 1950, only 2 hours 20 minutes of the 39 hours in the sample week was taken from gramophone records. Given the resulting significance of live or originally recorded music, especially from the BBC's house orchestras, where the BBCSO went today, it was likely that radio programme output would follow tomorrow; and, with Sargent at the helm of the orchestra, that would not be into modernist waters.

The Royal Festival Hall at the Festival of Britain site encapsulated the hopes of the early Fifties, and the BBC carried concerts from its inauguration. Two such concerts were broadcast during the 1951 sample week. The first featured the BBCSO under Malcolm Sargent playing Brahms, Vaughan Williams, Richard Strauss and Debussy on Sunday evening, and attracting a solid 2% of the audience; the second, on the Third Programme on Tuesday evening, was an all-Beethoven concert graced by Moiseiwitsch and Schwarzkopf, drawing 0.6%. This latter was firmly mainstream, with the *Piano Fantasia* followed by the *Choral Symphony*, and it is a mark of the reducing attraction of the Third Programme that even such a star-studded event could not draw nearly as many listeners as the more recondite Home Service concert two days before.

Two concerts stand out in terms of audience size in the sample week. The Light Programme broadcast excerpts from Puccini's *Madame Butterfly* on Tuesday evening to a remarkable 14% of the potential audience. That reach was almost matched by the Home Service the previous evening, with Gilbert and Sullivan's *Mikado* live from Sadler's Wells with 13%. These 5 million listeners were beyond question a mass audience, albeit for popular works. The potentially wide appeal of programmes generally is borne out by the overall audience for classical music radio, with the Home Service—an equal provider with the Third Programme of classical music—not infrequently reaching 1 million listeners for broadcasts, and the Third Programme itself quite often coming close to 200,000, not far below that of the Light Programme's routine output.

Yet doubts were growing. The Board of Governors at their meeting on 25 October 1951:

> expressed the view that the Third Programme was making an important contribution to culture and thought that it had fully justified itself. They

regretted that the numbers listening were not larger, and hoped that, now that the reception [quality] had been much improved, every effort will be made to increase the listening figure, with a very clear understanding that standards should not in any way be lowered.[iv]

Across Britain in 1952, change was in prospect but not yet accomplished. EMI announced that it would be replacing 78-rpm records with long-playing or extended play records,[v] yet two months later Decca issued a new recording of Stravinsky on 10 sides of 78s.[vi] It was the end of an era rather than the start of a new one. *The Times*' coverage of the funeral of George VI reflected an almost bygone age, but amid all the 'martial splendour and pageantry' the crowds were said to have been fewer than anticipated because of the impact of television.[vii] In classical music, Cage's *4'33"* was given its first performance in August, although BBC radio airwaves remained safe from any such ultra-minimalist silence.

The BBC's Charter was renewed in July 1952, at the start of a second Elizabethan age (Queen Elizabeth II had acceded to the throne on 6 February). Establishment figures continued to dominate. Haley resigned as BBC Director General to become editor of *The Times* in September, and was succeeded in December by the far less visionary Ian Jacob. Hugh Chignell notes the downside in the appointment for radio:

> Jacob ... had none of Haley's reservations about the value of television and was understandably focused on the need to deal with the newly arrived competition. Radio ... was neglected as a result. (2011: 60)

There were more changes at the BBC. Richard Howgill became Controller of Music in 1952, a post he was to hold until 1959. Lindsay Wellington replaced Basil Nicholls as Senior Controller, thus breaking the final senior link with the post-war settlement. Haley and Nicholls subsequently disputed who deserved the credit for the introduction of the Third Programme (Carpenter 1997: 8–9). Haley asserted that Nicholls was 'very anti-Third ... having said that he had got the original idea, he was then convinced that ... it was all wrong',[viii] but these two men shared a socio/cultural aspiration which Wellington was to set aside later in the decade.

The 1952 sample week confirms that, while the Home Service and the Light Programme continued to offer a good range of music, the Third Programme was starting to retreat almost into a caricature of its output. Monday evening scheduled a five-act opera, *Les Huguenots* by Meyerbeer and Friday evening offered Thomas Arne's *Love in a Village*, an 18th-century ballad opera in three acts which had gone unperformed since 1928. On Wednesday evening, a one-act opera *Volo di Notte* by Dallapiccola, preceded by a concert of Telemann's *Tafelmusik* were features of an evening of scant appeal. The audience never rose above 0.1% for Telemann, Poulenc, Busoni, Mozart or van Dieren, and was below recordable levels for the Italian opera. This meant that around or below 35,000 people were all that were attracted to the 3¼ hours of the Third Programme's classical music at any one time across the whole Wednesday evening.

It fell to the Home Service to provide mainstream afternoon and evening concerts. It achieved its best audience figures with a couple of concerts on the Sunday, with well over a million people listening to the *Sunday Symphony Concert* of Bach, Haydn, Dukas and Elsa Barraine, and the same number tuning into hear the BBC Scottish Orchestra play Tchaikovsky's *Pathétique* later in the evening.

The Light Programme meanwhile continued to sustain the popularity of middle-brow output. Its regular weekday *Lunchtime Concert* consistently attracted 1 or 2% of the potential audience (30 times the total listening to the Third Programme that Wednesday evening) without noticeably compromising on its output. Monday featured Schubert, Wagner and Haydn; Tuesday, Mozart, Mendelssohn and Schubert; Wednesday, Haydn, Strauss and Berners; Thursday, Weber, Lalo and Dvořák; and Friday, despite edging more to the light classical, included works by Bach, Gluck, Beethoven, Borodin and Glinka. This was a good central classical canonic repertoire, with respectable audiences. It even included an educational component: Tuesday afternoon saw a broadcast of *Talking of Music* by Sidney Harrison, discussing the *Music of the Masters* concert to be broadcast on the Light the following afternoon—both attracting some 250,000 listeners, and featuring Weber, Delius, Borodin and de Falla.

The Light Programme's Saturday evening concert, *The Hour of Music*, with the BBC Opera Orchestra, highlights the difficulties of too restrictive a taxonomy. The programme included an Elgar march, a von Suppé overture, one of Liszt's *Hungarian Rhapsodies* and Charles Mackerras' reworking of some of the music from the Gilbert and Sullivan operettas into the suite *Pineapple Poll*. This is light classical music, but still classical—and it achieved the Light Programme's highest audience of the week for classical music, 3% or almost 1.1 million adults.

Thus BBC output in 1952 embodied a relationship between the popular output of the Light, the middle brow of the Home and the high brow of the Third Programme. The small audience figures for the Third Programme on Wednesday would probably have been thought justified, since over on the Home Service the BBCSO, under Sargent, was presenting a featured concert of works by Sibelius, which sustained an audience of 1 million through the evening. However, it may be argued that such an approach only remained valid if the more challenging output was presented in a way accessible to a wider audience, and if the different platforms were linked by the kind of 'escalator' which Haley had envisaged—but there was little if any evidence of that happening by the early Fifties.

Jacob had thought that radio 'was in full flight' in late 1952 (presumably a positive comment, though potentially ambiguous).[ix] Yet whatever the excitements surrounding the impending Coronation, classical music output on the three BBC stations in 1953 was becoming less appealing. The new combination of Howgill as Controller of Music with John Morris as Controller of the Third Programme seemed to confirm the BBC in its growing conservatism. Jacob recalled that television got going in earnest after the Coronation on 2 June 1953, when it 'began to cover really big populations', and that questions arose whether the BBC was 'prepared to keep up the whole apparatus of radio just for a small population' of perhaps a million listeners in the evenings, which had been radio's prime time before the advent of television.[x] These questions started to condition the BBC's thinking about radio as a whole, not least about classical music radio.

Although the number of hours of classical music radio output was up slightly in 1953, the audiences reached by the top programmes were notably lower. With television—even before the competitive stimulus of ITV—now firmly established, there were not to be many more blockbuster evening classical concerts on the radio such as had featured even two years before. In the wider world political tectonic plates were shifting. Stalin died in March. In the USA, Copland appeared before the House Committee on un-American Activities in May. Yet while Messiaen's *Réveil des Oiseaux* was preparing for its first performance at the Donaueschingen Festival in southwest Germany, the Third Programme's approach was reflected in the sample week by just one outing each for Berg and

Honegger and a dusted-down performance of Elgar's *The Apostles* on Thursday evening, which barely attracted an audience at all. Hindemith enjoyed a couple of outings, including the performance of his *Symphony in B Flat* on the Third Programme by the band of the Irish Guards—a broadcast claimed by Arthur Jacobs to be 'the first time, surely, that a military band has been heard on the Third Programme'.[xi] William Glock made an appearance on the Third Programme, following up a concert of music by Stravinsky with a 45-minute *Study in Music Criticism*, which attracted barely a third of the concert's audience of 220,000.

There was plenty of more standard fare elsewhere. The Home Service offered concerts almost every evening, the Light Programme continued with its lunchtime and sometimes afternoon concerts. But audiences were shading down, the repertoire was rarely refreshed. The formality of presentation was starting to become a problem in an increasingly demotic society, as the Third Programme made few concessions to inexpert listeners. Percy Scholes wrote to *The Listener* in April urging that:

> if the Third Programme is to contribute, as it is surely intended to do, to the widening of the nation's love of the best music there must be daily application on the part of those who draft and those who announce the programmes of what we may call … ordinary commonsense.[xii]

The cost of radio was coming under close attention. The BBC's Finance Controller calculated the savings which would result from the closure of the Third Programme,[xiii] a total of £432,309 out of the BBC's total radio expenditure of £8,682,815, or 5%.[xiv] Radio expenditure actually rose to £9,387,166 in the year to 31 March 1954, thus qualifying slightly the contention that BBC resources for radio were ever more constrained.

If the Third Programme was starting to be questioned, that was partly because it was narrowing its target listening. An audience research study in May 1953 concluded that:

> the Third Programme's character is such that no one would expect it to appeal to more than a minority of the population. Though it is not designed to appeal to any particular strata of the population [*sic*], its level of sophistication effectively precludes its appeal from being catholic.[xv]

Audience figures were beginning to matter, spicing up the confrontation between the popularisers and the elitists. The father and founding figure of BBC audience research, Robert Silvey, wrote in the *BBC Quarterly* in 1953 that the Third Programme had a weekly audience of 4.8% of the adult population, 1.75 million, vaunting a widening of the radio franchise for this genre of music;[xvi] yet by 1953 BBC discourse was characterised by a concern for serving the elite rather than any widening of the audience:

> Two percent of the population might be regarded as, according to a consensus of judgements, 'good prospects' for the Third Programme, i.e. to be at home with its level of sophistication, and a further six percent as 'fair prospects'.[xvii]

The approach of the same BBC audience research report in 1953 was jarringly condescending towards the mass audience:

> Although the Third Programme reaches a much higher proportion of its 'primary market' ... than the rest of the population, yet it remains true that no less than three quarters of its patrons are drawn from outside this primary market. ... listeners who like to hear Third Programme broadcasts even though they are *unlikely to be able to meet them on equal terms* [my emphasis].

This is an extraordinary assertion, that listeners who are unable 'to meet the broadcasts on equal terms' lie outside the station's primary market and by implication somehow did not deserve to be tuning in. What better archetype could be found for the elitist, class-dominated Fifties? To continue the stereotyping, the same report notes that:

> the average educational and *intelligence* levels of the Third Programme patrons are, *as might be expected*, considerably higher than those of the population [both my emphases].

In his *BBC Quarterly* article, Silvey made specific observations on what makes people suitable 'prospects' for the Third Programme—educational level; intelligence level; degree of interest in a specified range of subjects or activities with which the Third Programme frequently deals; and 'the reading of periodicals of a level of sophistication similar to that of the Third Programme'.[xviii] All of this suggests that the reaction against Haley's aspirational inclusivity was gaining strength.

Conservatism and Retrenchment 1954–1955

By 1954, Morris as Controller of the Third Programme was acknowledging that increasing financial pressure on music output, as a consequence of the diversion of resources into television, was having its effect on Third Programme ambitions, and that 'the continuing need for economy has made it inadvisable for the Third Programme to embark upon any ambitious projects during the coming autumn and winter'.[xix] Morris also noted that 'a modest series of programmes devoted to contemporary German music, hitherto somewhat neglected, will also be broadcast'— arguably a level of attention to what was happening in the wider world which was overdue, but not necessarily something to set the pulses racing.

Elsewhere, the straitened times were producing a lack of ambition in the programmes. Output in 1954 was pretty conventional, the audiences consistently modest. The most popular programme of any classical music broadcast during the 1954 sample week was Anthony Hopkins introducing the BBC Northern Orchestra in *Music to Remember*, to which more than 1 million listeners tuned in for a not-too-challenging 45 min of Beethoven, Telemann, Wolf-Ferrari and Dvořák. This was the middle-brow, middle-taste and middle-class content which characterised Home Service music.

Across all the channels, the dominance of works by Beethoven and Mozart is very noticeable in the 1954 sample week. Twelve Beethoven works were performed, eight by Mozart; those apart, only Bach, Haydn and Schubert received multiple plays among the total of 69 composers represented in the schedules. Few of those composers were not readily recognisable by a middle-of-the-road British concert audience, and fewer still were themselves British, with only Elgar and Rawsthorne being felt worth a mention in the *Radio Times* review of the week's music.[xx] Yet 'serious' discourse continued to be concerned with the tastes of the elite. *The Listener* carried features on Bax, Hindemith and Schoenberg as well as on Dallapiccola, while the BBC broadcast in August a 'forgotten opera' by Spontini whose neglect was thought by *The Times'* critic to have been 'neither surprising nor mistaken'.[xxi] The growing disconnect between the taste of the broader audience and the aspiration of the providers of classical music radio was becoming increasingly hard to ignore.

By the start of 1955, mid-decade Britain was apparently comfortable in its post-war prosperity, and seemed disinclined to change much. Anthony Eden duly succeeded Winston Churchill, winning a General

Election in May which put the Conservatives more firmly in the policy seat. In the arts in Britain, the modern was the mainstream: Arthur Bliss—for two wartime years the BBC's Director of Music—was made Master of the Queen's Music and premiered a large-scale work for orchestra, *Meditation on a Theme of John Blow*. The British premiere of Samuel Beckett's *Waiting for Godot* was given in August at London's Arts Theatre. Such novelty however could be misleading. The nation was still dogged by 'complacency, parochialism and lack of serious structural change' (Marwick 1990: 81).

The Television Act had reached the statute book the previous year, with the first Independent Television (ITV) companies being appointed in October 1954 and beginning broadcasting in September 1955. Although its imminent arrival had already constrained radio budgets in 1955, the BBC had yet to understand the challenge to its self-referential approach, asserting in that year's *Handbook* that 'the BBC strives to discharge a threefold duty to music—that is, to the art itself, to this country's achievement in the art, and to those who practise it'.[xxii] There is nothing here about audiences, a point reinforced by Silvey's observation in the same issue that 'the size of audience is, on its own, by no means a complete indication of a broadcast's impact on the public'.[xxiii]

By 1955, hours of classical music output on the Third Programme were reduced—down from around 20 hours a week at the start of the decade to around 16 hours a week for the second half. This was part of the cost-cutting of radio in the face of the rise of television, and reflected the BBC's urgent need to combat ITV's success. That left the Home Service as the major provider of classical music, with a continuing contribution from the Light Programme. Yet even there, audience levels were surprisingly low, indeed often too low to be measured.[2] During the sample week, *Music Magazine* and a couple of other music feature programmes sit alongside otherwise unremarkable concert and record programmes. Most of the concerts seem rather routine: the BBCSO broadcast from Leeds Town Hall on Sunday for a little under an hour, the BBC Northern Orchestra an hour on Monday during the day and the BBC Scottish Orchestra *Music to Remember* on Monday evening.

---

[2] This is slightly distorted because the Daily Listening Barometer only uses whole percentage points for the Home Service and the Light Programme, but uses decimal points for the Third Programme where the audience otherwise would be mostly invisible.

The main concert for the week on the Home Service was the BBCSO from the Royal Festival Hall, conducted by Malcolm Sargent, starting with Bach and Bliss, and then devoting the second half to Sibelius.

The Third Programme equally seemed not to inspire listeners in any numbers. It offered two blockbuster operas: Smetana's *Dalibor* on Sunday, and Wagner's *Die Walküre* from Covent Garden on Saturday evening, the former attracting between 40,000 and 120,000 listeners, the latter finding an audience of around 40,000 for the second act but no measurable audiences for the first or third acts. Otherwise it was broadcasting mostly rather dull recitals. Even when, as on the sample Friday, Wilhelm Kempff played an attractive programme of Beethoven and Brahms, there was still no measurable audience. This seemed to be a channel now without a mission; there was certainly nothing which might attract or educate the uninformed listener. It has been convincingly suggested by Chignell that Morris, the station's Controller, 'didn't really believe in the Third' anyway.[xxiv] When questioned by the first Marriott Working Party, discussed below, Morris responded by saying that the Third Programme could be closed down because he had no control over the 'supply departments' and in particular over drama.

The Light Programme continued to offer classical music, with a daytime concert every weekday, featuring programmes from the mainstream broadcast canonic repertoire achieving respectable audience levels of around 400,000 listeners, but well below its appeal of earlier years. The great post-war renaissance of the BBC's classical music output had largely run out of steam, and had settled into a new and rather stale orthodoxy while new leisure pursuits arose and television gathered strength.

Reorganisation of Classical Music Radio 1956–1958

1956 was very much a pivotal year in the broader scheme of things. The Suez crisis in July, when 'the British people had been brought to the edge of an abyss' of division about the place of the UK in the wider world (Kyle 2011: 3), marked the start of an acknowledgement in sensible circles that Britain was now moving to a post-imperial state. The completion of the first phase of the introduction of ITV services in May confirmed the shift of attention and finance from radio to television and ushered in the new consumer society. In classical music radio, the dominant post-war idea that the BBC had a duty to lift the cultural tastes of its listeners, embodied in Haley's pyramid, was now open to challenge.

Lindsay Wellington had been Senior Controller of the Home Service for ten years from 1942, and took overall charge of BBC Radio from 1952 right up until 1963. He was surely unique among BBC 'suits' in being commemorated after his death at the end of 1984 in Alastair Cooke's *Letter from America*, a series he originally commissioned.[xxv] Wellington's radio counter-reformation began in July 1956. It was occasioned by the BBC's alarm over the inroads which ITV was making into its television audiences, and to radio listening to the Light Programme in the evenings, which reinforced the pre-existing intention to make economies in radio to fund competitive activities in television. It came about in an atmosphere where enthusiasm for Haley's pyramid of rising tastes had long since dissipated. And it was triggered by Richard D'Arcy Marriott, newly arrived from Northern Ireland to be Wellington's Chief Assistant and who was in Asa Briggs' opinion unsupportive of Haley's approach and 'had no sense of reverence' (Briggs 1995: 38).

'Future of Sound Broadcasting', a memorandum written by Marriott on 18 July 1956, set in motion a wholesale re-examination of the BBC's radio output, and a substantial challenge to the role and even existence of the Third Programme. Marriott's approach went very much with the grain of thinking in Jacob's BBC. By October, with the strong support of Wellington, a Working Party had been set up to consider how to cut costs and therefore the hours of radio broadcasting while at the same time giving the programmes greater popular appeal. This First Marriott Working Party (so-called to distinguish it from another related initiative in the late Sixties) reported in January 1957. It urged that sound broadcasting as a whole should be streamlined and that the hours of the Third Programme should be shortened significantly.

It was this latter proposal which attracted condemnation from the cultural elite, as discussed below, and has drawn most scholarly attention, but more significant was the effective end of the post-war *dirigiste* cultural ambitions. Marriott's report confirmed that the BBC had abandoned the underlying principle of Haley's cultural pyramid, and no longer expected to move listeners' taste and patronage from the ordinary to the exceptional.[xxvi] This is a key moment in the narrative. Marriott's central assertion consciously implied

> the rejection of an attitude that many of us have grown up with, about having a mission to educate, to up-lift, to lead people on to better things, to give them what we think they ought to want rather than what they do

want ... We ought to remember that about half the population consists of very simple people, with not very much education, who look to radio for their entertainment and relaxation (and who shall say that they are wrong?).[xxvii]

The proposals as a whole were largely endorsed by the Board of Management on 25 February 1957 and, despite every effort to keep them secret, they were leaked very quickly. The Cambridge social historian Peter Laslett brought together a group of luminaries from the elite with the purpose of defending 'their' radio channel, the Third Programme. Laslett's position was heavily tinged with irony. He was the historian who, more than any other at that time, pressed for scholars to address the activities, needs and stories of the mass of 'ordinary people', rather than just the elite few hundred at the top of society; yet he was also the leader and convenor of the Third Programme Defence Society, dedicated to protecting just that elite provision.

This was the mid-Fifties, and despite Laslett's embrace of the ordinary yeoman in his historical work, the argument was carried out through classic establishment channels. There were letters and statements to *The Times* and the *Manchester Guardian*, semi-private meetings at Broadcasting House and a booklet entitled *Unsound Broadcasting* published by T.S. Eliot.[xxviii] A deputation from what was now styled the Third Programme Defence Society, which met with the BBC's Deputy Chairman, included Laslett himself, Elliot, Ralph Vaughan Williams, Michael Tippett and Laurence Olivier. The story of the meetings and the intrigues, amply described by both Briggs (1995: 34–61) and Humphrey Carpenter (1997: 166–177), is fascinating in terms of institutional history but in truth had less impact in terms of the broadcasting of classical music than the *a priori* decision by Marriott and Wellington to abandon the thinking behind Haley's 'pyramid' of cultural taste.

The reorganisation of the BBC's radio services involved looking at the Home Service and Light Programme together, while allocating to the Third Programme 10% of radio hours. Despite that being disproportionately generous, by a factor of ten to one, given its relative audience size, the outraged reaction from the musical and cultural High Establishment revealed the entrenched elite.

Until the implementation of the new pattern in September 1957, classical music radio in 1956 and 1957 had continued largely unchanged, with its unexceptional character rather at odds with the turmoil behind the scenes. There were some strange programming decisions. The Third Programme broadcast different performances of Brahms' *Fourth Symphony* on Sunday and Monday of the sampled week, under the title *Composer and Interpreter*, going up against the major Home Service concert of the week. Marriott may well have had his eye on the continued failure of the Home Service *Morning Recital*, broadcast on weekdays, to achieve any measurable audience.

There was a levelling down in overall audience levels to classical music, with no broadcast in the 1957 sample week reaching more than 750,000 listeners and the Third Programme median falling to 0.1% of the total potential adult audience, or under 38,000. Over on the Home Service, the largest audience of the week was to a concert on Monday evening comprising only the César Franck *Symphony in D Minor*. On that channel on Sunday morning, *Music Magazine* reviewing Buxtehude and Joseph Marx was heard by 380,000 listeners, the same rating as the following *Your Concert Choice* with Ravel, Medina and Schoenberg. Yet a performance by the Philadelphia Orchestra of works by Wagner and Richard Strauss achieved no measurable audience. BBC classical music radio appeared to be drifting.

The eventual new pattern from September 1957 saw classical music banished from the Light Programme, slightly extended on the Home Service, and reduced but entrenched on the Third Programme. Using the Third Programme's frequencies in the early evening was a new service, Network 3, which combined coverage of a range of what might be termed 'leisure pursuits' in an uneasy melange of hobbies from bridge to pigeon-fancying, and what were supposed to be accessible cultural activities. It was derisively dubbed the 'fretwork network',[xxix] but it included some classical music-based material, including confirming a regular place for *Record Review*.

It was suggested at the time that Network 3 was introduced when the hours of broadcasting of the Third Programme were curtailed because 'the Corporation's conscience still demanded that something should be done to uphold its reputation as a source of "culture" as well as of entertainment'.[xxx] That does not seem to have been the view from inside the BBC where Controller of Sound Planning Rooney Pelletier wished to offer:

> 'good' but not necessarily 'serious' music. Nursery slope repertoire in impeccable performances. The 'brow' is somewhere between the best of light music and the most popular Prom. The afternoon would not have

the character I imagine for it unless it included good, familiar light music – waltzes by Strauss and Lehár, Edward German dances, operetta, etc. ... We are seeking to present – I must use a horrible phrase to make myself clear – 'familiar classics and near-classics'.[xxxi]

The entire process of reorganisation was an archetype for how the British Establishment dealt with such matters in the Fifties: the initial memorandum from Marriott; a Working Party established under Marriott's leadership by Wellington; proposals which were then leaked to and publicly challenged by the contemporary intellectual elite, gathered into the Third Programme Defence Society; leading to a new pattern of radio broadcasting, in which the 'nobs' turned out to have done rather well, after all.

The BBC asserted that the outcome represented 'better and more balanced radio programmes on a smaller budget'.[xxxii] The protesters regarded it as 'a disaster for sound broadcasting, a retreat on all fronts in the face of the advance of competitive television'.[xxxiii] What had really happened was the reassertion of elite intentions for the Third Programme (albeit on reduced hours) and the discarding of any significant mission to enhance popular appetite for classical music radio until the introduction of the Music Programme in August 1964. The removal of classical music from the Light Programme in daytime disenfranchised a potential audience of a million listeners or more, who were no longer going to stumble across this sort of output in an easily accessible radio environment, and for whom a tiny amount of such music on Network 3 was irrelevant. As for how the BBC might recover those who had been alienated by the elitist nature of the Third, Carpenter (1997: 170) observes 'nowhere was it suggested how this should be done'; arguably, because the elite in power saw no imbalance.

Much of the academic discourse about the affair has suggested that it was all about the Third Programme, and debates whether or not the changes were cultural 'vandalism', an accusation flung at the BBC by musical humourist Gerard Hoffnung.[xxxiv] However, other than from an institutional point of view, what is more significant about the outcome lies elsewhere. As Wellington was aware, the essence of the Working Party's argument was:

> that the Corporation's preoccupation with its cultural mission is wrong in principle and impracticable in a competitive world.[xxxv]

He preferred it to be expressed that the BBC:

> does not believe it right or sensible to try to dragoon taste, or compel it, by refraining from offering a straightforward programme of simple entertainment for those listeners – the majority of the community at any given time – who like and prefer it.

Either way, the BBC's acknowledgement that it was abandoning its previously embraced duty to lift the musical tastes of the whole of its audience was in effect the reassertion of the view that 'good' music was for the elite, and that the masses were better served by the pabulum of popular music.

It was not a new idea that such people had no right to be listening. These were the people who were 'unlikely to be able to meet [serious output] on equal terms'.[3] They were now to lose that opportunity. On the other hand, the high-brow elite—who had been so affronted by a reduction in the hours of output of the Third Programme—now had the guaranteed continued existence of their cultural radio channel until the end of the next decade. As Wellington wrote in the *Radio Times*, when the new pattern was launched:

> we are not 'fighting for the mass audience', but we do not forget that it is our responsibility to entertain as well as to inform and educate. We have been asked if we have abandoned our mission to educate and improve public taste. We see our task rather as to provide the opportunities for people to widen their experience and extend the range of their enjoyment ... in the belief that listeners are capable of choosing what they want.[xxxvi]

The 1958 sample week provides a good opportunity to consider what—after all that institutional turmoil and public argument—the new pattern for classical music output meant for the radio audience, and how they chose to exercise the choice which Wellington accorded to them.

The conclusion must be that they were unimpressed, not least by the overall reduction in classical music output to its lowest level since 1946. Listening to classical music on the Home Service (now by far the majority provider of the genre) failed to increase, with many programmes not registering a measurable audience, and only *Music to Remember* on

---

[3] See below p. 77.

Monday evening exceeding 400,000 listeners. Audiences to the Third Programme also remained static, while Network 3 made almost no impact at all on the music-listening public. Classical music had disappeared completely from the Light Programme, although the weekday *Concert Hour* shifted to the Home Service where it kept its audience numbers (although not necessarily the same listeners). The arrival of *Record Review* on Network 3 (Carpenter 1997: 182) did not compensate for the loss of hours on the Light Programme, although the new programme itself has remained a staple of the BBC's classical music radio offering until the present day.

Although the Home Service provided a respectable quantity of output, it did not become any sort of champion for popular appreciation of classical music. Efforts to expand the canonic repertoire meant that a few more British composers were featured, in what might be thought to be an act of appeasement to those who had lobbied against the BBC's changes. Although Elgar, Vaughan Williams and Walton barely got a look in, less celebrated composers (if it is fair to describe Ethel Smyth in that way) were scattered lightly through the schedules. On the sampled Thursday evening, the Home Service broadcast *Appointment with Music*, featuring living British composers, from Bliss to Ketelby and Torch. The following evening, *The Living Composer* featured works by Rawsthorne.

The Third Programme continued much along its usual track, albeit with fewer hours—around 13½ hours each week compared with 16½ the previous year. On the Saturday of the sample week, it linked with Finnish broadcasting to offer a joint concert of works by Sibelius, the first half from Helsinki, the second from London, and was rewarded by audiences of 115,000 and 150,000 for the two halves.

It may be argued that—the reduction of hours apart—the new arrangements served the demands of the elite while reducing provision for a mass, popular audience. Sunday on the Home Service offered Honegger's *King David* symphonic poem head-on in mid-afternoon. The high brow could continue to enjoy Bach cantatas and then quartets from Dvořák and Martinů one evening on the Third Programme, followed by a full Haydn opera the next. Those who might previously have stumbled upon the Light Programme *Concert Hour* would now have to make an appointment for destination listening on the Home Service.

There were some early examples of what would later become a more relaxed approach to radio programming. A Home Service feature, *The Story of the Proms*, was notable for playing one movement of Haydn's

'Surprise' Symphony, just the scherzo from Mendelssohn's *Midsummer Night's Dream* and generally looking much more like a modern sequence programme despite its purported purpose of 'tracing the development of this institution'.[xxxvii] The BBC ran a 'radio record week' from 11 to 17 May, although the elite touch immediately surfaced, with the *Radio Times* claiming that 'the record expresses, as Leopold Stokowski once predicted it would, the absolute soul and spirit of the music itself without any extraneous diversion'.[xxxviii]

Almost two decades since he wrote his essay on *The Symphony*, mentioned at the start of this chapter, would Theodor Adorno still have disagreed?

Changing the Guard

As the decade came to an end, there was something of a general changing of the classical music guard. The death of Ralph Vaughan Williams on 26 August 1959 was symbolic of a shift away from the post-war musical consensus. He had been a major figure in English music for the whole of the century so far, and he encapsulated 'a certain style, a certain place, and a certain time' (Pirie 1979: 213–214). Benjamin Britten was now not only the most admired modern British composer, but one who was changing the vocabulary of contemporary classical music in the UK. Nor was he now alone in this. The first performance at the Cheltenham Festival in July 1959 of Peter Maxwell Davies' *St Michael Sonata* for 17 wind instruments, introduced a composer who was to write a new kind of symphony. His contemporaries and friends at the Royal Manchester College of Music under Richard Hall were leaders of a new radical but not revolutionary style in British music. At this time also some more progressive composers began to receive a hearing in public concerts, including Elisabeth Lutyens and Alexander Goehr.

BBC classical music radio however was firmly in the grip of Wellington and Marriott's retrenchment. During the 1959 sample week there was not a single work from the Second Viennese School: no Schoenberg, Webern, Berg; and absolutely no *musique concrète*, no minimalism. The Home was now the majority provider of classical music radio and stolidly occupied the centre of the canonic repertoire. Much the same was true of what Alison Garnham has called Howgill's 'leaderless' Proms (Garnham 2007: 167).

In that sample week, the Home Service broadcast from the West of Ireland Music Festival on Wednesday evening a typical programme (in the sense of being firmly in the middle ground) of Wagner, Tchaikovsky, plus the first UK broadcast performance of Rimsky-Korsakov's orchestration of a work by Mussorgsky. There was little response in audience numbers, with listening continuing to decline, an impression confirmed by a BBC Audience Research decision to report tenths of a percentage point for the Home Service; previously, that had been done only for the Third Programme. The largest Home Service music audience for the week was Monday evening's *Music to Remember*, with just 1.5% of the adult audience for a concert of Liszt, Saint-Saëns and Falla given by the BBC Scottish Orchestra. One positive innovation was *Music at Night*, offered every evening for half an hour a little after 11 pm. These were original BBC recordings, again mostly of mainstream works, but their audience varied from not measurable to 0.1%.

The most striking feature of the Third Programme was the eighth in the series of Hans Keller's remarkable *Functional Analysis* programmes. These wordless programmes featured the performance of a musical score specially composed by Keller which was conceived as a discussion conducted only in music derived from an original, classical work. They were each a product of '[Keller's] instinct that music should be capable of being discovered in terms of itself, rather than through words' (Wood in Babbit et al. 1986: 401) and 'a most extraordinary (and probably rather un-English) creation' (Garnham 2003: 4). In one of a collection of 13 papers gathered together in *Music Analysis* as a Hans Keller Memorial in 1986, Alan Walker relates that the pianist Clifford Curzon studied Keller's 'Functional Analysis' of Beethoven's Piano Concerto in G Major. Having done that, he found that the original work and Keller's interpretation became so intermingled that he had difficulty separating them. 'Keller interpreted this episode as the best compliment that could possibly be offered to his scores' (Walker in Babbit et al. 1986: 396).

Otherwise, the Third Programme maintained a decent level of output and just about attracted a 'measurable' audience, but with the exception of Keller it was fairly unexciting, offering a wider range of contemporary composers than the Home Service but not going overboard about it. During the sample week, much was made of a series of concerts on Saturday evening starting with *Chamber Music of the Baroque*, moving on to Russian piano music and concluding with the Boccherini String Quartet. A BBCSO concert of Britten, Ravel, Prokofiev and von Essen represented the meat in the sandwich—although it was still only listened to by about 75,000 people.

3 THE FIFTIES: DEFENDING THE ELITE   89

There were already questions being asked about music on Network 3, which had taken the frequencies of the Third Programme in the early evening as part of the 1957 reorganisation. Marriot wrote to Wellington in January suggesting that:

> Network 3 had ... double the audience of the Third Programme a year before and, even now, is fractionally bigger than the Third Programme two years before. Nevertheless the drop is considerable and may well lead us to reconsider our plans for early evening broadcasting.[xxxix]

When challenged by Wellington that 'this is an area where size of audience, whether in itself or in comparison to another one, does not itself provide a conclusive answer',[xl] Marriott's reply was couched in terms of institutional tactics rather than audience needs:

> We have to keep firmly in mind that the Third Programme Defence Society's claims for the extension of Third Programme hours could only really be based on two things: that there is absolute value in the quantity of cultural and intellectual material broadcast, regardless of the time of day it goes out and who listens to it ... [and] that the potential audience is being deprived of the service that they really need at that time of day.[xli]

Classical music radio had not yet enjoyed its equivalent of the 'angry young men' who were reinventing literature and art, and during most of the Fifties it had been at the mercy of the conservatives and the anti-popularists. The risk of conceding dominance to the demands of the elite had not escaped Marriott, even though he was the commissioner of the new arrangements:

> It seems to me that we are, as so often is the case, tending to cater for the minority within a minority and that we are not doing enough for the middle range of the music public (which itself is well above the middle range of the general public). I mean specifically that we seem to be doing too much chamber music and difficult orchestral music in relation to the great well-known orchestral works which are undoubtedly what the majority of the music public want.[xlii]

In the autumn of 1959 William Glock took over as BBC Director of Music, as the next chapter will relate. He arrived at the end of a decade which had seen classical music radio decline from the high aspirations and achievements of the Forties, through a reorganisation of BBC radio which entailed the abandonment of earlier ambition, to a fairly workmanlike but mostly unexciting state. In that, it reflected the new conservatism of British society as a whole, as well as the reduction in budgets and attention for radio caused by the dominance of television. Classical music audience levels had fallen savagely, partly as a result of the competition for all radio from television and—with radio sets still lacking easy portability—from the growing range of other leisure opportunities. Programme planning had always been largely self-referential, but in the course of the Fifties—with the explicit abandonment of the socially redistributive role of the Third Programme—it became a matter dominated by the tastes of the cadre of radio producers. Those were not always for high-brow output, but they certainly did not allow much space for seeking to extend the popularity of this genre of music. The Fifties had been a time with few highlights for the mass audience, when only the demands of the elite received much attention. The Sixties were to change that eventually, by initiating a renewed experiment with popularity for classical music radio in the form of the Music Programme, while Glock set about redefining and then protecting the high brow.

Notes

i. *BBC Handbook* 1951, p. 12.
ii. BBC's New Music Chief. *Radio Times*, 12 May 1950, p. 14.
iii. C.B. Rees. Good luck, Sir Adrian ... Welcome, Sir Malcolm. *Radio Times*, 12 May 1950, p. 7.
iv. Memorandum from Director of Home Sound Broadcasting (Nicholls) to Controller Third Programme (Grisewood), 1 November 1951. BBC WAC R34/890/.
v. Long-Playing Records. *The Times*, 20 October 1950, p. 6.
vi. Orchestral Music. *The Times*, 23 December 1950, p. 9.
vii. *Radio Times*, 1 May 1953, p. 27.
viii. BBC Oral History. William Haley interviewed by Frank Gillard, 6 July 1976. BBC WAC R143/60/1.
ix. BBC Oral History. Ian Jacob interviewed by Frank Gillard, 6 July 1976. BBC WAC R143/3/1.
x. Ibid.
xi. *Radio Times*, 1 May 1953, p. 27.
xii. P.A. Scholes. Presenting Third Programme Music. *The Listener*, 2 April 1953, p. 564.

xiii. Memorandum from Controller Finance (Lochhead) to Deputy Head Sound Broadcasting (Wellington), 22 September 1953. BBC WAC R20/189.
xiv. *BBC Handbook* 1955, p. 132.
xv. The Third Programme, the size and character of its public. BBC Audience Research Department, 1 May 1953. BBC WAC R34/890/1.
xvi. Robert Silvey. The Third Programme and its market. *BBC Quarterly* Autumn 1953, vol. VIII, no. 3.
xvii. The Third Programme, the size and character of its public. BBC Audience Research Department, 1 May 1953. BBC WAC R34/890/1.
xviii. Robert Silvey. The Third Programme and its market. *BBC Quarterly* Autumn 1953, vol. VIII, no. 3.
xix. Third Programme; forthcoming plans for Autumn and Winter. Memorandum from Controller Third Programme (Morris) to Deputy Head Sound Broadcasting (Wellington), 13 August 1954. BBC WAC R34/890/1 and R9/13/99.
xx. *Radio Times* Music of the week, 30 April 1954, pp. 7–8.
xxi. A Forgotten Opera. *The Times*, 16 August 1954, p. 4.
xxii. *BBC Handbook* 1955, p. 60.
xxiii. *BBC Handbook* 1955, p. 42.
xxiv. Hugh Chignell, personal communication, 21 April 2017.
xxv. Letter from America, 18 January 1985. http://www.bbc.co.uk/programmes/p00ydpdq.
xxvi. Future of Sound Broadcasting. Memorandum from Director of Sound Broadcasting (Wellington) to Director General (Jacob), 18 October 1956. BBC WAC R34/1022/2.
xxvii. Memorandum from Assistant Director of Sound Broadcasting (Marriott) to Director of Sound Broadcasting (Wellington), July 1956. BBC WAC R34/1022/2.
xxviii. BBC hear plea for 'Third'. *The Times*, 19 July 1957, p. 6.
xxix. Our Radio Correspondent. Making 'Dates' On Network 3. *The Times*, 18 September 1957, p. 8.
xxx. How much does Network 3 matter? *The Times*, 14 October 1959, p. 4.
xxxi. Good music in Home Sound Broadcasting. Controller Programme Planning Sound (Pelletier) to Assistant Director of Sound Broadcasting (Marriott), 18 July 1957. BBC WAC R34/1035.
xxxii. Lindsay Wellington, Director of Sound Broadcasting. The New Pattern of Sound Broadcasting. *Radio Times*, 27 September 1957.
xxxiii. Retreat in face of television. *The Times*, 9 April 1957.
xxxiv. Letter from Gerard Hoffnung to Alexander Cadogan, BBC Chairman, 15 August 1957 (quoted in Carpenter and Doctor 1997: 158).

xxxv. Network 3 Listening Figures. Memorandum from Assistant Director of Sound Broadcasting (Marriott) to DSB (Wellington), 20 February 1959. BBC WAC R27/847/1.
xxxvi. Lindsay Wellington, Director of Sound Broadcasting. The New Pattern of Sound Broadcasting. *Radio Times*, 27 September 1957.
xxxvii. The story of the Proms. *Radio Times*, 2 May 1958, p. 32.
xxxviii. Supplement to *Radio Times*, 9 May 1958, front page.
xxxix. Network 3 Listening Figures. Memorandum from Assistant Director of Sound Broadcasting (Marriott) to DSB (Wellington), 20 February 1959. BBC WAC R27/847/1.
xl. Network 3 Listening Figures. Manuscript note on the memorandum [curiously, dated 19 February 1959, the day before the memorandum itself was dated]. BBC WAC R27/847/1.
xli. Network 3 Listening Figures. Memorandum from Assistant Director of Sound Broadcasting (Marriott) to DSB (Wellington), 20 February 1959. BBC WAC R27/847/1.
xlii. Music Output. Memorandum from Assistant Director of Sound Broadcasting (Marriott) to Director of Sound Broadcasting (Wellington), 15 January 1959. BBC WAC R27/847/1.

Bibliographic Sources

Adorno, T.W., and R. Leppert. 2002. *Essays on music: Theodor W. Adorno*. London: University of California Press.
Babbitt, M., S. Bradshaw, W. Glock, A. Goehr, M. Graubart, J. Harvey, et al. 1986. Hans Keller Memorial Symposium. *Music Analysis* 5 (2/3): 374–405.
Benjamin, W., and Underwood, J.A. 1936/2008. *The work of art in the age of mechanical reproduction*. London: Penguin.
Briggs, A. 1995. *The history of broadcasting in the United Kingdom, vol. 5, competition*. Oxford: Oxford University Press.
Carpenter, H., and J.R. Doctor. 1996. *The envy of the world: Fifty years of the BBC Third Programme and Radio 3, 1946–1996*. London: Weidenfeld & Nicolson.
Chignell, H. 2011. *Public issue radio: Talks, news and current affairs in the 20th century*. Basingstoke: Palgrave Macmillan.
Garnham, A. 2007. The BBC in possession. In *The Proms: A new history*, ed. N. Kenyon, J. Doctor, and D. Wright. London: Thames & Hudson.
Hennessy, P. 2006. *Having it so good: Britain in the fifties*. London: Allen Lane.
Kenyon, N. 1981. *The BBC Symphony Orchestra: The first fifty years 1930–1980*. London: British Broadcasting Corporation.
Kyle, K. 2011. *Suez: Britain's end of Empire in the Middle East*. Revised ed. London: I.B. Tauris.

Kynaston, D. 2009. *Family Britain, 1951–1957*. New York: Walker & Co.
Marwick, A. 1990. *British society since 1945*, 2nd ed. London: Penguin.
Pirie, P.J. 1979. *The English musical renaissance*. London: Gollancz.
Street, S. 2006. *Crossing the ether: British public service radio and commercial competition 1922–1945*. Eastleigh: John Libbey Publications.

CHAPTER 4

The Sixties: Simple and Conservative Tastes

Framing the Sixties—classical music radio in 1960—the impact of William Glock—classical music radio 1961–1964—the Music Programme—classical music radio in 1965—classical music radio 1966–1969—'Broadcasting in the Seventies'.

The Sixties were regarded at the time and since as a fabled decade, although they also included the days when—in the Cuban missile crisis of 1962—the world came closest yet to nuclear annihilation. These years were characterised by a revolution in popular cultural attitudes and social mores. For classical music radio, the narrative shows a determined effort by a reinvigorated BBC to reawaken widespread interest in classical music radio, just when offshore pirate radio was snatching away patronage of broadcast popular music. Until the management consultant-inspired changes set out in *Broadcasting in the Seventies*, classical music radio found itself on the crest of a new wave. In particular, the multi-channel pattern of output across BBC radio which accompanied the introduction of the Music Programme in the second half of the decade is the second high-water mark in the provision of accessible and classless classical music radio in the UK, which blended the high-brow with the popular.

Framing the Sixties

For the metropolitan sector of British society, and those younger people who were newly commercially empowered, the intense years from the middle Sixties until the early Seventies came to be seen as a time of popular cultural ferment, in which transistor radios, the beat poets, the contraceptive pill and the *Lady Chatterley* trial were all factors in, or symptoms of, social change. On the other hand, life as lived across most of the country was rather different from that, especially in provincial towns and the countryside. As Dominic Sandbrook notes, 'many of the best-known changes in the period, like the growth of television, the introduction of the mini-skirt or the development of the pill, provoked considerable unease or anger in some sections of the population' (2007: xvii).

Arthur Marwick (1998: 16–20) identifies a 'cultural revolution', discernible through the formation of new sub-cultures and movements; innovative entrepreneurialism; what he describes as the 'unprecedented influence of young people'; technological change, especially in broadcasting; the emerging dominance of 'spectacle' in entertainment; internationalism in youth culture; substantial improvements in material standards of living; major changes in attitudes to race and class, and in family relationships; 'permissiveness' in sexual matters; changes in fashion for clothing and personal presentation; a new popular culture, centred on rock music; the continuing liberal consensus contrasted with some extreme conservative reaction; concerns for personal rights; the advent of multiculturalism; and what he considers were 'original and striking (and sometimes absurd)' developments in elite thought.

There is a broader political perspective as well. Peter Hennessey regards 1960 as the 'moment that marked a change of period in British History'. He argues that in the first six months of the year, the combination of Prime Minister Macmillan's 'Wind of Change' speech, announcing the effective end of the British Empire, the collapse of the summit talks in Paris in May between Khrushchev, Eisenhower, de Gaulle and Macmillan, and the British Government's acceptance that it could no longer stand alone as a nuclear power, came together to 'illustrate a proud old political society on a tilt' (Hennessey 2006: 620).

For radio, the start of permanent stereophonic broadcasting in 1966 was a significant vindication of the growing importance of VHF transmission, but it was the introduction of the transistor that meant that during the Sixties radio was suddenly in its (then) modern state: portable, personal, freed from electrical supply wires. That was to be the dominant characteristic of radio until the full impact of digital and internet platforms began to be felt in the first and second decades of the twenty-first century.

Rock 'n' roll came to Nashville in 1956, and found its way to Britain with increasing impact as the Sixties began. The attempts of the BBC to keep it 'at arms length' (Barnard 1989: 38), set up a stand-off between the aspirations of the newly commercially enfranchised teenage cohort and those who saw themselves as guardians of the heritage of British radio, and the resulting dialectic was a driving force in radio broadcasting as a whole in the Sixties (and for much of the rest of the century). The most obvious manifestation of that stand-off was the brief three-year phenomenon when offshore pirate radio stations flourished without being directly illegal. They triggered—or, more probably, coincided with other forces that would anyway have produced—a resurgence in radio in the UK. Between 1964 and 1967, the offshore pirate stations demonstrated that radio could once again attract audiences of many millions, and that the medium could appeal to the newly enriched younger generation (Street 2006: 202–203). I have written elsewhere that 'for the mass audience of British teenagers ... it was the "top 40" sounds of the offshore stations ... which were the true sounds of their lives for those three years, and which created an expectation of what ought to be provided by legitimate stations' (Stoller 2010: 19).

There were winds of change, too, in English classical musical life, although the experimentation of rock music found only a few echoes in the classical music world, possibly because that had already undergone the genuine radical reappraisal of the early Darmstadt years. The effect on it of the tsunami of pop and rock music was chiefly to render classical music a minority taste even for most experimental musicians. Composers from the Royal Manchester College of Music—including Peter Maxwell Davies, Harrison Birtwistle and Alexander Goehr, together with pianist John Ogden—were beginning to make their mark, and there were hearings as well for progressive composers such as Thea Musgrave, Iain Hamilton and Humphrey Searle among others. The names of American and Continental avant-garde composers such as Stockhausen, Henze, Dallapiccola, Copland, Barber, Ives, Lutosławski and Penderecki started to become more familiar to UK concert audiences (Pirie 1979: 218), but they were often ill suited to radio. Contemporary classical music in the West as a whole had embraced modernist expressionism in the Forties and Fifties, followed in the Sixties by minimalism. Developed in both the visual arts and music as a reaction to the expressionism of the post-war years, and prizing objectivity rather than subjectivity, it offered little which was easy for radio to broadcast.

BBC classical music arrangements, although largely unaffected by the offshore pirates, had their own revolution with the arrival in the autumn of 1959 of William Glock as BBC Controller of Music. That nearly did not happen. The retiring Controller, Robert Howgill, wanted Glock to succeed him, and it seems that Glock was first approached about the job as early as March 1958 (Carpenter and Doctor 1996: 193). The BBC had delayed, however, and by the middle of 1959 Glock was on the point of being appointed as Principal of the Guildhall School of Music. At the last moment, partly on the advice of Michael Tippett, he declined to appear for a final interview at the Guildhall, and took the BBC job instead (Kenyon 1981: 290). Given that in these years popular music, and to a large degree popular culture generally, was dominated by transatlantic influences, it is significant that Glock substantially—and his sometime lieutenant, Hans Keller overwhelmingly—were themselves influenced more by European contemporary music than by American ultra-modernism.

CLASSICAL MUSIC RADIO IN 1960

In 1960, the BBC's classical music output was still relatively conservative. The Home Service remained the dominant provider, not just in terms of hours offered but also in consistency of accessible output. Much of the provision was firmly middle-brow. Sunday's Home Service programmes in the sample week in May 1960, for example, offered works by Handel, Mozart, Gounod, Bizet, Schumann, Haydn, Stravinsky, Nielsen, Smetana, Mozart and Bach, with only John Riviez managing a look-in from the fringes. On the Wednesday of the sample week, it broadcast the whole of Beethoven's *Fidelio* (rather incongruously broken by the *Nine O'Clock News*) from Sadler's Wells, supported by a *Radio Times* feature. Home Service concerts in general—and there were eleven of them during a week—almost always came in at less than one hour. Other musical programmes were usually around half an hour. Against this background, it is easy to understand why the idea of a continuous service of good music was to gain currency. There is a hint of things to come on the Saturday afternoon on Network 3. This was a two-hour programme

Music of the Masters, which was a BBC recorded concert featuring works from the mainstream classical canon.

The Third Programme still demonstrated its belief that it was catering for listeners of a level of musical education and discernment which would have been highly exclusive. *The Innocent Ear* comprised works broadcast without their title or composer being given in advance, challenging listeners to identify them:

> What a humbling experience is a guessing game called The Innocent Ear ... the four composers of last week's programme were Arne, Roussel, Schoenberg and Bax, and anyone [*sic*] might feel reasonably sure of spotting their distinctive styles. In fact you are not likely to unless you happen to know the work itself which presents an unusual and little-known view of the composer.[i]

The Third Programme could still seek to educate the high brow on occasions, but it was failing to address a wider public. To take one example: Hans Keller wrote brilliantly about *Schoenberg and the String Quartet* in *The Listener* ahead of a broadcast on the Third Programme on 27 April 1960,[ii] yet the programme itself received little audience support. Of the Third Programme's 16 hours of classical music output in the sample week, an hour and a half of those comprised a feature about Berlioz's opera *The Trojans* in *Birth of an Opera* on Monday. The opera itself then took up fully five and a half hours on Tuesday, in a relay of from Covent Garden. Yet the opera never reached more than 47,000 people at any one time, and there was no measurable audience for the previous day's feature.

The BBC continued to assert that it took its classical music very seriously, and to cross the line into self-satisfaction:

> No other organisation can compare with it in range of repertory. At the same time, the infinity of possible programmes is a tremendous challenge; a constant effort is made to ensure that only vital works, both past and present, shall be performed and, equally, that the standards of performance shall maintain a high level.[iii]

Overall, audience figures for the sample week in 1960, while reflecting what seemed to be the inevitability of smaller audiences for radio as television asserted itself, show the potential of reasonable audiences for approachable works, even those which are relatively challenging. *Fidelio* on the Home Service on Wednesday evening achieved the highest audiences for classical music during that week, not far short of 500,000. But the median audience across the Third Programme was just 50,000, the highest 100,000.

The Impact of William Glock

The Fifties had ended, as it were, with music radio's equivalent of Castro's almost simultaneous overthrow of Batista in Cuba, what Paul Kildea has called Glock's 'cultural *coup d'état*' (in Doctor, ed. 2007: 21). Glock was already a noted music critic and administrator. He had arrived from a spell as Director of the Dartington International Summer School—which he had founded—with the intention of starting 'a wide-ranging revolution in BBC music ... involving the revitalisation of music programmes, of the public concerts given by the BBC, and of the Symphony Orchestra' (Kenyon 1981: 291).

But if the impact of Glock on the BBC orchestras and on the Proms was indeed 'revolutionary' as Kildea asserts, for the generality of radio's music output the situation is less clear-cut. He was swiftly able to encourage a wider selection base for music, allowing more contemporary music through the net. The orchestral changes also had a knock-on effect on programme content, but Glock's influence on routine programme output was less draconian.

There are two contrasting views about Glock in this respect. Composer and music academic Alexander Goehr felt that Glock 'devoted all his attention to the Proms, the invitation concerts, and the BBCSO, leaving his staff to get on with the rest of the programmes without interference'.[iv] Critic and academic David Wright argued, on the other hand, that Glock was:

> the sole redeemer of an outdated and fusty department, the rejuvenator of broadcast music in Great Britain, without a wart in sight. (2010: 51)[v]

In reality, the institutional politics of the BBC meant that the Controller of Music was in constant 'dialogue' with the Controller of the Third Programme, and Glock's real impact was to ensure that, within the political maelstrom of the BBC, individual producers were given scope to commission performances and recordings and to make programmes. Leo Black, in his memoir of his time as a Third Programme producer, believes that this was the key to both the achievement and problems of BBC classical music output in the Sixties:

> The music output of Home and Third, as later of Radio 3, depended on the initiative and energy and knowledge of producers given every encouragement by line managers ... Which in turn brought out the balanced output in the profoundest sense, that of representing everything worthwhile and not merely what each individual producer thought worthwhile. (2010: 51–52)

Julian Lloyd Webber, by contrast, took the view that under the influence of Glock 'classical music turned its back on audiences and shot itself in the foot'.[vi]

Glock undoubtedly influenced the climate within BBC music radio as a whole. His championing of European modernism within the BBC was seminal, and its impact on the various set piece broadcasts and concerts was profound and wide ranging. The opening up of BBC radio to modern and European composers was overdue, and if it was led by his programming of the Proms and his championing of composers and conductors such as Pierre Boulez, it was still necessary and timely. Even so, Glock's early preoccupation with the Proms—and his real impact there and on the BBCSO too—was to an extent achieved by letting routine radio output alone, to the detriment of potentially vastly more listeners. As discussed earlier,[1] there is danger in allocating disproportionate significance and attention to the Proms.

CLASSICAL MUSIC RADIO 1961–1964

Early in 1961—before the arrival of the Music Programme—there were four clear strands of classical music output on BBC radio, not quite coinciding with the institutional arrangements:

- the Home Service, attracting significantly larger audiences than the Third Programme, offering mainly workaday programming with the occasional special concert;
- featured programmes on the Third Programme, often major concert major relays of opera performances, promoted in the *Radio Times* and covered in *The Listener* but hardly attracting an audience;

---

[1] See Introduction (Chap. 1), p. 9.

- more eclectic output, representing a small proportion even of the Third Programme's music time but attracting disproportionate coverage in *The Listener*; and
- a little popular classical output on the Light Programme and educative efforts on Network 3.

Classical music had returned to the Light Programme for one hour on Saturday evenings in 1961, with *Saturday Concert Hall*; and there was a short stereophonic experiment broadcast between Network 3 and BBC Television. Otherwise during the 1961 sample week, the Home Service continued to make the running, with *Music to Remember* on Tuesday evening attracting the largest classical music audience of the week. Sundays on the Home Service were particularly successful in audience terms, with *Music Magazine*, *Your Concert Choice* and the *Sunday Symphony Concert* each attracting three times as many listeners as the most popular programme on the Third Programme all week. Audiences for the Third Programme were by now very disappointing. They never reached 100,000, while there was no measurable audience at all for classical music on Thursday evening on the Third Programme, despite the *Thursday Invitation Concert* featuring the Amadeus String Quartet.

Some impact of Glock's greater openness to modernism was beginning to be felt during 1961 in terms of what was on offer to listeners. Contemporary British composers were heard in a song recital on Monday evening on the Third Programme: Thea Musgrave and Richard Rodney Bennett along with Schoenberg and Dallapiccola. A concert from Berlin on Sunday evening included Henze and Hartmann alongside Stravinsky and Britten (with Peter Pears singing Britten's *Nocturne*). A motet by Anton Heiller completed the evening.

Audiences might be absent, but the BBC Governors were impressed. At their Board meeting on 27 April 1961 they 'considered that Mr. Glock's contribution on music was highly encouraging' although one Governor:

> suggested that the policy, which had been successful last year, was right but it should not go too far in the way of excluding works which were very familiar to old people but which came fresh to each generation of young listeners.[vii]

There were by now some evident stirrings of interest in addressing the middle market in new ways. Rooney Pelletier, who had been appointed Controller of Programme Planning (Sound) after an earlier stint as

Controller of the Light Programme, rehearsed in January 1961 the possibility of an evening slot on Network 3 being given over to 'orchestral music of the Prom type'.[viii] He expressed a general wish 'to increase the amount of orchestral music broadcast in the daytime if possible'. It is reasonable to see this as illustrating the general thinking which was to lead to the institution of the new daytime channel, the Music Programme, later in the decade, which in turn owed something to the success of popular classical music on the Light Programme in earlier years.

While the Cuban missile crisis raged, and—appropriately—Britten's *War Requiem* received its first performance in Coventry Cathedral, such of the BBC's attention in 1962 as could be spared from the new television sensation of *That Was The Week That Was* turned to introducing a daytime radio service of 'good music'. The Pilkington Committee, which had been set up by the Macmillan Government in 1960 to consider the future of broadcasting, reported in June 1962. It recommended colour television and a second BBC TV channel and dismissed the prospect of commercial competition to the BBC in radio, but it allowed the BBC to float the idea for what was to become the Music Programme in 1964.[ix]

Meanwhile, if the years between 1960 and 1962 represented the time when Glock was 'testing the waters' at the Proms as David Wright describes (in Doctor, ed., 2007: 178), for radio output as a whole they were unremarkable. Indeed, BBC radio was now being sidelined even in respect of broadcasting classical music. The dominant classical musical broadcast in November 1962 was Ken Russell's film about Elgar, in the BBC TV *Monitor* series. This was ground-breaking, almost epic broadcasting which resonates to this day. It could have been matched by equivalent genuine popular exposure of the high art of music on the radio, but it was not. A different response was to come in the form of a new radio service of accessible classical music through the daytime, but not until the end of the following year.

There were two obvious destination programmes during the 1962 sample week. The only opera was von Einem's *Dantons Tod* relayed from Germany with support from Norddeutscher Rundfunk (NDR) on the Third Programme through Sunday evening. The *Radio Times* was at pains to point out that although the composer:

> was born as recently as 1918 his music is not 'modern' in the currently accepted sense. His score is liberally sprinkled with accidentals but not atonal. Nobody who enjoys Richard Strauss and Mahler need shy away from Dantons Tod.[x]

Listeners took the publication at its word, with an unusually high 100,000 audience which carried across to a BBC recording of the Dartington String Quartet playing Schubert and Haydn later in the evening.

Bach's *B Minor Mass* broadcast on Monday evening on the Third Programme did even better, with nearly 200,000 people listening to the cream of English soloists, singers and chamber players. The major Home Service offering was a BBCSO concert on Wednesday evening, which drew 250,000 listeners to a choral concert of works by Gabrieli, Mozart and Kodály. *Concert Hour* consistently attracted this level of audience for mainstream works, even though it was deprived of a regular slot and jumped around the schedules.

Frank Gillard, who had returned from being an outstanding war correspondent to build a management career initially in BBC regional radio, became Director of Sound Broadcasting in 1963, and the scene was set for change in BBC radio. 1963 was in the centre of Glock's 're-invention' of the Proms (Wright in Doctor, ed., 2007: 168) but not yet of the democratisation of the radio output. Elsewhere in Britain, change was happening, not just prefigured: the National Theatre opened, John Robinson wrote *Honest to God* and E.P. Thompson published *The Making of the English Working Class*. For radio, the patterns of the early Sixties continued into 1963, with the balance of power shifting still further away from the Third Programme towards the Home Service in terms of classical music output.

With a few exceptions, the Third Programme was generally having a hard time attracting listeners. The sample week's seemingly most spectacular offering, Verdi's *Macbeth*, in an Italian recording supplied by Radiotelevisione Italiana to the Third Programme on Sunday, attracted no measurable audience. Friday evening's cycle of works by Beethoven, Ravel and Webern recorded no listening, but then nor did any of the programmes broadcast across that entire evening on the Third Programme or on Network 3. It requires a particular view of the nature of a public good to see this failure to attract an audience as valid public service use of a broadcasting frequency. For a few people in the Fellows' Dining Rooms at Balliol or All Souls—for whom Harold Nicholson had thought the Third Programme was intended[2]—Val Gielgud's production of Sophocles' *Electra* no doubt seemed deeply worthwhile, as did the reflections of the foreign editor of the *Economist* on the Moscow-Peking

---

[2] See Chap. 2, p. 59.

schism which followed the short music programme. This was 1963, when the Sixties 'revolution' was about to break out and reach a new, youthful population. But not, it seems, on the BBC Third Programme.

1964 was the pivotal year for radio in many ways. The launch of Radio Caroline in April 1964 changed the game for popular radio. In a vaguely analogous move, the BBC introduced a brand new service, the Music Programme, during daytime on the frequencies of the Third Programme, an 'almost continuous service of good music' in the phraseology of the Marriott Working Party report in 1959.[xi] There may be no direct causal linkage between the changes in popular radio and classical music radio, but the social, cultural, political and economic forces of the Sixties worked in different but comparable ways across the whole cultural field in the UK. Director of Sound Broadcasting Gillard acknowledged in a lecture in 1964 that radio could not remain as it had been before the '"almost fully arrived" television age'.[xii] It was by now abundantly clear that the pattern of musical offerings between the Home Service, the Light Programme, the Third Programme and Network 3 still needed sorting out, despite the attempts of 1957 to do just that.

The Music Programme

It was therefore more than time for the reinvigoration of classical music output. Consequently—20 years after the process was begun to provide a cultural channel in the post-war settlement, the Third Programme, and a decade after the abandonment of Hayley's pyramidal approach to elevating listener taste—the BBC launched the Music Programme in August 1964. This was a dedicated daytime service of serious music, serving the identifiable but for too long largely ignored middle-market appetite for the type of music which the Third Programme had steadily abandoned, within a single channel rather than part of mixed programming output.

The genesis of the Music Programme is traced back by Carpenter (1996: 222) to the perception of senior management in 1959 that the introduction of Network 3 in September 1957 had been a failure. However, Marriott had already floated the notion with Wellington in 1956 at the start of that review process.[xiii] Marriott is arguably as convincing a candidate as Glock as the most significant figure in late Fifties and Sixties classical music radio, being involved at this point and then again in at the end of the decade ahead of *Broadcasting in the Seventies*.

A good part of the institutional impetus towards change came from Marriott's dissatisfaction with the serious music output well before 1959. He had been on the receiving end, for example, of complaints from the Music Department about the planning of classical music on the Home Service in the middle of 1957, with evidence that this major channel was going its own way irrespective of 'pleas for regular relays of standard opera', and that it showed 'a reluctance to accommodate chamber music'.[xiv]

Marriott's response had been to press for the relatively popular rather than concede to the elite. He asked that:

> there should be every day in the best listening time, at sometime between 7 and 10 pm, a concert of good music which is primarily orchestral in character ... There is no doubt that orchestral music is more popular than chamber music and recitals among the general public that takes pleasure in good music[xv]

although this was an approach greeted unenthusiastically by the Music Department of the time.[xvi] It is reasonable to infer that Marriott had this type of exchange and dissatisfaction in mind, when framing his 1959 memorandum to Wellington (discussed in the previous chapter):

> I am somewhat worried by the nature of our music output but before pursuing the matter further with those concerned, I would be grateful for any advice you can give from your greater personal knowledge of the subject. It seems to me that we are, as so often is the case, tending to cater for the minority within a minority and that we are not doing enough for the middle range of the music public. (which itself is well above the middle range of the general public)[xvii]

The end of the second quoted sentence might serve as a draft manifesto for the Music Programme. At that stage, Marriott was careful not to propose any substantial change in the institutional arrangements, but the Area and Local Broadcasting Committee (which Marriott chaired) recommended that the unoccupied daytime frequencies used for the Third Programme and Network 3 should carry 'throughout the daytime an almost continuous service of good music'.[xviii]

Humphrey Carpenter asserts (1996: 225) that Glock was privately dubious about the idea of the Music Programme. Glock indeed recalled some twenty years later that he had 'in the back of one's mind ... the danger of musical wallpaper', but even then his actual recollection when interviewed by Gillard in March 1983 as part of the Oral History of the BBC, was much more nuanced:

> I felt two things about it, one really reminding me of criticisms by people like Benjamin Britten that one shouldn't be able to hear the B minor Mass on 3 July, or any time, or St Matthew Passion say would be a better example, but one must go at Easter time and it should be the right occasion and the only occasion. And the other of WH Auden that we've become a society of consumers. Consumers who really didn't take things in any more than we took in the newspapers, in other words by the next day even the greatest things had been forgotten. There is that uncomfortable feeling in the back of one's mind and I shared it a little bit and called it the danger of musical wallpaper. On the other hand it gave the listener the chance to experience an entirely new kind of programme, a new kind of musical succession.[xix]

Writing in 1963, however, as the Music Programme was gearing up towards its launch, Glock had seemed unequivocal in his support:

> [the Music Programme] will certainly double our output and just as certainly confront us with a tremendous challenge to whatever resourcefulness we may possess ... It is an exciting prospect that lies ahead, a prospect not without its dangers, including that of musical saturation. But whatever else may happen, there is one thing we intend to maintain; and that is liveliness.[xx]

In helping the station to get started, Glock was unswayed by Benjamin Britten's plea when speaking at Aspen, Colorado, in 1964 that using classical music as a background accompaniment to daily tasks was 'a devaluation of the currency of sublime art'.[xxi]

The BBC had proposed to the Pilkington Committee in February 1961 that it should use the frequencies of the Third Programme for classical music during the daytime, and the Committee had noted the scheme and concluded in June 1962 that it should be allowed to go ahead.[xxii] Wellington and Marriott could now plan what was very much their programme idea, rather than that of either Glock or of the Controller of the Third Programme, the novelist Howard Newby (who was to rise from being a radio producer to become Managing Director Radio in 1976).

As Glock himself recalled in his interview with Gillard 20 years later, the Music Programme was from the beginning an example of the commodification of classical music radio.[xxiii] Reflecting on a name for the new service, Pelletier was even driven to talk about 'the core of the brand image' and although Marriott was sceptical about the idea that an advertising agency might be involved,[xxiv] they were both addressing a new relationship between producer and consumer, characteristic of Sixties broadcasting.

As they moved closer to the point when the Music Programme would happen, BBC reflections on its purpose are revealing in their historical context, but also in how the new service offered an opportunity to rethink that relationship between producer and consumer. Controller of the Home Service Ronald Lewin believed that:

> the appeal of the Music Programme should be to the 'general listener' with genuine but not necessarily highly sophisticated musical interests who will welcome the opportunity of a service which provides him, from morning to evening, with a continuous alternative to Home and Light. It is not a service intended to cater simply or even primarily for the listener with a specialised sophisticated musical taste ... We must recognise that the greater part of the time we should be providing background music, and that the majority of our listeners will be those who prefer good music as a background rather than pop music or speech.[xxv]

Negotiations with the Musicians' Union (MU) to secure more 'needletime'—the term for the amount of commercially recorded music a radio station is licensed to play—continued until the summer of 1964, so that the new Music Programme was not able to launch until the end of August that year, initially on Sundays only. The issue of needletime was central to the success of the Music Programme. Glock believed that 50% of the programme output needed to come from gramophone records to ensure a sustained quality of output,[xxvi] although analysis demonstrates that figure was never even closely approached once the station went on air. The eventual agreement, reported in *Music and Musicians*, was that 'in return for an increase in needletime, the BBC would maintain its house orchestras "for the foreseeable future"' (quoted in Carpenter 1996: 227). This was part of the general understanding between the BBC and the MU which Aubrey Singer was to rip apart in 1980.[3]

---

[3] See Chap. 6, pp. 158ff.

4 THE SIXTIES: SIMPLE AND CONSERVATIVE TASTES   109

As negotiations with the MU dragged on, BBC management sought the support of the Central Music Advisory Committee, and in doing so set out the broader public benefits which they argued it would bring:

> A regular Music Programme devoted wholly to good music – including good light music – would be an important development in itself which would in the course of time attract many new adherents to music and must render great service to the art and practice of music.[xxvii]

This was to be a familiar argument in the early years of Classic FM, that bringing people to classical music through its more accessible aspects would in time enhance public appreciation of serious music as a whole. Arguably, the Music Programme—like Haley's pyramid before it, and the aspirational stage of Classic FM after it—was not given enough time to validate these claims. However, it reveals a wish to spread the understanding and appreciation of culture beyond the *cognoscenti*, and as such reflects a Sixties attitude which—Haley apart—had not been much in evidence in the BBC's approach to classical music radio hitherto.

Even the approach to presentation was to be different. Rather than typical formality, it was agreed that:

> the object of the presentation is to add to the enjoyment and understanding of listeners ... the personal contribution of the announcer is needed to create a relaxed and friendly presentation which is essential if we are to involve a distinctive Music Programme style and avoid the 'awed' approach.[xxviii]

Here again is a ground-breaking shift in the relationship between the BBC and its listeners, as mediated through the presentation staff, who were even urged to include back-announcements because 'it is expected that people will be tuning into this new programme throughout the day. Many are bound to do so while music is being played'.

Gillard was forthright in demanding that the Music Programme 'should not be regarded as a channel for new, difficult and advanced music', on the grounds that it had to attract a decent size of audience. Gillard endorsed Marriott's view that:

> we shall have to keep firmly in mind that the majority of the potential audience for [the Music Programme] are music lovers with fairly *simple*

and conservative tastes [my italics], and that our first task is to attract and build up an audience for this new programme venture.^xxix

As a way of ensuring that, the Chief Assistant who planned and then took responsibility for the Music Programme—John Manduell—reported to the Controller of the Home Service and not the Third Programme, in order 'to keep the service firmly in the "middlebrow" range' (Garnham 2003: 84). Manduell (2016: 101) recalls receiving a memo from Gillard saying 'no Bartok before breakfast', which catches the BBC's intentions nicely.[4]

Manduell's working definition for the Music Programme was that it would offer:

> music capable of affording a degree of aesthetic satisfaction [which was] interpreted as excluding popular music which can only be regarded as entertainment music in the commercial sense but including a wide range of music composition that can legitimately be regarded as stemming from a genuinely artistic impulse.^xxx

That allowed the Music Programme to include jazz, brass band music and operetta as well as chamber music, orchestral music and opera. However, he also recalls that although:

> there had been comfortable expectations in certain quarters that we would only broadcast 'agreeable' music which people could enjoy without undue effort. Naturally within BBC Music Division such limited assumptions were resolutely contested. (Manduell 2016: 101)

The Music Programme came on air in three phases: from 30 August 1964, just on Sundays; from 12 December 1964, extending to weekdays from 8 am to 2 pm, and Saturdays up to the start of sports coverage usually at 12.30 am; and then from 20 March 1965 with the weekday hours increased to run from 7 am to 6.30 pm, when *Study Session* retained some elements of the old Network 3 until the Third Programme itself began at 7 pm. It absorbed a number of programmes from the Home

---

[4] The phrase provided Manduell with a title for his memoirs. *No Bartok before Breakfast* published in 2016 goes some way towards making up for the unavailability of the interview conducted with him for the BBC's Oral History project.

Service—the *Sunday Symphony Concert, Music Magazine, Your Concert Choice* and *Talking About Music*. The intention was to find 'various ways in which the expansion in our music broadcasting can assist and strengthen the general position of music and the musician in this country'. Alongside material provided by European broadcasting organisations, plus of course the new needletime allowance, Manduell was confident of 'the successful execution of this whole vast project'.[xxxi] The BBC's efforts to bring the new service 'to the attention of the music-loving public' focussed on competitions in Cardiff (for Mozart piano performances) and at Dartington (works by Beethoven), plus a series of mini-festivals starting at Cambridge University (Manduell 2016: 102–103).

What was offered even on the first Sunday morning was revelatory for classical music radio. Throughout the morning, the Music Programme provided the envisaged continuous service of serious music, beginning with a sequence programme entitled *What's New* and moving through a mixture of gramophone records and original recordings. The popular daytime service ranged from Gluck to Handel, Haydn to Bach and Mozart to Verdi and Vaughan Williams. Although consciously accessible, this was not to be a soft touch, with a short Puccini opera, *Gianni Schicchi*, filling the middle of the following Sunday morning, an approach followed on subsequent Sundays with *Pagliacci* and then the *Barber of Seville*. The show was on the road, and can be considered in its full form in 1965.

The Music Programme would provide a pattern for the decisive shift to genre radio across BBC national services as a whole at the end of the decade. It was one critical part (and in audience terms by far the largest) of how Radio 3 was to be put together following *Broadcasting in the Seventies*. It was the legitimate parent of the recast Radio 3, which Nicholas Kenyon developed in the early Nineties, and arguably also the begetter of Classic FM—albeit on the wrong side of the blanket. Classical music radio as we understand it today in the UK is in a direct line from the Music Programme between 1964 and 1970.

Classical Music Radio in 1965

Whether you came from the intellectual elite or the broad middle brow—or even, however counter-intuitive for the BBC, from among those uneducated in the genre—1965 was a good year to be a consumer of classical music on the radio. It represents one of those peaks—along with the late Forties and the early Nineties—when the range, quantity and accessibility of classical music radio demonstrated what could be done if everyone and everything came together in a positive symbiosis. For the first time on UK radio, it was possible to listen to classical music radio virtually all day long, between the Home Service, Third Programme and Music Programme. In the 1965 sample week that meant on Sunday all the way from 8 am until 11.30 pm, apart from 30 minutes early evening and an hour and 20 minutes mid-evening. On weekdays, classical music was on offer from 7 am until the Study Session began at 6.30 pm. It resumed with the Third Programme at 7.30 pm together with not inconsiderable Home Service output in the evening. On Saturdays, there was classical music from 8 am to 11.40 pm, interrupted only by sports coverage in the afternoon before the Home Service *Music of the Masters* concert came to the rescue at 4.30 pm.

The Music Programme was meeting its brief to be accessible but not slight. On Monday of the sample week in 1965, for example, it opened with *Overture*, with records of Scarlatti, Gluck, Rodrigo; moved through a string orchestra performance of Ferguson, Handel and Schoenberg; before coming to Fauré as *This Week's Composer*. Turning away briefly to music by Noel Coward, it came back at lunchtime to a *Midday Prom* of Haydn and Schumann. A 10-minute *Concert Calendar* reviewed the British musical scene, before programming records of William Walton's First Symphony, *Music in Miniature* and then an *Intermezzo* of British baroque music. David Oistrakh playing Beethoven preceded half an hour of world music, returning to the classical canon with Bach cantatas from 4 pm. At 5 pm, *Further Hearing* included what the *Radio Times* billed as 'music that might perhaps be heard more often than it is'—in this instance that was Tippett's *Concerto for Orchestra* and Messiaen's *Chronochromie*. The final half-hour of the Music Programme featured *Scores from the Films*, which in the sample week was excerpts from Prokofiev's music for Eisenstein's *Alexander Nevsky* (an example of film music justifiably being included within the classical canonic repertoire).

The Home Service carried *Music to Remember* in the evening, when there was speech programming on the Third Programme (and attracted the largest classical music audience of the week in the process, almost 300,000) before the Third Programme broadcast the first half of an ambitious BBCSO concert of Stravinsky, Bartók and Webern from its American tour. During the interval of that concert, listeners could switch across to hear records of John Ogden playing Bach, Mozart, Schumann and Liszt on the Home Service, before coming back to the Third Programme for the second half of the concert including Stravinsky, Schoenberg and Debussy. The Third Programme then offered a Campra motet, before broadcasts closed with a Smetana string quartet in *Music at Night* on the Home Service.

This was the approach adopted right through the week, so that classical music output on the BBC can be seen as having been cut from a single piece of cloth. That was part of its great strength. The producer/consumer relationship was enhanced because classical music was not confined within a single ghetto channel, but was available to both specialists and non-specialists. The listener could stumble across it on the Home Service, have the opportunity to sample it at any time during the day on the Music Programme, but still not be denied a genuinely high-brow offering on the Third Programme in the evening. The Music Programme and the Home Service also did not shy away from programming more challenging works: Schoenberg, Webern, Tippett and Messiaen on that single Monday, for example.

Furthermore, the abundance of output empowered and liberated the Third Programme to undertake some ambitious programmes. It broadcast two major operas during the sample week: *Moses* by Rossini by the Welsh National Opera on Sunday evening; and *Hippolytus and Aricia* by Rameau on Thursday evening from Birmingham University (the Music Programme chipped in with Purcell's *Dido and Aeneas* across lunchtime on Sunday). As well as covering two concerts of the BBCSO's American tour, the Third Programme also featured works by Gerhard in the *Tuesday Invitation Concert*.

The Home Service kept a firm place for classical music. On Saturday afternoon of the sample week there was a series of attractive programmes, starting with a song recital on gramophone records, and moving on to *Music of the Masters*, with the BBC Scottish Orchestra playing an attractive, mid-market programme of Berlioz, Elgar, Dvořák and Beethoven's Fifth Symphony. *Gala Concert Hall* in the evening, with the BBC Concert Orchestra, offered 'a programme of works for all the family'. It featured extracts rather than full works: from Humperdinck's *Hansel and Gretel*, from Herold's *La Fille mal gardée* and the last movement of Beethoven's Third Piano Concerto. Whatever the purists might have thought about failing to play entire works, the audience responded well, with 200,000 and then 250,000 listening to these programmes.

Overall, however, audience levels were not particularly exciting. The Home Service with a top audience of 300,000 and the Music Programme at around 250,000 were attracting some of the potential audience but without hitting the high notes. Third Programme audiences remained stubbornly at or below 100,000 for all the programmes broadcast during the sample week. The BBC claimed in its 1966/1967 Annual Report a listening hinterland of around 5 million,[xxxii] which is closely in line with the underlying classical music radio audience identified throughout this history but hard to reconcile with the actual, much lower audience figures measured for individual programmes.

The reaction to the new service within the BBC was mostly positive, although—possibly because of the absence through illness of Manduell in these early months—many people within the BBC hierarchy wanted their own twopenny-worth from the Music Programme. Assistant Controller of Music Gerald Abraham was not happy about the representation of British orchestral music in the schedule. Marriott himself tried to ensure that there was light music 'of the widest possible appeal' when the Home Service and the Light Programme were carrying schools broadcasting and *Woman's Hour*, respectively. Hans Keller, despite having been in acting charge of the Music Programme at the time, complained that it was 'faceless' and then pressed for the inclusion of a programme of Beatles music.[xxxiii]

Once back in his normal role after covering for Manduell's illness, Keller's interventions became scatological:

> what the bloody hell is the first Symphony, which is not comparable to Beethoven 9, to do with the second, which admittedly isn't either, yet is a jolly sight better? What the still bloodier hell have Hummel and Moscheles to do with Leo? Who cares anyway? And when did he spring from that background? It must have been while I wasn't looking. What, the bloodiest conceivable hell, has Leo to do with the hacks?[xxxiv]

The engineers wanted more stereo broadcasts, while the record industry was pressing for a different recent releases programme.[xxxv] The 'advice' continued, covering the interval in the *Midday Concert*, the amount of biographical detail to be included in announcements, the appeal of afternoon programming, the sequencing of works chosen for broadcast—virtually all as a result of internal BBC views, almost none responding to the expressed or perceived needs of the listener.

Of all of these interventions, perhaps the most interesting (and certainly the most powerful institutionally) was that of Senior Controller Frank Gillard on the subject of the length of items to be included in breakfast-time programmes. Responding to a request from Manduell, he set out a policy which was reasonably similar to that which would be adopted by Radio 3 in the early Nineties, and then by Classic FM:

> You ask about the length of items in the breakfast-time programmes. The answer is of course that ideally they should not be too lengthy. If the repertoire is all that much restricted, we should copy the Italians and not hesitate to repeat suitable works at frequent intervals. But if a more popular policy involves acceptance of longer works, we should not shrink from it. Far better to speed the worker on his way with regret in his heart at having to miss a movement of music than start off his day with a fit of annoyance and irritation because of the altogether unsuitable choice of item.[xxxvi]

It had been Gillard's view from the outset that 'if we fail to find an audience of reasonable size of the programme, we shall before long become embarrassed by it'.[xxxvii] The BBC conducted a separate research study into the Music Programme in September 1965.[xxxviii] From that it deduced that 5.5% of the population listened 'fairly regularly' to the Music Programme on weekdays and weekends, with another 4.5% listening fairly regularly at weekends only, giving a total of 10% as the Music Programme's 'following' or 5 million people. That is improbable. It was based on data derived from a questionnaire given to those who *had already* expressed an interest in the output. Total patronage, extrapolating from the median audience figures in the Daily Listening Barometer,[5] was much more likely to have been of the order of 2.5 to 3 million, which allied to the audiences for classical music on the three other channels would come closer to the consistent 5 million figure.

Demographic data from this survey suggested that Music Programme listeners were more middle aged and slightly better educated than the population as a whole, but 'they are very far from being all "music lovers"'. The research study concluded that:

> the Music Programme's audience will always contain a fairly significant proportion listening, not because of their interest in serious music as such,

---

[5] See Appendix B, pp. 255ff.

but because they preferred it to any of the other radio services available to them.

Despite the steps it was taking towards a new, accessible way of presenting classical music radio, the BBC continued to debate what Glock had spoken of as 'musical wallpaper'. At the very time that he was directly responsible for the Music Programme, covering for Manduell's illness in the early months of 1965, Keller was writing that:

> although he himself was 'constitutionally incapable of background listening', not enough was yet known about 'musical perception and cognition' to be able to say that such listening is always a bad thing ... People who assimilate a musical language pre-consciously may thus learn to absorb the musical substance more readily.[xxxix]

The Times summarised well the divided views of the late Sixties:

> A seven-day all-day service of broadcast music must largely cater for the housewife who is not content with Housewives Choice as an accompaniment to the washing of the breakfast dishes, and who would rather make the beds to Mozart than to Music While You Work. Also in mind are husbands driving to and from work through slow-moving traffic, people who work more efficiently with a background of congenial music, people of all kinds who cannot, and perhaps are not minded to, devote complete attention to what they hear, but prefer Bach or Bartók to the Pops.
>
> Some high-minded souls firmly believe that music is too sacred art—'Eine Heilige Kunst'[6]—to be degraded into any background role ... but in our own age, when so much of the music we hear is long familiar, there are two ways of listening: the way of complete surrender for special occasions, the intellectual way; and the sympathetic but not completely engaged receptive faculty, which may extend to no more than sensuous apprehension of the music.[xl]

The argument continues to this day—not least in respect of the arrival of Classic FM in 1992 and Radio 3's pre-emptive response to that. Nor was it merely a British concern. The French had a word for 'musical

---

[6]The words sung by a soprano in the role of 'the Composer' in the prologue to Richard Strauss' opera *Ariadne Auf Naxos*.

wallpaper'; they called it 'musique d'ameublement'. At the same time as the Music Programme was being launched in the UK, the Director General of the French state radio and television service was dismissing fears expressed by French intellectuals that high-minded programming would suffer as its new France Culture network set out to attract larger audiences.[xli] In Germany, Corinna Lüthje (2008) has demonstrated similar arguments surrounding the arrival of Klassik Radio in 1992.

CLASSICAL MUSIC RADIO 1966–1969

From 1965 onwards, until subverted by *Broadcasting in the Seventies* and the implementation of 'generic' structures, the multi-channel pattern continued to the benefit of all. Glock's influence over the general content was now more evident, and although the focus remained firmly as usual in the canonic centre there were an increasing number of exceptions. A concert on the Third Programme on the sampled Monday evening was built around a new Boulez work conducted by the composer—whom Glock championed avidly—and began with works by Berger. The *Monday Concert* the same day on the Music Programme included a work by Walter Goehr, part of Boulez' circle. Henze appeared late on Thursday evening on the Third Programme and there were outings for Stockhausen and Webern. This was not to be allowed to go too far. Noting a reference in a meeting between Glock and the Composers Guild about 'the possibility of placing substantial quantities of contemporary music in the Music Programme', Marriott stressed to Glock that 'it is very clear from audience research ... that new music has a very small following among listeners to this programme'.[xlii]

In 1967, the issues surrounding the future of radio began to crystallise, although the implementation of changes was not synchronous. The offshore pirate radio services were outlawed by the Marine, &c., Broadcasting (Offences) Act in August 1967, and on 30 September 1967 the BBC launched its own pop music service, Radio 1. The Light Programme and the Home Service became Radios 2 and 4, respectively. The Music Programme, Network 3 and the Third Programme were lumped together under the portmanteau title of 'Radio 3', but without any real change in their respective outputs until 1970. For classical music radio, therefore, listeners might barely have noticed any difference—except, that is, at the 1967 Proms where Boulez conducted Stockhausen's *Gruppen*. Later that season, a mortally ill Malcolm Sargent appeared at the Last Night of the Proms on 16 September 1967, his innately conservative approach to the music festival dying with him 17 days later.

For the Third Programme, the Music Programme and Network 3, despite being billed under the umbrella name of 'Radio 3' from 1967, there was to be little actual change in output until 1970. It was the re-labelled Radio 4 which showed the most ambition in classical music broadcasting in these final years of the old dispensation. In the sample week of 1968, for example, a programme of music performed by American orchestras on Saturday afternoon reached 300,000 listeners, while *Gala Concert Hall* that evening attracted 450,000, as did *Music to Remember* on Tuesday evening. There were classical music features during the weekdays: *This is Ballet* on Monday afternoon and *Opera Round the Clock* on Tuesday afternoon, both attracting good audiences. Perhaps the most aspirational programming of the week was a three-hour performance of Mozart's *Idomeneo* in a concert performance from the Festival Hall on Wednesday evening. This was rewarded with an audience of close to 500,000 listeners, a significant figure for an evening radio broadcast of opera in the television and pop music radio age. The Home Service maintained its ambition on the following evening with a concert performed by the London Philharmonic Orchestra at the Festival Hall of works by Beethoven and Stravinsky; and then again on Friday evening, with the Hallé Orchestra offering Glinka, Schubert and Tchaikovsky. Both were heard by audiences in excess of 300,000.

In 1969, as the BBC prepared for the full implementation of Radio 3, output on Radio 4 was reduced, although the station once again achieved the highest audiences for classical music of the sample week: 300,000 heard *A Man and His Music* on Saturday evening and *Music to Remember* on Tuesday evening. Radio 4 also broadcast features on Italian tenor Enrico Caruso, one of the first operatic stars of the gramophone record era, early on Sunday evening, and on Bartók on Thursday evening. Completing the offering, the Music Programme continued to provide a good range of music, mostly from the centre of the canonic repertoire, but introducing some early and some contemporary music from time to time. The range of composers during the sample week in 1969 was reduced a little from the previous year, but still allowed for the introduction here and there of some contemporary works. Nevertheless, coming to the end of this multi-channel period, the First Viennese School remained dominant, with the most played composers in order Beethoven, Mozart,

Schubert, Brahms, and Haydn. Other composers receiving multiple plays were Bach, Wagner, Tchaikovsky and Elgar.

Debates about 'popularity' continued. Robert Silvey's BBC Research Department produced a report in 1969 examining the tastes and opinions of Music Programme listeners.[xliii] Sampling in Greater London only, it suggested unsurprisingly that listeners were more comfortable with composers from the centre of the canonic repertoire—Beethoven, Tchaikovsky and Chopin—than with the 'moderns'—Bartók, Stravinsky, Prokofiev and Britten. The dominant finding was a wish among those who patronised the Music Programme to be able to find music whenever they wanted it, rather than being inconvenienced by too much speech.

P.J. Dodd, Manduell's opposite number in the Gramophone Department, challenged the populist interpretation:

> We should not aim to give the majority of listeners exactly what they want ... If we were to do this we should only need a dozen or so discs: the Nutcracker Suite, Beethoven's Fifth and a few others (separate movements only, of course) would keep us going, repeated ad nauseam. In other words by giving the majority exactly what they want we could easily make the Music Programme more 'popular'.[xliv]

As the Sixties came to a close, and the time for the full implementation of an integrated, generic Radio 3 approached, the impression persists for the second half of the decade that the BBC across its three classical music services was offering a good range of music, both accessible and challenging, and scheduling at least some of it where listeners might come across it serendipitously. With the addition of a little feature and educative material, this was a creditable fusion of mass and elite, of popular and high brow, and firmly outside any single classical music ghetto—an inclusive and relatively classless approach which was about to be discarded.

'Broadcasting in the Seventies'

Broadcasting in the Seventies was the title of the report published by the BBC in July 1969, which was informed by and followed the report from McKinsey Management Consultants commissioned by new BBC Chairman Charles Hill in February 1968. The phrase is also used as shorthand for the fundamental shift of BBC radio into four generic networks, thus abandoning the mixed programming approach which had applied since the launch of the BBC itself. It therefore represented the final shedding of the notion that listeners might come across material—such as classical music—by accident, and as a consequence be enlightened and educated.

The document, and its implementation, changed BBC radio to a degree unprecedented since at least the post-war reorganisation and arguably since broadcasting began in the UK. The irreversible shift away from 'mixed' towards 'genre' programme services aped the 'brand' approach of American commercial radio, but was damagingly disruptive to the British tradition of integrated rather than segregated output. Hugh Chignell notes that 'the message contained in the document, and the extraordinary and significant reaction to it … [are] essential … in understanding what happened in the 1970s—a decade profoundly influenced by the pamphlet and its impact' (2011: 92).

Asa Briggs (1995: 721–810) identifies the start of the process with concerns over BBC finances felt by Charles Hill when he was controversially appointed as Chairman in September 1967, while noting that its origins reach back into the work of Marriott and his first Working Party in the Fifties. David Hendy considers that the initiative arose from 'acute' financial pressure and a sense that radio had ceded centre stage to television, but he also judges that Hill's role was substantial and surprisingly personal. Introducing dramatic change at the end of the Sixties greatly appealed to Hill as a major event to mark his time as Chairman, and radio provided him with his opportunity. That in turn 'made *Broadcasting in the Seventies* needlessly provocative' (Hendy 2007: 56).

It would have been more than surprising if there had not also been a defensive reaction to the unprecedented success of the offshore pirate radio services between 1964 and 1967. Just as with the audience inroads made by the Continental English-language stations before the war, such as Radio Luxembourg, the BBC was rattled by uncouth intruders like Radio Caroline, which deployed modern output with skill and scarce respect for tradition. Rather than stick to what it could do well, adjusting to meet contemporary circumstances, the Corporation was railroaded into copying the approach of the newcomers. That may have been all very well for popular music, but for classical music it represented abandoning a real high point of achievement in multi-channel programming.

An initial internal review was carried out by a Working Group, once again under the guidance of Marriott, which met between 14 December

1967 and 15 November 1968, when it was replaced by a Policy Study Group chaired by Gillard himself. As with his first Working Group in the Fifties, Marriott's work set the tone for the eventual outcome, recommending that the Music Programme and the Third Programme should be 'brought together under single controllership', 'dropping the names Third Programme and Music Programme and uniting the whole network programme service under the single title Radio 3'.[xlv] Both Marriott's and Gillard's groups were considerably exercised by available resources and uncertain whether the BBC could sustain four national networks. They debated whether the new Radio 3 should become in time an all-music programme, rather than retaining some elements of speech, and if so whether it should be under the control of the Music Department. In the event, some speech remained, and Howard Newby—who had been Controller of the Third Programme since 1958—became from 1970 to 1971 the Controller of Radio 3.

The whole issue of *Broadcasting in the Seventies* was one of those *causes célèbres* which dominate institutional histories of UK broadcasting. There was extensive and acrimonious debate about the report: inside the BBC, among the *cognoscenti*, in Parliament and in the press. Briggs discusses the widespread 'staff discontent' expressed through 'angry speeches at meetings ... [and] letters to *The Times*'.[7] Public discussion was corralled by the Campaign for Better Broadcasting—an organisation in direct lineage from the Third Programme Defence Society in the Fifties—which was again mainly concerned to protect the elite provision of the Third Programme; and by self-styled Free Communications Groups, which pressed for democratic control of broadcasting with a view to achieving 'a radical change in the present state of society'.[xlvi] Parliamentary discussion framed itself in terms of a wish to protect the quality of BBC broadcasting,[xlvii] but was conducted against a keen awareness of increasing pressure within the Conservative Party for the introduction of commercial radio to break the BBC's final broadcasting monopoly. These debates also prompted Minister of Technology Anthony Wedgwood Benn's loaded statement about 'broadcasting being really too important to be left to the broadcasters'.[xlviii]

Yet for all the distinguished academic examination of *Broadcasting in the Seventies*, that discourse has focussed largely on the politics of right

---

[7] See Chap. 5, p. 131.

Table 4.1 Audience comparison between Music Programme and Radio 3

	Maximum audience	Median audience
1968—Music Programme sample, week commencing 4 May	250,000	150,000
1971—Radio 3 sample, week commencing 8 May	202,000	101,000

and left, and the even more byzantine internal institutional politics of the BBC. The likely wishes or interests of the listeners to classical music—as individuals rather than members of class-based action groups—featured very little if at all in the discussions within and outside the BBC in the late Sixties. Hendy (2007: 148) notes only the BBC's expectation that listeners would move between different generic services, tuning to 'a little [sic] Radio 3 when they felt in the mood for classical music'. That was not to happen, despite Briggs' assertion that, for Radio 3, 'listeners, while still asking questions, showed that they did not object to the new programming pattern. Audiences rose slightly' (1995: 803–804). The audience figures for 1968 and 1971 actually show a shading down in patronage (Table 4.1).

For classical music in particular, as this narrative history demonstrates, listeners were well accustomed to moving as the deckchairs were repositioned on the BBC liner. Early in the Sixties, programmes such as the lunchtime *Concert Hour*—one of the most popular BBC classical music offerings—would move from the Light Programme to the Home Service, and then on to the Music Programme which was housed on the daytime frequencies of the Third Programme. Thus when the new Radio 3 began broadcasting on 4 April 1970, a listener who was not a keen student of the *Radio Times* might well not have noticed the difference, or have been bothered about it in any event at this stage.

The problem is the disjuncture between actual listener behaviour, on the one hand, and, on the other, the preoccupations of those within the Third Programme/Radio 3—together with those commentators and academics at the time who felt they had a particular *locus* in this matter. Chignell (2011: 95) notes that 'the uproar in the letters pages of *The Times* and elsewhere', especially in respect of the supposed end of the Third Programme, was almost more important than the changes themselves. As audience figures demonstrate, listening to classical music radio did not shift greatly over the supposed watershed of *Broadcasting in the Seventies*.

For the average listener to classical music radio on the BBC, the main impact of the reorganisation of services which followed *Broadcasting in the Seventies* was reduced availability. There were fewer hours of classical music broadcasting on offer (a reduction of around one third) and as a consequence fewer composers featured (in the 1970 sample week, down around one fifth from 1968). Most critical of all, in terms of the accessibility of classical music to the non-specialist listener, for the first time since the BBC began, regular classical music was provided only on one single station.

The short period between 1965 and the end of the decade was one of the highpoints in the provision of classical music radio. There was a wide range of output, embracing the high brow and the middle brow. Educative attempts linked elite and popular material, which was available without too many class-based assumptions. And classical music was offered across three or four channels, meaning that those listeners who knew where it was could find it, while those who might enjoy it if they heard it could still stumble across it. It was one of the damaging consequences of the theory and practice of *Broadcasting in the Seventies* that this achievement was cut off before it had a full opportunity to yield fruit. It did, however, leave the field clear for the surprising entry of private radio into what had been the BBC's own walled garden, as the new Independent Local Radio stations from 1973 onwards offered classical music within just such mixed programming as the BBC had abandoned in 1970.

Notes

i. *The Listener*, 21 April 1960, p. 731.
ii. *The Listener*, 12 May 1960, p. 858.
iii. *BBC Handbook* 1960, p. 58.
iv. Quoted in Carpenter and Doctor (1996: 206).
v. Quoted in Black (2010: 51).
vi. Edmunds (2006: 252) quoting Julian Lloyd Webber: 'why classical music lost out to Elvis and Buddy'. http://www.music.gla.ac.uk/tfowler/articles/Webber.html.
vii. Memorandum from Director Sound Broadcasting (Wellington) to Controller Music (Glock), 10 May 1961. BBC WAC R27/847/1.

viii. Home Service day-time. Memorandum from Controller Programme Planning (Sound) (Pelletier) to Assistant Director Sound Broadcasting (Marriott), 11 January 1961. BBC WAC R27/847/1.
ix. Report of the Committee on Broadcasting, Cmnd. 1753. London: HMSO, 1962.
x. *Radio Times*, 12 May 1962, p. 10.
xi. Area and Local Broadcasting Final Report 1959. BBC WAC R34/1585/1.
xii. Frank Gillard. Sound Radio in the Television Age. BBC Lunchtime Lecture, 11 March 1964.
xiii. Memorandum from Assistant Director Sound Broadcasting (Marriott) to Director Sound Broadcasting (Wellington), 8 October 1956. BBC WAC R34/1022/2.
xiv. Good music in home sound broadcasting. Memorandum from Head Music Programme (Sound) (Johnstone) to Assistant Director Sound Broadcasting (Marriott), 15 July 1957. BBC WAC R27/847/1.
xv. Orchestral Music. Memorandum from Assistant Director of Sound Broadcasting (Marriott) to Controller Music (Howgill), 27 November 1957. BBC WAC R27/847/1.
xvi. Orchestral Music. Memorandum from Controller Music (Howgill) to Assistant Director Sound Broadcasting (Marriott), 6 December 1957. BBC WAC R27/847/1.
xvii. Music Output. Note from Assistant Director Sound Broadcasting (Marriott) to Director Sound Broadcasting (Wellington), 15 January 1959. BBC WAC R27/847/1.
xviii. Area and Local Broadcasting Final Report 1959. BBC WAC R34/1585/1.
xix. Glock interviewed by Gillard. BBC Oral History, March 1983. BBC WAC R143/51/1.
xx. William Glock (Controller Music). The BBC's music policy, probably late January 1963. BBC WAC R27/847/1.
xxi. B. Britten, 1964. On receiving the first Aspen award; a speech.
xxii. Report of the Committee on Broadcasting, 27 June 1962, Cmnd 1753.
xxiii. Orchestral Music. Memorandum from Controller Music (Howgill) to Assistant Director Sound Broadcasting (Marriott), 6 December 1957. BBC WAC R27/847/1.
xxiv. Third Network Music Programme. Memorandum from Assistant Director Sound Broadcasting (Marriott) to Head Home Service (Lewin), 16 June 1960. BBC WAC R27/818/1.
xxv. Music Programme. Memorandum from Head Home Service (Lewin) to Controller Music (Glock) and others, 17 December 1962. BBC WAC R27/818/1.

4 THE SIXTIES: SIMPLE AND CONSERVATIVE TASTES   125

xxvi. Music Network and Needletime. Memorandum from Controller Music (Glock) to Assistant Director Sound Broadcasting (Marriott), 15 February 1963. BBC WAC R27/847/1.
xxvii. Music Programme. Memorandum from Head Home Service (Lewin) to Controller Music (Glock) and others, 17 December 1962. BBC WAC R27/818/1.
xxviii. *Ibid.*
xxix. Music Programme. Memorandum from Director Sound Broadcasting (Gillard) to Controller Music (Glock), 30 July 1964. BBC WAC R27/818/1.
xxx. John Manduell. The Music Programme, 11 November 1964. BBC WAC R27/847/1.
xxxi. *Ibid.*
xxxii. Quoted in Briggs (1995: 579).
xxxiii. From a range of comments archived in BBC WAC R27 818/2.
xxxiv. Memorandum from Chief Assistant (Orchestral and Choral) (Keller) to Chief Assistant Music Programme (Manduell), 13 May 1965. BBC WAC R 27/818/2.
xxxv. From a range of comments archived in BBC WAC R27 818/2.
xxxvi. Early morning programmes. Memorandum from Director Sound Broadcasting (Gillard) to Chief Assistant Music Programme (Manduell), 10 November 1965. BBC WAC R21/818/2.
xxxvii. Music Programme. Memorandum from Director Sound Broadcasting (Gillard) to Controller Music (Glock), 30 July 1964. BBC WAC R27/818/1.
xxxviii. Music Programme. Report on a survey made in September 1965 into the nature and opinions of Music Programme listeners and BBC Audience Research Report, March 1966. BBC WAC R9/9/30.
xxxix. *New Statesman*, 8 January 1965, p. 41. Quoted in Garnham (2003: 84).
xl. Our Music Critic. Listening with Half an Ear to Music All Day Long. *The Times*, 27 November 1964, p. 15.
xli. Wider audience for cultural broadcasts. *The Times*, 15 January 1964, p. 11.
xlii. New music in the Music Programme. Memorandum from Assistant Director Sound Broadcasting (Marriott) to Controller Music (Glock), 18 March 1966. BBC WAC R27/818/3.
xliii. The Tastes and Opinions of Music Programme Listeners. BBC Audience Research Report 1969. BBC WAC R9/9/33.
xliv. Haydn: Bach. Memorandum from Chief Assistant Gramophone Programme (Dodd) to Chief Assistant Music Programme (Manduell), 27 March 1969. BBC WAC R27/818/4.
xlv. Policy Study Group. The Future of Network Radio, second progress review. BBC WAC R78/548/2.

xlvi. Notice of the Meeting of the 76 Group. Quoted in Briggs (1995: 796).
xlvii. *Hansard* (1969) House of Commons, vol. 792 cols 1496–1632, 3 December 1969.
xlviii. George Clark. Gunter broadside at Benn's 'frightening' attack on BBC. *The Times*, 21 October 1968, p. 1.

Bibliographic Sources

Barnard, S. 1989. *On the radio: Music radio in Britain*. Milton Keynes: Open University Press.
Black, L., C. Wintle, and K. Hopkins. 2010. *BBC music in the Glock era and after: A memoir*. London: Cosman Keller Art and Music Trust in association with Plumbago Books.
Briggs, A. 1995. *The history of broadcasting in the United Kingdom, vol. 5, competition*. Oxford: Oxford University Press.
Carpenter, H., and J.R. Doctor. 1996. *The envy of the world: Fifty years of the BBC Third Programme and Radio 3, 1946–1996*. London: Weidenfeld & Nicolson.
Chignell, H. 2011. *Public issue radio: Talks, news and current affairs in the 20th century*. Basingstoke: Palgrave Macmillan.
Doctor, J.R., A. Garnham, D.A. Wright, and N. Kenyon. 2007. *The Proms: A new history*. London: Thames & Hudson.
Garnham, A.M. 2003. *Hans Keller and the BBC: The musical conscience of British broadcasting, 1959–79*. Aldershot: Ashgate.
Hendy, D. 2007. *Life on air: A history of Radio Four*. Oxford: Oxford University Press.
Hennessy, P. 2006. *Having it so good: Britain in the fifties*. London: Allen Lane.
Kenyon, N. 1981. *The BBC Symphony Orchestra: The first fifty years 1930–1980*. London: British Broadcasting Corporation.
Lüthje, C. 2008. *Das Medium als symbolische Macht: Untersuchung zur soziokulturellen Wirkung von Medien am Beispiel von Klassik Radio*. Norderstedt: Books on Demand.
Manduell, J. 2016. *No Bartok before breakfast*. Todmorden: Arc Publications.
Marwick, A. 1998. *The Sixties: Cultural revolution in Britain, France, Italy, and the United States*. Oxford: Oxford University Press.
Pirie, P.J. 1979. *The English musical renaissance*. London: Gollancz.
Sandbrook, D. 2007. *White heat: A history of Britain in the swinging sixties*. London: Penguin Books.
Stoller, T. 2010. *Sounds of your life: The history of independent radio in the UK*. New Barnet: John Libbey.
Street, S. 2006. *Crossing the ether: British public service radio and commercial competition 1922–1945*. Eastleigh: John Libbey Publications.

CHAPTER 5

The Seventies: Breaking the Monopoly

The arrival of Radio 3—'An Alternative Service of Radio Broadcasting'—Classical music radio 1973–1976—ILR's programming approach—classical music radio 1977–1979—rumours of war.

The Seventies get a bad press, although in broadcasting these years were remarkably fruitful. There is now an emerging corpus of general British history which regards the Seventies as a disturbed decade, beset by violence and confrontation. Politically, these years saw relatively little systemic change until 1979, as the task of dealing with an increasingly fractured society flip-flopped between the two major parties. The key historical event was economic. The oil price shock, which was a consequence of the Arab-Israeli war of 1973, brought to an end the long post-war boom and therefore exposed the unresolved elements from the churn of the Sixties. These showed themselves in financial and industrial turmoil, characterised by the so-called 'Winter of Discontent' and the International Monetary Fund bailout in 1978/1979, and would lead to unanticipated right-wing radicalism which then set the tone for the Eighties.

The UK finally succeeded in joining what was then called the Common Market in 1973, but spent most of the rest of the decade handling financial crises, coping with armed insurrection and facing industrial relations discord. The 'Troubles' in Northern Ireland flared up with Bloody Sunday in January 1972, and British society became both more fearful and more repressive. Perhaps as a consequence, these were also barren years for liberal experimentation, with the Open University getting into its stride[1] but few other social initiatives. Generally, these seemed drab and depressing years, rocked by oil shocks, terrorism and industrial unrest, seen in 1973 by Christopher Booker—one of the founders of *Private Eye*—as a 'long, dispiriting interlude' between the iconoclastic Sixties and the rise of Margaret Thatcher's Britain, when 'the prevailing mood was one of a somewhat weary, increasingly conservative, increasingly apprehensive disenchantment'.[i]

The excitement of pirate and new pop radio in the late Sixties had dulled down as the Seventies began. The previous decade bequeathed a mixed legacy to radio in the Seventies, as it did to British society as a whole. Television and radio came under scrutiny from almost the last of the grand public enquiries into broadcasting, which had begun as far back as the Sykes Committee in 1923. In the Seventies, this took the form of the Annan Committee. That paved the way for Channel 4 to come into existence as a liberal and permissive publisher of television, but most of its other proposals—especially for the democratisation of radio—were side-lined by the election of Thatcher's Conservative Government in May 1979.

However, two seminal changes during the Seventies reshaped the ecology of radio, and with it the classical music offering. The first has been considered in the previous chapter's examination of *Broadcasting in the Seventies*, which completed in 1970 the reshaping of BBC network radio. Moving from mixed programming to generic output produced an unprecedented new structure for BBC classical music radio.

The second tectonic shift saw the BBC's monopoly of radio broadcasting finally broken, and replaced by a duopoly akin to that which had applied in television since the mid-Fifties. *An Alternative Service of Radio Broadcasting* was the title of the 1971 White Paper,[ii] and under the auspices of a reconstituted Independent Broadcasting Authority (IBA), the first Independent Local Radio (ILR) stations came on air from October 1973. ILR made major contributions to radio, including competition in the provision of classical music radio to the BBC's single cultural channel, but has received little academic attention. This history of ILR's notably successful efforts in the field of classical music radio is just one example of a largely unexplored phenomenon in British

---

[1] The first Open University radio broadcast was on 3 January 1971.

broadcasting and overall social history, which both represents and illustrates the aspiration but eventual failure of a late-flowering social market enterprise.

The new radio duopoly presented in a fresh guise the long debate over whether classical music could and should be opened up to a wider public, or needed to be grounded in the tastes and demands of a cultural elite. BBC classical music radio retreated at the start of the Seventies from multi-channel provision into a single channel of output, the new Radio 3, and its relevance to the wider audience diminished accordingly, while the departure of William Glock in 1972 allowed conservatism to reassert itself in the BBC's approach. Unexpectedly however, ILR—which had a statutory public service remit to be *independent*, public service radio, rather than merely *commercial* radio—fulfilled that obligation in part through the broadcasting and patronage of classical music. ILR stations attracted large audiences and became significant players in their individual localities. The excitement at its innovative provision of programmes and concerts and the audience response so far as can be ascertained illustrate the extent to which the BBC's change to generic networks had left space in the musical middle ground.

THE ARRIVAL OF RADIO 3

As discussed in the previous chapter, *Broadcasting in the Seventies*[iii] was published by the BBC in July 1969. The phrase is also a metonym for the fundamental shift of BBC radio into four generic networks, thus abandoning the mixed programming approach which had applied since the launch of the BBC itself. It therefore represented the final shedding of the ambition that listeners might come across material—such as classical music—by accident, and as a consequence be enlightened and educated.

The full new form of Radio 3 began on Saturday 4 April 1970, just before the General Election whose unexpected result was to start the process towards commercial radio for the UK, as discussed below. Edward Heath's new Government was addressing the widespread disenchantment of the youth audience with the BBC's popular music output; meanwhile, the dissatisfaction of the elite with the BBC's classical music output rumbled on long after the conclusions of *Broadcasting in the Seventies* were established beyond revision in January 1970.

A letter published in *The Times* the following month, from 134 members of the BBC's radio programme staff, argued that with the replacement of the Third Programme 'the outstanding creative achievement of BBC radio will be abolished, and no project of comparable vision will take its place'.[iv] Gerard Mansell, who as deputy to the outgoing Managing Director Radio Frank Gillard had led the implementation team for the change, urged complainants to wait and see, relying on continuance of 'the provision of high quality programmes for minorities'.[v] However, *The Listener* carried letters headed 'dissatisfied' across the early months of the year, and that dissatisfaction did not go away when the schedules appeared. The BBC's new Managing Director Radio Ian Trethowan reacted furiously to criticism of the new plans from an anonymous 'well-known broadcaster' in *The Times* in March.[vi] Despite this level of noise, it is notable that the complainants seem to have been either BBC insiders or the self-appointed intellectual elite, from Leo Black to Oliver Zangwill.[vii] There is no evidence of expressions of discontent from listeners, who had so recently enjoyed one of the high periods for classical music radio. They simply stopped listening.

It might almost be seen as wish-fulfilment for those uneasy at the democratisation of classical music output in the preceding years that, from April 1970—for the first time since the war—classical music was provided by the BBC only on one single station. For Stephen Walsh writing in *The Listener* on New Year's Day 1970, the entire output of the Home Service, the Music Programme and the Light Programme over previous years might not have existed. He estimated an *increase* in classical music output of around 10% brought about by the arrival of Radio 3.[viii] In fact, the *fall* between 1967 and 1971 was of the order of 6%.

The new Director General from 1969, Charles Curran, thought of classical music within the BBC from the point of view of a patron of the arts. He was pressed by Government to spend money on keeping orchestras going, but wondered 'a little ruefully whether its dedication to the tasks which it shouldered nearly 50 years ago is not too readily taken for granted'.[ix] After flourishing in the late Sixties, led by the Music Programme, the BBC, in its planning, assumptions and public utterances about classical music, returned to being self-referential. When it glanced outside, that was chiefly to meet the insistent demands of the elite. The wider audience remained largely unknown to the Corporation or its intellectual critics.

What did the first year of this now fully-fledged new service offer to the generality of listeners? The output in the 1970 sample week was still dominated by the First Viennese School of composers. Of the 88 composers featured in the sample week, most were heard only once and only five of them enjoyed more than four plays. However, those five—Beethoven, Mozart, Bach, Haydn and Schubert—could not have been more central in the canonic classical music repertoire. By contrast, the Second Viennese School enjoyed only two performances of works by Webern in *Twentieth Century Music* on Monday evening. Compositions by Stockhausen and the British eccentric Havergal Brian were both given one outing.

Equally striking is the move away from live music or relays of live performances towards what the BBC still mostly called 'gramophone record' output. Commercially released recordings comprised around 36% of the musical output, despite a number of repeated concerts by the BBC orchestras, compared with just 13% ten years previously. That rough proportion applied too in the customary three operas broadcast over the course of the sample week. Monteverdi's *Vespers* from 1610 was relayed from the Queen Elizabeth Hall on Sunday evening to a barely measurable audience; Bizet's comic opera *Don Procopio* in a repeated studio recording was offered on Sunday afternoon, but heard by only 0.1% of the potential audience; while Wagner's *Tannhäuser* on Thursday afternoon on gramophone records did no better.

Radio 3 sustained a little educational effort; the *Ernest Read Concert for Children* on Sunday morning was simply a relay of an external event. On Friday evening, *Interpretations on Record* considered different performances of the first movement of Beethoven's *Emperor Concerto*, while the repeated *Talking about Music* and Sunday's *Music Magazine* provided a small amount of speech-based feature programming. Across on Radio 4 on Saturday evening, though, there was a harbinger of the future. Robin Ray—later to be one of the creators of Classic FM—was hosting a panel show, the *Clever Stupid Game*, while Radio 3 was deep in Monteverdi. Ray's audience was four times that of Radio 3.

The inheritance from the Music Programme of middle-brow output during the day mostly continued into Radio 3 in 1970, but with little spark. Mornings, particularly at weekends, attracted the largest audiences, but otherwise it was unusual for more than 100,000 people to be listening to the station at any time. The highest audience of the sample week early on Saturday morning was 350,000 adults (while ten years earlier, even up against a dominant television medium, the Light Programme equivalent had attracted almost 1 million).

Radio audiences had of course fallen sharply after the arrival of television in the Forties, a process accelerated by competitive television from the mid-Fifties onwards, but this was not a constant or irreversible decline. Radio listening in Britain had been revived by the combination of the transistor set and the arrival of the offshore pirate radio stations, and that reversal of previous trends was confirmed subsequently by Radio 1, and then by ILR. As the performance of the independent local sector and then Classic FM were to demonstrate, that new growth was available for classical music radio as well as pop music, although the BBC was late in coming to understand and exploit that opportunity. Arguably, so much energy had gone into institutional infighting about the creation of Radio 3 that not enough was left for the programming output, at least not for the popularising of the genre which is scarcely evident in the output.

As the decade began to advance, the BBC's routine classical music on Radio 3 remained just that—mostly routine. There were plenty of exceptions, but none shifted the overall tone or appeared to have much if any impact on the general audience. In May 1971, the newly appointed Chief Conductor of the BBCSO Pierre Boulez was interviewed briefly one Friday lunchtime on a talk billed in the *Radio Times* as 'about Germany's musical life—and his own role in it'. If any measurable number of Radio 3 listeners had tuned in, they might have learned about BBC Controller of Music William Glock's 'bold choice' for the new maestro of the BBCSO (Kenyon 1981: 345) and Boulez' aspirations; but they did not listen in measurable numbers, nor to an hour and a half of experimental modern music by Shepherd, Messiaen, Birtwistle and Satie on *Evening Sequence* later that day.

The gulf between the populariser and the elitists seemed as wide as ever. In November, Richard Hoggart in the second of his 1971 Reith Lectures asserted that 'ideas should be made as available as possible without unnecessary obscurity or dilution'.[x] Director General Charles Curran however thought that the BBC was 'in many respects ... like a university',[xi] and BBC classical music output remained firmly in Curran's camp, not Hoggart's. Even though during 1971 there was much to-ing and fro-ing among the elite (and self-interested newspapers) over the plans for 'commercial radio', so that the BBC faced a 'gathering storm over the future of radio',[xii] that addressed only popular music radio.

The fact that ILR when it came would broadcast classical music as well as never mentioned during the Parliamentary debates about the 1971 White Paper.

One significant innovation on Radio 3 in 1971 was David Munrow's *Pied Piper* programme of 'tales and music for younger listeners', broadcast most weekday afternoons. Munrow was widely acknowledged as 'one of the most brilliant and appealing broadcasters in the BBC's history' (Carpenter and Doctor 1997: 265) although these programmes cannot really be counted as classical music. Even so, for all their appeal to the *cognoscenti*, by the time audience data were available—in 1972—on three sample occasions the programme failed to achieve a measurable audience, on the fourth it reached just 50,000 people.

Bloody Sunday convulsed Derry and then Britain in January 1972. The Sound Broadcasting Act creating radio competition was enacted in July, but in classical music and its radio representation the direction of gaze was mostly retrospective. New British music was exemplified by Tippett's Third Symphony, concluding his 'visionary trinity of major works' (Pirie 1979: 237), along with the *Vision of St Augustin* (1966), and the *Knot Garden* (1971). Tippett represented the epitome of the Third Programme's legacy, both in his compositions and also in his activism within the Third Programme Defence Society in the Fifties, and the Campaign for Better Broadcasting in the late Sixties.

1972 was marked also by the departure of William Glock, after 13 years as Controller of Music. His successor, Robert Ponsonby, was a man of a very different stamp, identified by Black (2010: 93) as 'Eton and the Guards' and someone who—unlike Glock—'wanted to be involved in day-to-day decisions'. He held this key post right through the rest of this decade and into the next, partly by learning to accommodate the views of subsequent Managing Directors Radio, although towards the end he was by his own admission very nearly broken in spirit by the musicians' strike at the end of his 14-year tenure (Ponsonby 2009: 55). BBC 'turf wars' continued right through the decade. In 1975 Ponsonby was apologising for giving 'professional offence' to BBC Managing Director Ian Trethowan for insisting that 'if a public performance is damaged by the requirements of TV or radio, we shall broadcast something second-rate. The opening night of the Proms was at risk in this respect ... I think you believe that I am putting the public concert, as such, before the broadcast, as such. I'm not. I'm simply saying that the broadcast can only be as good as the public concert'.[xiii]

Howard Newby moved to become Director of Programmes Radio, and was replaced as Controller, Radio 3 by Stephen Hearst, another 'abrasive, Viennese-born ex-television executive', initially given to insisting 'on programmes which listeners would understand and not switch off', in which stance he alarmed the Music Division (Black et al. 2010: 93). The BBC's 50th Anniversary Concert on 11 November was the first concert to be broadcast simultaneously (simulcast) by BBC2 television and Radio 3.

There was little sign by 1972 that Radio 3, even after a couple of years to settle down, was meeting the needs of the general audience. Rather to the contrary, there was another extended spat about what one letter writer to *The Times* called 'the creeping vulgarisation of Radio 3'.[xiv] This was once again a debate among the few, ignoring—indeed consciously rejecting—any participation by a wider franchise. Regular *Listener* critic, Steven Walsh, argued that 'the central problem is as usual one of control. There is a feeling ... that the people best-qualified to run a musical operation, i.e. musicians, are given insufficient power to do so'.[xv] What was lost was any awareness of the legitimate interests of the middle-brow audience which the Music Programme had identified, but which Radio 3 at that time seemed too dominated by the various vested interests to continue to serve effectively.

Serious music fared much less well than serious speech in the aftermath of the controversy over *Broadcasting in the Seventies*. Hugh Chignell (2011: 105) notes that the BBC in these years displayed a new ambition and seriousness in spoken word programming, which 'provided fertile ground for some of the most interesting programmes ever produced on BBC radio'. He cites the current affairs documentary series *Analysis* and the rise of the radio feature, such as *The Long March of Everyman*, both on Radio 4. Yet *Analysis* when introduced in 1970 was reaching audiences of 250,000, higher than even the most popular Radio 3 programme across the whole sample week. There were those within the BBC who wished to demonstrate a seriousness of purpose in defiance of the popularising tendencies of Mansell and Gillard (Chignell 2011: 108), but in Radio 3 that very largely meant elitist conservatism in programming judgements.

Meanwhile, plans for the introduction of what the BBC resolutely termed 'commercial radio' were proceeding apace. What nobody had spotted was that these new stations might provide competition in classical music radio. But that was about to happen.

'An Alternative Service of Radio Broadcasting'

As the Seventies began, a medium which had appeared to be largely supplanted by television found new opportunities amid the societal change of the Sixties and as a consequence of new technology. The offshore pirate radio stations, with Radio Caroline from Easter Day 1964 in the vanguard, had demonstrated that radio could be once again an innovative, mass appeal medium. The BBC's response to the reawakening of popular music radio in the Sixties, the new Radios 1 and 2, was in part intended to head off such competition. However, the relatively unexpected Conservative victory in the June 1970 General Election brought to power a Government which had 'commercial radio' as a central plank in its manifesto. Heath's Government began at once to shape a network of radio broadcasting to end the BBC's monopoly. This service was to mirror the very successful pattern of ITV. It was to be public service radio, funded by advertising, locally owned and tightly regulated by the IBA—the old Independent Television Authority with an additional duty, which it had accepted only reluctantly (Stoller 2010: 30–31).

Although it had demonstrated an appetite for innovative radio, Britain was not yet ready for full *commercial* radio, even if there was a substantial potential audience for it. As I have argued elsewhere, the nation's leaders 'contemplated vistas of radical change only through the frosted glass of tradition, caution and deference, which had characterised their society' (Stoller 2010: 24). The resulting system of *independent* radio was a bold experiment. Even though it was introduced in economically unpropitious times, it proved to be successful until new socio-economic and political forces overwhelmed it during the late Eighties.

The ILR stations came on air in a series of phases from the autumn of 1973, dictated by the emerging political view of the system. The first batch of licences were awarded in London to LBC and Capital Radio, followed by Glasgow (Radio Clyde), Birmingham (BRMB), Manchester (Piccadilly Radio), Newcastle (Metro Radio), Swansea (Swansea Sound), Sheffield (Radio Hallam), Edinburgh (Radio Forth), Plymouth (Plymouth Sound), Nottingham (Radio Trent) and Teesside (Radio Tees). The Sound Broadcasting Act 1972 required the IBA to ensure that each station broadcast 'a wide range of programmes', which the Authority interpreted as applying to the music output of the stations as well. The effect was virtually to mandate classical music output on every station.

When Heath's administration was replaced by a minority Labour Government under Harold Wilson in 1974, the IBA was given a limit of 19 stations while the Annan Committee considered the future of broadcasting in the UK (Stoller 2010: 63). These stations operated within a specific public service remit. After the Annan Committee's report in March 1977, the system was allowed to expand from 1979 onwards. By the end of the Eighties, it had grown to 60 stations, covering all the major towns and cities in the UK. Those new stations came on air with the same obligations of public service broadcasting as the first 19, and therefore reflected the same approach to classical music programming as the pioneers had done.

When the ILR system was being devised, Government and regulators had come under considerable pressure from the powerful Musicians' Union (MU). Without the MU's agreement, it was felt, it would not be possible to build the necessary consensus to allow the system to be introduced.[xvi] The Union also had considerable influence over the copyright societies,[2] with whom negotiations needed to be concluded to allow the ILR stations enough needletime to play commercial records. As a consequence, a requirement was included through the legislation that stations must spend 3% of their net advertising receipts on the employment of musicians. The effect of this was to ensure that within each ILR station there was a pot of money waiting to be spent. Bringing that together with the wish to gain regulatory approval, the effective obligation to broadcast classical music and—as may be discerned—a genuine wish on the part of at least some of the stations to take a lead in this radio genre, meant that music initiatives could be funded even when the stations were experiencing significant commercial constraints in other respects.

The statutory regime for ILR also included provision for 'secondary rental', in effect a tax on profits which might be excessive. Once profits exceeded 5% of net advertising revenue, after preoperational costs and accumulated losses had been paid off, as much as 50% of that profit was skimmed off into a central fund administered by the IBA. It yielded significant sums, 40% of which was used by the IBA to develop ILR,

---

[2] Phonographic Performance Limited (PPL) represented the rights interests of the record companies. The Performing Rights Society (PRS) did so for composers, arrangers and performers of music. For more details about this long-running issue see Stoller (2010: 181–196).

leaving 60% 'to be spent by the contractors on projects agreed with the Authority'.[xvii] As early as 1979, the IBA had £1.9 million to allocate; the following year this had risen to £2.7 million.[xviii]

Partly through its own inclinations, and partly as a result of continuing pressure from the MU, the IBA determined that much of this money was to be spent on classical music projects. IBA Director of Radio John Thompson explained that, although this was never actually a requirement, most of those involved in the discussions ahead of ILR:

> hoped there'd be some elements of classical music because they thought that dealing with orchestras was actually going to be administratively less difficult ... there wasn't much earnest discussion of types of music. Occasionally, both the Union people and indeed the copyright societies would josh me about it, saying 'of course it's going to be popular music', but I think they actually were not taken by surprise when it emerged that there was going to be what you and I would broadly describe as classical music.[xix]

The members of the IBA were drawn from that administrative class for whom classical music was part of the desired 'fabric of culture' as Matthew Arnold would have understood it. Thompson himself agrees that 'from the outset, if I had any individual role, I certainly hoped there would be elements of classical music'.[xx] The same was true of most of the Authority's senior staff (including this author). Despite the network's substantial reliance on pop music, the IBA celebrated the 10th anniversary of the ILR system with a string quartet concert.[xxi]

CLASSICAL MUSIC RADIO 1973–1976

Although competition was starting to arrive, for BBC radio little changed in 1973 in its classical output. One new programme, each weekday evening, was *Homeward Bound*, a sequence of light classics and gramophone records nominally for car-bound listeners. Not that they responded to it with huge enthusiasm. The audience in the sampled week varied from 0.1% to unmeasurable. The other innovation was the arrival of a classical record requests programme, *Your Concert Choice*, broadcast for nearly 2 hours on Sunday morning. That was backed up by Wednesday morning's *Your Midweek Choice*, requests again, although in that instance comprising less popular works: with a J.C. Bach symphony, a Handel organ concerto and an Ireland concertino, this was not instantly accessible popular radio.

The BBC Music Department had become ever-more self-referential. Glock's final promotion was a series of Winter Proms at the Royal Albert Hall and elsewhere over the New Year of 1973, where 'the paying audience at several of the nine concerts was only about one tenth of the Hall's capacity'.[xxii] If accurate, that means that only around 600 people paid to attend each concert. Despite that, it was only 'under heavy pressure' that Glock's successor, Ponsonby, agreed to abandon the Winter Proms for the following year. He felt this 'a deplorably retrograde step, and an abdication of the BBC's role of patron toward contemporary music' and—possibly even more significant—something that would 'disappoint Pierre Boulez'.[xxiii]

On television, BBC2's success with Joseph Cooper's *Face the Music* demonstrated once again the existence of a substantial potential audience for classical music broadcasting if presented in an accessible form. Cooper took particular pleasure from 'making music appeal to a wide audience' and getting people to attend concerts as a result. He noted that:

> professional musicians get very snooty about 'bleeding chunks'[3]–that's where you play a little and stop. But those are what drive people to the record shops.[xxiv]

BBC Director General Ian Trethowan seemed insouciant towards both parts of his potential audience for Radio 3:

> Radio 3 has not justified the fears of most of those who were so concerned at the disappearance of the Third. The cornerstone of the network is still the service of serious music during the daytime to the car-bound and house-bound who so bombarded us with their anxieties when it was reported (quite wrongly) that the Music Programme was going to be axed. In the evenings we broadcast regular concerts of mainstream serious music … as well as providing a platform for contemporary music.[xxv]

---

[3] The phrase 'bleeding chunks' had probably been coined by Sir Donald Tovey in 1935: 'Defects of form are not a justifiable ground for criticism from listeners who profess to enjoy the bleeding chunks of butcher's meat chopped from Wagner's operas and served up on Wagner nights as *Waldweben* and *Walkürenritt*' (*Essays on Musical Analysis* 1935 vol. II p. 71).

The quality Trethowan missed was *integration*. Of course Radio 3 could broadcast *outré* music in the evenings to no audience; and equally it could peddle standard repertoire to the 'house-bound' during the daytime. The point was about making the connection between the two, and as a consequence energising the audience. Haley in the Forties had understood with great clarity that this was the BBC's duty and therefore mission. Joseph Cooper in the Seventies did so as well. Trethowan seemingly did not.

The challenge of ILR was not being felt by the BBC in classical music at this stage, even though it was gaining momentum. Some critics who also earned their living broadcasting for the BBC were quick to disparage the efforts of the new stations. Broadcaster and journalist Fritz Spiegel jeered at ILR's 'unserious' musical offering,[xxvi] allowing Gillian Reynolds (then Programme Director of Radio City) to make the point that the Liverpool station:

> presents an hour every Friday of local classical music; there is a half hour programme every Saturday evening on the coming week's musical calendar; one and a half hours on Sunday nights are devoted to recorded classical music.[xxvii]

In a sign of what was to come in the Nineties, Robin Ray—who was to be one of the leading spirits behind Classic FM—hosted a lengthy classical music record programme on Capital Radio, although not without incident, as on one occasion when the last minute or two of Mozart's G Minor Symphony disappeared to make room for 'a lugubrious voice and spooky noises which advised us to buy the Evening News'.[xxviii]

1975 provided further evidence of Radio 3 drawing back. Fewer composers featured in the sample week, despite a notable level of exposure for Bach and evidence of the emergence of enthusiasm for French composers. Apart from specific programmes such as *Music in Our Time*, there was less evidence of European modernism, and almost none of the more experimental American composers. The 1975 sample week provided examples of Radio 3 indulging its own higher ground taste while relinquishing any claim upon a mass audience. *Record Review* on Saturday featured records of German harpsichord music. Saturday, Sunday and Monday saw the broadcasting of three successive operas: *Il Trovatore* from Covent Garden; Berlioz' *The Damnation of Faust* from the Birmingham Town Hall (in recording); and then an unfinished

Mozart opera, *Zaide,* live from the Congress Hall in Saarbrücken. Apart from half an hour of Berlioz on Sunday afternoon, none attracted more than 50,000 listeners. The *Midday Concerts,* which in the Fifties were attracting at times 500,000 listeners or more, by 1974 reached only a tenth as many. Yet a sizeable potential middle-brow audience still existed: one broadcast of Mozart's *Requiem,* preceded by Alfred Brendel playing Mozart's F major piano concerto on records, peaked at an audience of 400,000 against mainstream evening television.

Meanwhile, the ILR stations were beginning to get into their stride. Metro Radio in Newcastle, for example, broadcast five hours of classical music each week. Capital Radio's *The Collection* programme started its long run, Radio Clyde relayed the Cleveland Quartet and the Scottish Proms, and there were even *lieder* recitals on Radio City.[xxix]

Ill-fortune dogged Radio 3 during 1976. Pierre Boulez had returned to France in 1975 to head up a new musical centre in Paris, but his successor as Chief Conductor of the BBCSO, Rudolf Kempe, fell mortally ill in March 1976 and died in May. Given the importance of the BBCSO repertoire for imaginative programming on Radio 3, the loss of Boulez and then Kempe, and the subsequent interregnum, was another factor reducing innovation and originality. David Munrow of *Pied Piper* fame committed suicide also in May, depriving the network of one of its brightest innovators and listeners of decades of unfulfilled potential programming.

There was however a brief serendipitous shift in 1976. Financial pressures obliged Radio 3 and Radio 4 to share some programmes in 1976, thus reintroducing classical music to Radio 4 after a gap of six years. This unlooked-for return of multi-channel BBC classical music (along with ILR) showed what the radio audiences had been missing when forced into the ghetto of Radio 3, and how they would respond in greater numbers to freer access with fewer prior assumptions about their 'right' to listen. The second-largest classical music audience of the 1976 sample week was for 'a weekly selection of popular classics' presented by Robin Ray at Saturday lunchtime and broadcast on both Radios 3 and 4—another indicator, unremarked at the time, of the potential for this type of output which Classic FM was later to exploit so successfully. There was further sharing on Saturday afternoon of *Music of the Masters,* a record sequence again. Indeed, the proportion of live or relayed original recordings fell further; record-based programmes represented 33% of all music output across the sample week.

The celebration of the 30th anniversary of the Third Programme in September 1976 revealed that Radio 3 was still resting on the laurels of its predecessor. Stephen Hearst, the station's Controller from 1972 to 1978, felt that the linking of the Music Programme with the Third Programme had:

> provided the new network, Radio 3, with so solid a base of cultural, intellectual and political support that its future was made as secure as anything can be in our unstable world ... Moreover, British musical life had, and has, an excellence and vitality that transferred to broadcasting, and brought added strength.[xxx]

Few agreed with him. For some commentators, Radio 3 represented 'The Fall'.[xxxi] The leading radio critic of the day, David Wade, talked about it as being 'son of the Third', predicting 'premature senility: fiddling on innumerable violins while Rome—which is now smouldering—burns'.[xxxii] Nor was there genuine evidence of a wide audience. Hearst claimed in 1976 that 'nearly five million listeners ... listen at least once a week to Radio 3'[xxxiii] but independent research the following year suggests a weekly audience of around 2.7 million adults, and 2.6 million in 1978.[xxxiv]

For BBC radio in 1977, it was chiefly the shared classical music programming with Radio 3 which yielded strikingly high audiences. Robin Ray's eponymous Saturday record programme on Radio 3 plus Radio 4 was heard by 555,000 listeners in the sample week. As well as sharing with Radio 3 a concert with Pinkas Zuckerman playing and conducting Mozart on Tuesday evening, Radio 4 broadcast the time-honoured light-music programme, *These You Have Loved*, on Saturday evening to just under 500,000 listeners, repeated on Thursday morning to a striking 900,000 listeners. The other simulcast was with BBC2: Strauss' *Salome* attracted 100,000 listeners to Radio 3 on Saturday evening, and four times that number of viewers to BBC2, where the programme was watched by between 350,000 and 450,000 viewers.[xxxv]

These audience levels illustrate once again what was lost when classical music was deported to the ghetto of Radio 3. A larger and broader audience existed for this genre of output, if only it could be made available on a platform and in a style with which they felt comfortable. The achievement of ILR in reaching a wider audience offers further evidence to this effect. There, Radio Clyde was reporting a 'substantial listening audience' attracted to its classical music programmes, leading it to increase the time devoted to these.[xxxvi] Other major city stations were starting to record their local orchestras for broadcast: the Birmingham Symphony Orchestra by BRMB (Birmingham) and the Royal Liverpool Philharmonic Orchestra by Radio City (Liverpool).[xxxvii]

Homeward Bound, a new-sequence programme on Radio 3 in drive-time,[4] however, failed to find a measurable audience all week. This failure to connect with the popular audience is all the more notable given the evidence of Ray's success. Similarly, although all the 1977 Proms were broadcast on Radio 3, that was in the belief spelt out by Hugo Cole in *the Listener* that:

> the need to educate Proms audiences has passed. Today's music-lovers, educated by radio and record, have a far wider experience of music of all sorts than even the critics and performers of 50 years ago.[xxxviii]

By contrast, across in the private sector the Managing Director of Capital Radio, John Whitney, was pointing out that:

> a popular radio station with a large audience drawn to it by pop ... has ... an ability to educate far beyond anything that could be achieved by a station catering exclusively to minority interests. We at Capital Radio can – and do – use our ability to introduce our listeners to, for example, classical music. The result is that more Londoners listen to *The Collection*, our classical music programme, than to any classical music programme on Radio 3.[xxxix]

Whitney's audience claims stand up during the sample week, with the exception of the Robin Ray programme which was simulcast on Radios 3 and 4 and attracted a larger audience than Capital's *The Collection*.

For the elitists, the repertoire of Capital Radio's Wren Orchestra,[5] ILR's major single classical music initiative, 'consisted of what Radio 3 normally regards as shaving-time fare: genial suites, symphonies and concertos'.[xl] Yet ILR was extending its audiences, the ambition of its repertoire, and its promotion of classical music performances in its localities.

---

[4] Late afternoons on weekdays, typically the period between 4 and 7 pm.
[5] See Chap. 6, p. 172.

ILR's Programming Approach

By 1977, all of the ILR stations scheduled regular classical music programmes—apart from the news franchise in London, LBC—although the content of individual stations' programmes varied hugely. In the BBC, programme content was dictated by:

> the BBC producers' extraordinary cultural power to choose what goes on air, and so have a controlling influence on the shape of national culture across all the boundaries of national political debate. (Hendy 2000: 78)

In ILR, the programme presenter was left entirely to his or her own devices. This applied even in a major station like Capital Radio, where presenter Peter James recalls:

> I did what I liked. They let me spend all this money, and commission these great orchestras. I had a completely free hand, and could programme whatever I thought the audience would like. A typical response was after I broadcast a live recording of Richard Strauss' *Alpine Symphony* and wondered how the audience would react. The following day a taxi driver came into the station to say how much he had liked it and to ask where he could get a recording of it, and also to ask if Strauss had written other symphonies.[xli]

It was even more so in smaller stations like Radio 210 in Reading, as Fiona Talkington—then a presenter on Radio 210, later a BBC Radio 3 presenter and joint originator of its remarkable *Late Junction* programme—remembers:

> ILR wasn't playlist driven and was only constrained by what was in the station library and one's own collection. But, if you can call it a constraint, there was also the sensitivity to station sound and audience profile, at the same time recognising the interaction listeners enjoyed and the sorts of pieces they asked to hear ... this could range from the most popular – which people just enjoy – to the most obscure – which they enjoy often because it enables them to show off their knowledge.[xlii]

ILR's ambition ran beyond routine output of record programmes. Many stations sponsored significant local concerts by orchestras. Piccadilly Radio broadcast the final night of the Hallé Proms from the Free

Trade Hall in Manchester and also a Hallé performance of the *Messiah* at Christmas, as well as the Manchester midday concerts. Radio Clyde, as part of its 'Clyde 76' Festival, sponsored concerts by the Scottish National Orchestra in May; Radio City broadcast a series of Sunday evening concerts with the Royal Liverpool Philharmonic Orchestra; and BRMB Radio sponsored free concerts by the City of Birmingham Symphony Orchestra, including a notably successful 'Young People's concert'.[xliii]

The ILR companies were still very much in thrall to the IBA, at least until the relationships began to break down in the mid-Eighties. The Chairmen and Managing Directors of each station—very much the dominant figures—understood early on that they could win the IBA's approval by offering some good local classical music either in local concert promotion, or on-air broadcasts, or both. This was not only, as has been suggested—a little unkindly, given that this author was one of them—because at least two ILR Managing Directors, of Radio Hallam and Radio 210, were themselves the programme presenters. This approach pleased the cultural expectations of the Members of the Authority, its senior staff and also politicians and Government officials; it enabled the IBA's ambitious decision to broadcast all programmes in stereo to be heard to good effect; and it gave each company a standing among the opinion formers within its local area who might be won over to provide political support and advertising bookings. These were times when those who made up the most influential strata in society regarded classical music as an unalloyed virtue, and were prepared to give credence to the public service assertions of a medium which provided it.

In his study of American commercial radio, David Goodman has explained how a very similar situation pertained in the United States, at least up until the Second World War:

> Classical music, most of it broadcast live, was by all later standards astonishingly available to listeners to mainstream American commercial radio in the 1930s. (2011: 118)

He relates how, as someone who had enjoyed publicly funded broadcasting on Australian radio, he:

> took for granted an association of classical music with high culture and the sense that it is somehow above all opposed to commercialism ... the

mixture of classical music and commercialism seemed transgressive to me, some kind of cultural mistake. American friends were surprised at my surprise. They had grown up accustomed to just that kind of linking of classical music with up market consumerism that I was hearing. (2001: 116)

Part of this was what Goodman describes as a 'regulatory artefact', and it is reasonable to deduce that a similar situation pertained in the UK during the years when the regulator showed a concern for such matters. However, as Goodman observes, that by itself did not fully explain—in the USA any more than for ILR fifty years later—the widespread and ambitious presence of classical music:

[Commercial] broadcasters wanted and even needed classical music because it was so indisputably highbrow, sacralized, high status, and self evidently in the public interest. Classical music was a crucial part of the civic paradigms, and its ambition to create modern citizens with a developed capacity to absorb information, empathize across cultural borders, experience and control emotion, and arrive at reasoned personal opinions. (2001: 118)

CLASSICAL MUSIC RADIO 1977–1979

Although the BBC had begun by 1977 to notice ILR's classical music activities, there is no evidence that they influenced BBC output at all. Rather, the BBC sought to damn them with faint praise. Capital presenter Peter James recalls the station's outstanding broadcast on 9 March 1977 of Verdi's *Otello* from Covent Garden, which was broadcast across the ILR network:

Ian McIntyre, the BBC's then Controller of Radio 3, wrote in the *Evening Standard* acknowledging 'the splendid recording' but then proceeded to say that 'it was easy for Capital Radio to do this once while the BBC was broadcasting high quality music every day of every week.'[xliv]

The week-by-week output of each ILR station was indeed more mundane than the highlights which the IBA chose to report, but it was nevertheless consistent, popular and effective programming, albeit for only a few hours each week. By this time also, ILR output began to benefit from funding from secondary rental, remitted back to it by the IBA for 'worthwhile projects' which, as discussed further in the next chapter, paid for programmes which were then shared among the local stations.⁶ Nor were these programmes played out into the unheard air, an observation which could have been made about much of the Radio 3 output. A new audience was established for classical music (as well as, arguably, the old middle-brow audience better served).

There was one poignant indicator that ILR felt itself to be part of a long tradition of classical music radio in the UK. Capital Radio offered an annual award of £2,500 in memory of Anna Instone, who—with her husband, Julian Herbage—had been for so long a stalwart of the BBC's Gramophone Department, but had moved across to Capital shortly before her death in 1978. The award was designed to assist a musician's postgraduate studies, and continued until beyond the end of the period covered by this history, even though classical music was no longer broadcast by the station.

For those who regard the history of broadcasting through a corporate, strategic lens, it was as if during 1978 the BBC generals were being quietly moved into place for a major assault. Ian Trethowan had become Director General in 1977, and radio was to be run from 1978 by a new Managing Director, Aubrey Singer, who had most recently been Controller of BBC2 television and who 'did not love music' (Seaton 2015: 94). He set about marshalling his forces for an attack on the cost of the BBC house orchestras.⁷ That same year, Ian McIntyre, who was essentially concerned with speech radio, assumed the controllership of Radio 3 after a tough time at Radio 4 (Hendy 2007: 176) and Gennady Rozhdestvensky became Chief Conductor of the BBCSO after a long 'courtship' by Ponsonby (Kenyon 1981: 412). Neither of them was yet aware of the storm which Singer and Trethowan were brewing.

Barry Fantoni wrote slightingly in January 1978 in *The Times* of the 'appalling condescension' of Radio 3, arguing that:

> woven into the fabric of the BBC's cultural policy is the idea that what we hear on the radio should improve our minds and that those who plan broadcasting know what is best for us. We are to be lifted from the murky depths of Frank Sinatra and Lionel Bart to the celestial heights of Peter Peers and Hugo Wolf.[xlv]

---

⁶See Chap. 6, pp. 170ff.

⁷See Chap. 6, pp. 159ff.

His article immediately drew a furious response from those who wished to protect the elite position of Radio 3 as 'an island of normality in a media ocean of unreal trivia'.[xlvi] There was a range of letters similarly supporting the status quo in *The Times* correspondence columns throughout the spring of 1978.

In national politics, any prospect of the survival of the social-liberal consensus was snuffed out by the impact of the 'Winter of Discontent'. The Annan Committee's report in 1977 was destined to become an anachronism after the ensuing General Election, but at least it freed the IBA to expand the ILR system with 41 new stations, which would all expect and be expected to broadcast some classical music programming and be active in their local musical scene. The Annan Committee also argued for the superiority of good concerts over gramophone records, while urging that extra finance should be provided to the Arts Council to help with the funding of the BBC orchestras, especially outside London.[xlvii] Little attention was paid to these recommendations, although they were a hint of the impending battle over BBC orchestras at the end of the decade. Meanwhile, the ILR companies made their first reference to the Copyright Tribunal in the misplaced expectation of better terms for playing commercially recorded music.

For ILR, Capital Radio secured a considerable coup by recording and broadcasting a concert by Leonard Bernstein and the Vienna Philharmonic at the Royal Festival Hall on 18 February 1978, a programme relayed by virtually all of the other ILR stations. Radio City promoted and broadcast an experimental transmission in quadraphonic sound of a performance of Mahler's *Eighth Symphony* from Liverpool's Anglican Cathedral. The performance featured a specially augmented Royal Liverpool Philharmonic Orchestra and six choirs, conducted by Charles Groves.[xlviii] Secondary rental payable to the IBA reached £1 million, and was used to fund *inter alia* Capital Radio's concert series *Great Orchestras of the World*. The series was not without incident, as the music establishment hesitated about their new funders. Sean Street (2005: 122) relates how conductor Herbert von Karajan demanded that his fee be delivered to him in cash backstage during the interval before he was prepared to go out and conduct the second half of a concert.

There is evidence of the ILR companies embracing classical music broadcasting in ways that went well beyond their statutory and regulatory obligations. For instance, writing its own pages in the *IBA Yearbook* for 1979, the Birmingham station BRMB vaunted its community involvement with this genre of music:

> The station has sponsored a series of highly successful youth concerts with the City of Birmingham Symphony Orchestra in Birmingham town Hall. Held on eight Saturday mornings throughout the year, the concerts were recorded and subsequently broadcast on the station's Sunday evening classical music show. The BRMB radio music scholarship was held for the first time in 1978 and over 70 young musicians from all over the Midlands entered the competition.[xlix]

The implication for concerts of the scheduling of advertisements on radio was sufficiently widespread for the IBA to amend its regulations to facilitate such output:

> there will be occasions when a particular programme – perhaps an opera, classical concert or Parliamentary broadcast – will not lend itself to advertising interruptions and on those occasions the Authority is prepared to consider a reasonable redistribution of displaced advertising, provided that twelve minutes is not exceeded in any one clock hour.[l]

Radio 3 changed its medium-wave frequency on 23 November 1978, but the Radio 3 schedule during the 1979 sample week shows little change from 1978, although there were 111 different composers broadcast, the most for the decade. The increased importance of records in Radio 3's output is the other notable feature emerging from the analysis of the sample week. Excluding feature programmes, record-based programmes were around 40% of the total music output of the station, the highest percentage for the decade.

The weekend for Radio 3 was again built around record-based output all morning, with *Record Review*, focused upon Holst's *Planets Suite*, achieving the top audience of the sample week, 313,000. The featured opera on Saturday evening, *Rigoletto* performed by the Scottish Philharmonia and the Scottish Opera Chorus, remarkably received a sponsorship credit in the *Radio Times* listings for Commercial Union Assurance. The audience on Saturday peaked at 52,500 early in the afternoon and then remained unmeasurable for the whole of the rest of the day. Predictably, there was no popular audience for a music drama in two acts by Rutland Boulton, *The Immortal Hour*; nor, more surprisingly, for

Schubert, Kreutzer and Paganini in a recording of *Southbank Summer Music*; disappointingly for a concert of Walton, Stravinsky, Hindemith and Tchaikovsky; and probably inevitably for a late-night concert of Birtwistle, Stravinsky and Sackman.

This raises once again the worth or otherwise of an extensive and expensive period of network radio, on a peak day for radio listening, being devoted to material which only a disappearingly small percentage of the audience chose to listen to. Certainly, Boughton's opera 'set in the Hebrides, deep in the mists of time, amid the fairy world of Celtic mythology'[li] might arguably only ever have received public exposure in a Radio 3 broadcast. Yet, the reality that so few listeners tuned in for that programme and for the rest of the evening calls into question whether this is proportionate public service to society as a whole—or even a specialist part of it.

Arguably, the exposure of difficult music was and remains a legitimate public service aim. That can be said to be the case for the first performance of Hoddinott's *Job* on Tuesday afternoon of the sample week, even if it was not achieving a measurable audience, not least as it—like Boughton's work—was supported by a *Radio Times* feature. But how does that argument stand up in the case of the extended drivetime sequence of *Homeward Bound* and *At Home*, rarely achieving a measurable audience all week? It is reasonable to conclude that BBC's radio management continued to mistrust anything smacking of seeking popularity. As one specific example, the decision to drop from the 1980 Proms programme the 'Viennese night', which was to have been introduced by Richard Baker and Esther Rantzen, left those in BBC television feeling that the decision 'will deprive millions of a programme they enormously enjoy, apparently because a few people believe Esther Rantzen in some way belittles music'. Perhaps confirming their suspicions, Ponsonby riposted that 'the Proms really cannot dance to the tune of television's ratings'.[lii]

It might have been expected that Radio 3's music output would start to change when the new Controller, Ian McIntyre, announced his new schedules in July 1979. In a paper to the Governors entitled 'Pleasure and enlargement', on his appointment as Controller, Radio 3, he had asked 'should we be concerned about [increasing the audiences for Radio 3] and seek to broadcast a format which would fit the lifestyle of the busy housewife with a taste for classical music?' before concluding that 'the temptation to turn Radio 3 into a "top 100 (or 500) Classics" must be resisted'.[liii]

McIntyre was at heart a patrician, as is illustrated by his choice of title for his 'manifesto' paper. It was drawn from his recollection of an anecdote about his predecessor-but-one, Howard Newby:

> who presided so lovingly over this area of broadcasting for so long, [telling] the story of going to the States and describing the Third Programme to Americans he met. 'Oh I see' they said, 'it's educational broadcasting'. 'No' said Howard, 'it's putting out good minority programmes for people who like that sort of thing. No ulterior motive. Just pleasure and enlargement'.[liv]

McIntyre compared Radio 3 to a stately home which did not need the popularisation of a Safari Park in the grounds. Whatever his approach, however, his detailed plans 'were concerned solely with speech' (Carpenter and Doctor 1996: 300), and he implemented little dramatic change in the music format or schedule.

Rumours of War

The General Election victory on 3 May 1979 for a radicalised Conservative party was an inflection point for the UK, marking the end of post-war social liberalism and the arrival of the market liberalism which was to rule the roost until well beyond the end of the century. That was also to change the climate in which broadcasting operated by the end of the Eighties, as well as having a direct impact on the pattern of radio and television broadcasting, as the next chapter describes. For ILR, the shift in the *zeitgeist* was to overturn the settlement which had engendered its classical music broadcasting, so that by the end of Eighties that was to disappear entirely.

For BBC classical music, storm clouds were gathering. As early as February 1979, the new Managing Director Radio, Aubrey Singer, had informed the Governors that he was 'grasping the nettle of the orchestral problem' although 'he could not help feeling that he was doing so while wearing gloves'.[lv] According to Jean Seaton (2015: 103), Singer and Trethowan—who in his rise to the top of the BBC had been Managing Director Radio from 1970 to 1975—had already cooked up their plan for radio while travelling together in China, well away from other senior BBC music figures. Singer decided to start by tackling the Scottish orchestras, and in May he was reporting 'that in the face of Scottish resistance to the idea of devolving regional orchestras to their regions he was considering an alternative approach, which was to disband the Scottish Radio Orchestra'.[lvi] His forthright approach led Patrick Ramsay, Controller, Scotland to try to set up working channels and gentler negotiations.[lvii] Meanwhile, Singer was in discussions with the BBC legal team about what obligations they had towards the MU and what chance they would have of moving ahead without detailed discussions with the Union.[lviii]

Even at this early stage, the BBC Governors should not have doubted his determination. He told their June 1979 meeting 'that he was not prepared to continue spending five million pounds a year without producing one world-class orchestra'.[lix] By early July 1979 he felt that 'at last the orchestral strategy matter might be on the move', asking Deputy Managing Director Radio Douglas Muggeridge to take on responsibility for the task.[lx] Singer used a resolution at the MU conference on 23 July 1979 to persuade the Governors to agree that he could move ahead more quickly than originally planned,[lxi] starting the events that were to convulse BBC radio's classical music as the Eighties began.

There were moments during the Seventies—especially during the enforced simulcasting of Radios 3 and 4 which briefly widened the classical music radio franchise for the BBC—when some of the peaks of the late Sixties were glimpsed again. From 1973 onwards, classical music radio was alive and well, and living—albeit modestly—in ILR too. But the Eighties were destined to be different. It is not unreasonable to see a link between Prime Minister Thatcher's confrontational style and that of Singer, in their decisions to tackle those trade unions which seemed most to symbolise the restrictive practices they especially abhorred. That carried over to the ILR companies, as they sought to drop their public service remit, and they too challenged the power and influence of the MU. External pressures of labour relations, finance and the market would undermine classical music radio at the start and the end of the Eighties.

NOTES

i. Christopher Booker. Quoted in Sandbrook (2010: 9) but unsourced.
ii. *An Alternative Service of Radio Broadcasting*. 1971 White Paper, Cmnd 4636. London: HMSO.

iii. *Broadcasting in the Seventies*: the BBC's plan for network radio and non-*metropolitan broadcasting* 1969. London: British Broadcasting Corporation.
iv. William Ash, Archie Campbell, Susanna Capon, Douglas Cleverdon, Betty Davies, David Davis, Margaret Etall, H.B. Fortuin, Graham Gauld, Martin Jenkins, Gerry Jones, Charles Lefeaux, Ronald Mason, Nesta Pain, Marie Parotte, John Powell, Raymond Raikes. R.D. Smith, Hallam Tennyson, Terence Tiller, Colin Tucker, John Tydeman, Guy Vaesen, Keith Williams, Norman Wright et al. Policy On Radio Broadcasts: Opposition From Staff. *The Times*, 14 February 1970, p. 9.
v. *The Listener*, 1 January 1970, p. 18.
vi. Ian Trethowan. Future of Radio Broadcasts: Seeking Wider Audiences. *The Times*, 28 January 1970, p. 11.
vii. See for example a letter in *The Listener*, 29 January 1970, p. 150 signed by 28 intellectual luminaries including E.M. Forster and Bernard Williams.
viii. Stephen Walsh. *The Listener*, 26 March 1970, p. 425.
ix. Charles Curran. Music and the BBC. *The Listener*, 11 June 1970, p. 779.
x. Richard Hoggart. *Only connect: on culture and communication: the BBC Reith lectures 1971*.
xi. Michael Hatfield. The balance and bureaucrats of broadcasting. *The Times*, 4 March 1971, p. 14.
xii. The gathering storm over the future of radio. *The Times*, 6 March 1971, p. 12.
xiii. Controller Music (Ponsonby) to Managing Director Radio (Trethowan), 31 July 1975. BBC WAC R101/302/1.
xiv. Letter. *The Times*, 6 June 1972, p. 15.
xv. Stephen Walsh. *The Listener*, Thursday 15 June 1972, p. 798.
xvi. Interview with John Thompson, 16 December 2013.
xvii. ITA/IBA/Cable Authority Archive, Bournemouth University. IBA Minutes 397(76) of a meeting on 2 December 1976.
xviii. ITA/IBA/Cable Authority Archive, Bournemouth University. IBA Paper 357(79), 12 December 1979.
xix. Interview with John Thompson, 16 December 2013.
xx. *Ibid.*
xxi. *IBA Annual Report 1983/4*, p. 51.
xxii. The fiasco of the Winter Proms. *The Times Diary*, 9 February 1973, p. 14.
xxiii. Public concerts financial estimates: winter proms. Memorandum from Controller Music (Ponsonby) to Director of Programmes Radio (Newby), 7 February 1973. BBC WAC R101/302/1.
xxiv. Ann Morrow. Bringing bleeding chunks to the masses. *The Times*, 4 August 1973, p. 12.
xxv. Ian Trethowan (Managing Director Radio). On the future of radio. *The Listener*, 3 May 1973, p. 569.

xxvi. Fritz Spiegel. Music. *The Listener*, 14 November 1973, p. 643.
xxvii. Gillian Reynolds. Not serious. *The Listener* 5 December 1973, p. 737.
xxviii. Henry Raynor. Commercial stations seek to involve the public. *The Times*, 8 April 1974, p. 12.
xxix. *ITV 1975* (ILR supplement). London: Independent Broadcasting Authority.
xxx. Stephen Hearst. Three cheers for the Third. *The Listener*, 30 September 1976, p. 390.
xxxi. Jack Lonsdale. The rise and fall of the Third. *The Times*, 29 September 1976, p. 16.
xxxii. David Wade. Son of the Third. *The Times*, 25 September 1976, p. 6.
xxxiii. Stephen Hearst. Three cheers for the Third. *The Listener*, 30 September 1976, p. 390.
xxxiv. Joint Industry Committee for Radio Audience Research (JICRAR).
xxxv. BBC Daily Viewing Barometer, May 1977.
xxxvi. *TV & Radio 1976*. London: Independent Broadcasting Authority, p. 149.
xxxvii. *IBA Annual Report 1975/6*, p. 35.
xxxviii. Hugo Cole. A 55-course banquet. *The Listener*, 7 July 1977, p. 20.
xxxix. Letter. *The Times*, 7 April 1977, p. 17.
xl. Paul Griffiths. *The Times*, 6 May 1977, p. 15.
xli. Interview with Peter James, 30 May 2013.
xlii. Fiona Talkington, personal communication, 30 May 2013.
xliii. *IBA Annual Report 1976/7*, p. 35.
xliv. Interview with Peter James, 30 May 2013.
xlv. Barry Fantoni. Music hath charms, but can the same be said of Radio 3? *The Times*, 21 January 1978, p. 14.
xlvi. David Shayer. Music on Radio 3. *The Times*, 18 February 1978, p. 15.
xlvii. Annan Committee. *Report of the Committee on the Future of Broadcasting*, March 1977, Cmnd 6753: paras. 21.12 and 21.64.
xlviii. *IBA Annual Report 1977/8*, p. 35.
xlix. *TV & Radio 1979*. London: Independent Broadcasting Authority, p. 146.
l. *IBA Annual Report 1978/9*, p. 169.
li. *Radio Times*, 6 May 1979, p. 38.
lii. Memorandum from David Buckton (producer) to Head Music Arts Television (Humphrey Burton), 3 December 1979, sent on to Ponsonby by Burton on 10 December 1979. BBC WAC R27/1081/1.
liii. Radio programme policy paper prepared for the General Advisory Committee 7 December 1978 and discussed at the General Advisory Committee 7 February 1979, 7 December 1978. BBC WAC R92/69/1.
liv. *Ibid.*
lv. BBC Board of Governors minutes, 8 February 1979. BBC WAC R78/2258/1.
lvi. *Ibid.*

lvii. Letter from Controller Scotland (Ramsay) to Managing Director Radio (Singer), 14 May 1979. BBC WAC R78/2258/1.
lviii. Memorandum from Legal Adviser (Jennings) to Managing Director Radio (Singer), 12 June 1979. BBC WAC R78/2258/1.
lix. BBC Board of Management minutes, 26 June 1979. BBC WAC R78/2258/1.
lx. Memorandum from Managing Director Radio (Singer) to Deputy Managing Director Radio (Muggeridge), 3 July 1979. BBC WAC R78/2258/1.
lxi. BBC Board of Management minutes, 9 July 1979. BBC WAC R78/2258/1.

Bibliographic Sources

Black, L., C. Wintle, and K. Hopkins. 2010. *BBC music in the Glock era and after: A memoir*. London: Cosman Keller Art and Music Trust in association with Plumbago Books.
Carpenter, H., and J.R. Doctor. 1996. *The envy of the world: Fifty years of the BBC Third Programme and Radio 3, 1946–1996*. London: Weidenfeld & Nicolson.
Chignell, H. 2011. *Public issue radio: Talks, news and current affairs in the 20th century*. Basingstoke: Palgrave Macmillan.
Goodman, D. 2011. *Radio's civic ambition: American broadcasting and democracy in the 1930s*. Oxford: Oxford University Press.
Hendy, D. 2000. *Radio in the global age*. Cambridge: Polity.
Hendy, D. 2007. *Life on air: A history of Radio Four*. Oxford: Oxford University Press.
Kenyon, N. 1981. *The BBC Symphony Orchestra: The first fifty years 1930–1980*. London: British Broadcasting Corporation.
Pirie, P.J. 1979. *The English musical renaissance*. London: Gollancz.
Ponsonby, R. 2009. *Musical heroes: A personal view of music and the musical world over sixty years*. London: DLM.
Seaton, J. 2015. *Pinkoes and traitors. The BBC and the nation 1974–1987*. London: Profile Books.
Stoller, T. 2010. *Sounds of your life: The history of independent radio in the UK*. New Barnet: John Libbey.
Street, S. 2005. *A concise historical dictionary of British radio*, 2nd ed. Tiverton: Kelly Publications.

CHAPTER 6

The Eighties: Keeping the Philistines at Bay

Classical music radio in 1980—BBC musicians' strike and its impact—BBC classical music output 1981–1984—the apex of ILR classical music output 1980–1984; audiences for classical music on ILR; secondary rental and programme sharing; the 'Heathrow Conference'—classical music radio 1985–1989.

The Eighties began with the BBC preparing with some relish for a trial of industrial strength with their strongest trade union. They ended with the sounds of Beethoven's Choral Symphony filling what had been the no-man's-land between East and West Berlin, and the European radio airwaves too. Change in these years seemed dramatic and definitive at the time. Yet the perspective of history shows it as the culmination of forces emerging in an apparently sudden *bouleversement*, akin to an earthquake following long years of tension along pre-existing fault lines.

The years between the election victory of Margaret Thatcher in 1979 (or arguably from her confirmation in power as well as office following the Falklands War of 1982) until her resignation in 1990, were revolutionary for British society, politics, economics and culture. The breakdown of the 40-year social democratic consensus had seemingly been foreshadowed by the rise of the Militant Left, but the true change was the moving of the centre of gravity towards the political Right, from a planning-dominated to a market-dominated economic and political nexus. The public confrontations—with the miners at Orgreave Colliery, the IRA in Brighton's Grand Hotel or amid the Poll Tax riots—may be seen as the discarding of the comfort-blanket of the past in untypical and ultimately cathartic violence. These were in many ways the Thatcher years, dominated—at least in the public mind—by one individual to a degree wholly unusual for Britain in peacetime.

Throughout the decade, the broadcasting initiatives were mostly with television. Channel 4 began broadcasting in 1982, and both daytime and breakfast television started in the middle of the decade, prompting ILR to reconsider its commitment to a public service remit. Towards the end of the decade the prospect of new national radio services—commercial analogue, and digital for all—started to be discussed, although at that stage a new classical music service was not seriously in prospect.

It was the elevation of market considerations above the old socio-cultural priorities which led classical music radio in the Eighties into its two major upheavals: at the BBC as the decade began, and then in ILR as it came to an end. For the BBC, deliberate confrontation with the Musicians Union (MU) in 1980 thrust it into the turmoil of an industrial dispute, closely analogous with what was happening in UK industry as a whole. For ILR, the commercial freedoms of the decade lured it away from public service-based *independent* radio towards full-scale *commercial* radio in 1990, in which it seemed there was to be no place for this genre of music.

From the start of the decade, the two sectors approached their classical music tasks with differing intent. The BBC settled into relatively unambitious classical music service for its middle-brow audience, with virtually segregated attention to the higher brow; ILR shone with ambition in classical music for a few years, attracting a new, younger and more diverse audience, before being dimmed and eventually extinguished by the pursuit of the easier commerce of popular music radio.

Classical Music Radio in 1980

BBC radio entered the Eighties with little fanfare. It was dominated not only by the need for economies, but also by personal rivalries. Robert Ponsonby (2009), who succeeded William Glock as Controller of Music in 1972, reveals in his autobiography the depth of personal feelings both positive and negative. In his memoir, *Musical Heroes* (2009), he writes warmly of Glock, as being 'a man with a mission' (p. 112) and 'a hard act to follow'; that Controller of Music John Drummond 'could be arrogant and vain and intolerant' (p. 110); and that Aubrey Singer 'adopted a deeply offensive, sabre-rattling posture' (p. 55). Jean Seaton notes of Singer that in one significant aspect of the reorganisation which combined the Gramophone and Music Departments 'many thought he took revenge as well' (2015: 105). There is a sense that classical music was being 'demoted' within the BBC through much of the Eighties, its *esprit de corps* severely shaken by 'bitter negotiations' with the MU over the proposed closure of BBC orchestras in 1980, exacerbated by BBC management's 'inhumane' approach (Kenyon 1981: 432).

The other main contextual constraint was finance, with the BBC cancelling all live opera relays in 1980 as an economy measure (Carpenter and Doctor 1996: 306), and continued sharing of programmes between Radio 3 and Radio 4. However, the extension of classical music across wider platforms seems in retrospect to have been an advantage to listeners less at home on the 'higher plane' of Radio 3. During the 1980 sample week, Radio 4 broadcast nearly 7 hours of classical music programming. The shared concert on Thursday evening simulcast by Radio 3 and Radio 4 of the Bournemouth Symphony Orchestra playing Sibelius, Britten and Brahms, was billed in the *Radio Times* as being a Radio 4 programme. Another shared programme, *Play It Again* on Saturday afternoons, 'a personal selection of outstanding music broadcasts of the past week' achieved the highest audience for Radio 3 of the sample week.

Two major works were simulcast between radio and BBC2 television. Lehár's opera *The Merry Widow* was a May Bank Holiday treat, with its radio output—on Radio 4 rather than Radio 3—attracting the highest classical music audience of the week of 313,000. A performance of Britten's *War Requiem* on Friday evening, again a radio/television simulcast, drew 200,000 listeners to Radio 3. The success among listeners of this enforced multi-channel approach highlights once again the error of the new structure in seeking to operate Radio 3 as the only classical music radio channel. Radio 4 was showing itself fully capable of maintaining some solid classical output, even though this heresy went against the orthodoxy of *Broadcasting in the Seventies* and was suppressed a couple of years later. As well as the two simulcasts, both *Music to Remember* on Sunday night and the feature *Music for a Living* on Tuesday evening point to a clear opportunity for the network of Radio 4 to venture into musical output.

On Radio 3, mainstream morning output—mostly specified sequence programmes played from records—regularly attracted a decent audience of 100,000–200,000 listeners and sat firmly in the centre of the canonic repertoire. The number of composers featured differed little from previous years, with very few surprising entrants among the just under 100 composers whose works were broadcast. Even among those, when Brahms and Schumann—who may be thought as being among the less accessible of the canonic composers—are featured more than Beethoven and Mozart, respectively, it suggests a rather academic turn of mind among the programme-makers.

Mainly for Pleasure replaced *Homeward Bound* as continuous stream programming on the early evenings from the start of the year, with sequence programmes both specified and unspecified now a staple part of the output. Humphrey Carpenter regards this revised sequence programme as the major event of the early Eighties, using the new programme's title for a chapter title (1996: 298). Yet for the listener, there seems to have been little perceived difference, and no marked change in audience levels.

BBC Musicians' Strike and Its Impact

In a climate of cost-cutting for BBC radio, the strike of musicians in the BBC orchestras dominated the early years of the Eighties. Recently released archive evidence shows that Singer was intending from the outset to be confrontational. The minutes of the BBC Board of Management in January 1980 are specific about Singer's intention, and the extent to which he was supported in this by Trethowan:

> MDR [Singer] was proposing to disband the London Studio Players, the Northern Radio Orchestra and the Midland Radio Orchestra, to disband the Scottish Symphony and Radio Orchestras and to create a new Concert Orchestra of 50 players.
>
> MDR explained what he was trying to achieve. In the present financial climate he wanted not only to improve the musical quality of programmes but also to go to the Board with some real savings. He had taken into account the possibility of industrial action, and was convinced that this nettle must be grasped. DG [Trethowan] strongly endorsed what he said. The BBC had been talking about its orchestral problems for 11 years, and the time had come to do something; it was a now or never orchestral strategy.[i]

Others within the BBC were less supportive than Trethowan. Those same minutes record that:

> the national regional controllers ... were aggrieved by what they saw as the lack of consultation (and trust) between MDR and them on this issue.

The tensions between Ponsonby and Singer were also evident from an early stage. When Ponsonby made so bold as to suggest that the issue of quality needed to be addressed in the context of the Welsh Symphony Orchestra,[ii] Singer jumped in offensively:

> You are being tedious! Insofar as it is possible I will enhance the symphony orchestras. However, I have to have room for manoeuvre. Meanwhile, do you think you could send your memoranda on this delicate subject under confidential cover?[iii]

Equally, Singer could have had little doubt that the powerful MU would be prepared to take industrial action. It is reasonable to infer that he welcomed a 'trial of strength', which was very much in line with the new Thatcherite mood of the times. Carpenter and Doctor (1996: 306) report Ponsonby as saying that 'by the time the proposals were put to the MU, "the light of battle" gleamed in Aubrey Singer's eyes'. According to his own account, Singer met with the two leading officials of the MU to discuss cutting the numbers of full-time contracts for BBC musicians between September and November 1979, and was told then that moving from permanent to 'first-call' contracts in the popular music orchestras 'was completely unacceptable and would be strongly contested if we put it to them formally'.[iv] By January the following year, Singer's assistant, Michael Starks, was examining the wide range of implications of serious strike action by the MU.[v] When the proposals were formally put to the musicians, on 22 April 1980, the BBC was already dug in for a strike.[vi]

After delaying strike action for a month, in the hope of reaching a negotiated settlement, the MU called out its musicians in the BBC orchestras on 1 June 1980. This was to be a classic early Eighties industrial confrontation—strange words to use between orchestral musicians and the great cultural institution of the country, but wholly apt. The BBC Board of Management noted that the Union 'was mustering its forces in preparation for a long slog' and, worrying about the effect of all this on the Proms, 'agreed that much would depend on the timing of the playing of certain cards in negotiation on both sides'.[vii] The Union wrote to the BBC chairman, Michael Swann, on 18 June 1980 alleging 'irresponsible' and 'dishonourable' behaviour by the BBC's management.[viii]

Kenyon (1981: 432) recounts how the cancellation of the First Night of the Proms on 18 July 1980, and of the opening 20 concerts, hit traditionalists within the BBC hard. Carpenter and Doctor (1996: 307) consider it a 'traumatic episode'. The loss of the Proms had been envisaged earlier by the Board of Management as a risk they would not welcome.[ix] There are anecdotes about the reactions of BBC Governors—most significantly, according to Seaton (2015: 104), the Chairman's wife. Tessa Swann was herself a professional and prize-winning musician—which induced greater BBC willingness to negotiate. Chairman Michael Swann contacted Arnold Goodman, who had gained a reputation for mediating in intractable industrial disputes and who had told Ponsonby that the Arts Council—which Goodman chaired—would consider promoting the Proms if the BBC and the MU were still in dispute.[x]

It was Goodman's mediation which broke the deadlock. The Proms resumed on 7 August 1980, and although the detailed negotiations were to drag on in respect of the Scottish and Ulster Orchestras until the middle of 1981, by then (and perhaps only by then) 'the heat had gone out of the dispute so far as the musical world as a whole is concerned'.[xi] When all was concluded, the BBC had indeed made some modest savings but nothing like the draconian changes envisaged at the outset. The settlement of 24 July 1980 involved the withdrawal of all notices of dismissal. The Northern and Midland Radio Orchestras were to be retained until the spring of 1981, and the Scottish Symphony Orchestra was saved, although the Scottish Radio Orchestra would go in its place. The full-time numbers of the BBCSO were actually increased.

Human relations between different factions within BBC management were severely damaged. David Wright (in Doctor et al. 2007: 204) noted that 'Ponsonby's honourable position with regard to the Proms ... further confirmed him as "not one of us" in BBC terms' so far as Singer was concerned. Ponsonby himself believed that the staff of the Music Division were 'outraged' by the way in which Singer conducted the negotiations (Carpenter and Doctor 1996: 307) and that morale plummeted. He personally found the strike anguishing (Seaton 2015: 104). On what was now firmly 'the other side', Singer 'seethed at the thought that Radio 3 had broadcast a talk by a member of staff attacking the "Philistinism" of the BBC'.[xii]

What then of the listeners? They were deprived of many Prom relays. The MU arranged 'unofficial Proms' to be performed at Wembley Stadium, and the striking musicians staged lunchtime concerts outside Broadcasting House, but self-evidently these would not be broadcast. The BBC had to dip deep into its needletime allowance, and to use tapes of recorded music from other broadcasters, but this latter was not unusual. The real impact was on the morale of the service and those who produced it, reflected in the years immediately afterwards in a flatness of output and ambition. The events also 'compromised the BBC's image as a disinterested guardian of the nation's music' (Wright in Doctor et al. 2007: 205). As well as provoking challenges from such as BBC producer and notable composer Robert Simpson, it was a further step in the demystifying of the BBC (as Walter Bagehot would have understood it), which now descended into the slew of commonplace industrial relations confrontations. Reducing the BBC's status in the sense of the sacralisation of classical music also prepared the way for the great revolution of the Nineties with Classic FM, and the democratisation of Radio 3 which accompanied it.

BBC Classical Music Output 1981–1984

BBC output of classical music in 1981 continued along rather unexciting lines, arguably the effect of continued economies and lowered morale. Records made up an unprecedented 46% of the total music output in the 1981 sample week, which featured few outstanding programmes. The most noteworthy contemporary broadcast was of Robert Simpson's Sixth Quartet, and his arrangement of Bach, on Sunday evening. Given Simpson's place as a senior figure within the BBC music hierarchy, and his increasingly controversial role in public debate, it is reasonable to query why his compositions received such prominence. Part of the answer lies in Radio 3's continuing self-referential approach to programme decisions, especially where high-brow music was concerned.

The issue of elitist defence was never far away from public debate. Simpson himself published *The Proms and Natural Justice* in the autumn of 1981, effectively attacking Ponsonby for being too long at the helm of the Proms and failing to give exposure to more obscure contemporary composers.[xiii] That provoked complaints about the 'curiously narrow and prescribed views about contemporary and modern music' supposedly implemented by 'the Glock-Keller regime'.[xiv] In vain might Ponsonby assert 'Isaac Stern's immortal dictum about unpopular concerts: "if nobody wants to come, nothing will stop them"'.[xv] The debate dominated the correspondence columns of *The Listener*, but the potential audience seemed wholly uninterested. Former Controller, Radio 3 Steven Hearst reported on behalf of the Radio Network Working Party that Radio 3 was dominated by:

> a tone and style that, we believe, deter thousands of music lovers from listening in, out of a vague but deeply felt conviction that this particular service is 'not for them'.[xvi]

Even so, new Controller Ian McIntyre was said to have been set the task of 'keeping the radio Philistines at bay'.[xvii]

In the event, they showed little interest in entering the Promised Land. Just 1% of the population listened to Radio 3 in a typical day,[xviii] equating on the BBC's own measure to just over 500,000 adults. Compared with the known potential audience for this radio genre of some 5 or 6 million, it is little wonder that Singer agreed 'that a service of popular classical music was exactly what was needed',[xix] although the Board of Management had accepted *Broadcasting in the Seventies* and the consequential replacement of the Music Programme, which had provided just that.

Singer left radio in 1982 to become Managing Director Television, before leaving that post two years later.[xx] That year, with a new Director General in Alasdair Milne, and a new Managing Director Radio in Richard Francis, the BBC once again changed the boundaries of the music radio empires. The Gramophone Department and Music Division were combined into a single Radio 3 Music Department headed by Christine Hardwick, who reported to Controller, Radio 3 McIntyre, not to Controller of Music Ponsonby. Carpenter regards this as a matter of institutional politics (1996: 309), as no doubt it was, but it also reflected the growing importance of records *vis-à-vis* live or originally recorded music in the BBC's output. In the 1982 sample week, 90 hours of output on Radio 3 were made possible by some extensive use of records, representing two fifths of the total music output, while to exploit the brand opportunity the *Radio 3 Magazine* appeared in October, archly named *3*.

Perhaps strangely, in view of the pain which the events of the previous years had caused him, Ponsonby told the Governors in 1982 that:

> When, in 1980, we embarked, after long and careful reflection, upon our present orchestral strategy (accepting that this would almost certainly involve an MU strike) we had two original objectives: the disbandment of five orchestras in the field of light in popular music ... [and] the reorganisation and improvement ... of our symphony orchestras.[xxi]

He claimed that standards had risen, duplication had been cut out and that with an extra £300,000 allocated 'for improvements to the BBCSO', and with the renaming of the Northern Symphony Orchestra as the BBC Philharmonic Orchestra, a new and agreeable pattern had been set. Certainly, Radio 3 had the confidence to offer three operas in the 1982 sample week: Walton's *Troilus and Cressida* on Saturday early evening; Chabrier's *L'etoile* on Monday at the same time; and Verdi's *Luisa Miller* on Thursday afternoon. This was an interesting range, especially as all apart from Walton were original performances. There were several programmes of modern music in different guises. *Music in Our Time* remained on Thursday evening, but it is noticeable that through the week there were programmes featuring contemporary works, such as performances of Ligeti and then modern British music on Radio 3 on Sunday evening; and a concert given by the Boulder Wind Ensemble on Wednesday afternoon of works—fittingly for an American Youth Orchestra—by Krommer, Toensing, Dahl and Ives.

It is not usually possible to find the detail behind the content of sequence programming in these years. However, listings for Radio 3's *Mainly for Pleasure* were more extensive in 1982. The programme on the Tuesday evening of the sample week, presented by composer and author Michael Berkeley, revealed the essentially light nature of the output, blending arias and excerpts from compositions by Chabrier, Rossellini and Handel, with accessible works by Schubert, Rachmaninov, Haydn and Schumann. This was the type of popular and undemanding fare which made Classic FM such an audience success a decade later, yet in 1982 *Mainly for Pleasure* attracted no measurable audience, a fairly unusual feature for daytime Radio 3 in the sample week. It seems reasonable to conclude that listeners were not expecting such easy access, so that significantly fewer than 50,000 of them would turn to Radio 3 when 10 years later—in a more fiercely competitive situation, with increased presence of daytime television—Classic FM was achieving audiences of 100,000–150,000 with similar output at the same time.[xxii] Radio 3 audiences generally were settling to a fairly discouraging level. Although few programmes during the day failed to attract an audience, the largest audience for any programme was 200,000, and daily patronage was just 400,000.

In 1983, Radio 3 still did not quite have a monopoly of BBC output. Radio 4 carried an attractive programme of Haydn and Purcell on the Thursday evening of the 1983 sample week, a repeat of an earlier Radio 3 broadcast, and its own *Music to Remember* on Sunday evening of the Chicago Symphony Orchestra playing Tchaikovsky's Suite No. 3 in G. On Radio 4 on Wednesday, the chat-and-book-plugging programme *Midweek* was being presented by Henry Kelly, who would go on to be a prominent Classic FM presenter when the commercial competitor launched in 1992.

Radio 3 was heavily dependent upon music supplied by European broadcasting organisations, to ease pressures on needletime allocation. A European Broadcasting Union (EBU) concert from Radio Bremen on Monday evening, music of Mozart and Hindemith from Norddeutscher Rundfunk in Hamburg on Tuesday morning, *Music of Eastern Europe* from Sender Freies Berlin on Wednesday afternoon and an Austrian Radio recording of Handel's *Acis und Galatea* from January's Salzburg Festival on Thursday afternoon were typical examples. A further EBU feature, of recordings made by the BBC itself during the EBU's *International String Quartet Days* earlier in the year, and broadcast on Thursday evening, was given little prominence—possibly because the ILR entry, the Brodsky Quartet, had won the competition.

The works of 133 different composers were broadcast in the sample week in 1983. That is a remarkably high figure compared with typically around 100 composers in the Seventies or around 110 in the Nineties, and hints at a change of course. For example, Sunday afternoon's Nielsen broadcasts were part of a series of 16 programmes, while *The English Madrigal* programmes on Saturday, Sunday and Friday were from a 34-part series. *This Week's Composer* was Lennox Berkeley, justly celebrated on his 80th birthday, although not increasing the accessibility of the network. The First Viennese School of composers were still the most played on Radio 3, but the output of two dozen composers whose names were barely familiar—such as Stenhammer, Muffat, and Kunhau—arguably deterred potential listeners beyond those of the highest brow.

Humourist Miles Kington captured the general perception of Radio 3 in a satirical piece in April in *The Times*:

> There will be a procession to the Tomb of the Unknown Composer, who is responsible for so much of Radio 3's output. Wreaths will be laid by the Baroque Society, the Friends of French Opera Overtures, the Society for the Preservation of Rural English Song Writers and CAMRA (the Campaign for Real Albinoni). There will then be a performance of the song-cycle 'on Warlock edge' and six concerti grossi by Galtieri. They will then be played again at the right speed.[xxiii]

By the following year, Radio 3 had the field to itself apart from ILR. Radio 4 had nominally quit classical music, although *Desert Island Discs* on Friday morning of the sample week featured soprano Rosalind Plowright, who chose works by Vaughan Williams, Schubert, Wagner, Verdi, Bellini and Bruckner. As if aware of its isolation, Radio 3 had tracked back to the centre ground. Hardly any of the composers played in the 1984 sample week would not have been recognised by a mainstream audience. The overwhelming dominance of the First Viennese School was especially striking, with Mozart, Haydn, Beethoven, Brahms and Schubert all receiving a high number of plays. Following them in number were Elgar, Shostakovich and Handel, with Dvořák and Britten also well featured. Opera was mostly mainstream Mozart, with *Die Zauberflöte* on Bank Holiday Monday afternoon and an historic Glyndebourne recording of *Idomeneo* on Thursday afternoon, to mark that opera house's 50th anniversary.

Audience levels for Radio 3 recovered as well, surely as a consequence of offering more accessible music. Daytime programmes steadily attracted some 100,000 listeners, rising to 200,000 for *Your Concert Choice* on Sunday morning and part of *Morning Concert* on Thursday. There was still audience potential in the evenings, with a concert of Walton, Haydn and Bruckner by the London Philharmonic Orchestra on Thursday evening live from the Royal Festival Hall reaching 150,000 listeners. Equally, that audience could not be relied upon; right across the sampled month of May 1984 there was no measurable audience at all for Radio 3 on Saturday evenings from 6 pm or on Friday evenings from 6.30 pm.

Why this change? Perhaps the BBC was stung by charges of obscurantism, shying away from the hostility directed at it from Margaret

Thatcher, for whom the BBC was 'her greatest bête noire' (Turner 2010: 196). Conservative cabinet minister, Norman Tebbitt, perhaps the arch-Thatcherite, regarded the BBC as being 'a sunset home for the insufferable, smug, sanctimonious, naïve, guilt-ridden, weak and pink' (Turner 2010: 301)—a grotesque picture, but one perhaps recognisable here and there within Radio 3. With increasing scrutiny—and hostility—towards the BBC from an assertive and iconoclastic Government, there was a sense of Radio 3 swinging away from obscurity a little too far towards familiar output, arguably to protect the station from the charge of irrelevance in the context of an emerging and new market-based political mood.

By the time that the Peacock Committee was set up in March 1985, *inter alia* to examine prospects for part-funding the BBC through advertising or sponsorship, or indeed a measure of privatisation, Radio 3 had good reason to be fearful. 1984 had seen the first of a long series of privatisations—such as British Telecom—and the Thatcher Government was in its most militant stage of confrontation with the National Union of Mineworkers. In May and June, outside the Orgreave Coke Works, in a Staffordshire hamlet just north of Lichfield, thousands of police and pickets fought a series of running battles. In the early hours of 12 October 1984, the IRA bombed the Conservative Conference in the seaside resort of Brighton. The attempt to murder the Prime Minister was unprecedented in the twentieth century, and took the Northern Ireland War to new levels. Alwyn Turner notes that 'one had to look back to the gunpowder plot or the Cato Street Conspiracy for a parallel' (2010: 188). As discussed later in this chapter, one indirect consequence of the assassination attempt was the dismantling of the system of independent, public service radio and television following Thames Television's documentary, *Death on the Rock*. It would have seemed a minor matter to do away with a classical music radio network which had become too detached from its audience.

The Apex of ILR Classical Music Output 1980–1984

While the BBC had languished in the aftermath of the musicians' strike, ILR in 1980 was advancing to the apex of its classical music output, boosted by secondary rental of £2.7 million funding classical music concerts in London, at Snape Maltings and in Aberdeen, Sheffield and Belfast (Stoller 2010: 134). The IBA was jubilant, lauding:

many memorable occasions of exciting programmes ... including the first of Capital's *Great Orchestras of the World* series and the same station's recording of a splendid performance of Verdi's *Otello* from Covent Garden.

The IBA reported in 1980 that many ILR stations had their own orchestras. The Swansea Sound Sinfonia was at that time Wales' only professional chamber orchestra, with an inaugural concert in 1979 in Brangwyn Hall in Swansea, of a programme including Handel, Warlock and Bach. Capital's Wren Orchestra took concerts out around London in its *Music on Your Doorstep* series. Piccadilly Radio supported local and regional orchestras in Greater Manchester, notably the Hallé (sponsoring the last night of the Hallé Proms) and its own Piccadilly Concert Orchestra.

With the first tranche of new stations coming on air, each with the expectation that they would broadcast classical music and be active in their local music scenes, it seemed that ILR might go on to achieve the salience of pre-war stations in the USA (Goodman 2011), which made significant commitments to classical music, beyond regulatory expectations.

The role of Lyndon Jenkins at one of the new stations, Mercia Sound in Coventry, is illustrative that some at least of the ILR stations had taken this aspect of their programme output very much to heart. He was a classical music presenter at Mercia Sound from 1980 until the ending of such output in 1989. A specialist in British music, British artists and British musical history, Jenkins was also a regular contributor to specialist music journals and a writer of CD booklets for many leading record labels including EMI, Testament and Dutton. He broadcast regularly on Finnish and Danish radio about Sibelius and Nielsen, and his promotion of Danish music led to him being awarded a knighthood from the Queen of Denmark for services to Anglo-Danish cultural relations. Jenkins gave the first Adrian Boult Lecture in Birmingham in 1986, was Chairman of the Delius Society from 1994 to 2000, latterly Vice-President and Chairman of the Federation of Recorded Music Societies.[xxiv]

In the early years of the decade, there is a real sense of ILR commitment building to a high point. ILR by 1981 was actively participating in British musical life, especially in the localities and often through serious participants such as Jenkins. Many musical bodies increasingly turned to ILR for help and support, not least in the form of sponsorship of local musicians. Radio Clyde continued to sponsor and record for broadcast the baroque ensemble *Catalina*, sponsored a series of factory lunchtime concerts by Scottish Opera and began to commission work from composers resident in Scotland. The station's Head of Programmes Andy Hickey was a member of the Council of the Scottish Society of Composers. Capital Radio entered cellist Robert Cohen and soprano Janice Kelly for a competition run by the UNESCO International Music Council, Britain's first-ever entries into the competition. The two competitors were placed first and fourth, respectively.[xxv]

The following year, although the secondary rental pot had shrunk, the established companies continued to be active in promoting and broadcasting concerts, and together with the new stations maintained their classical output with a certain swagger and ambition. ILR achieved exclusive broadcast rights to the Royal Opera's *Madame Butterfly*, to Luciano Pavarotti's UK performance (in Manchester), and to the Edinburgh Festival production of the *Barber of Seville*.[xxvi] CBC in Cardiff, the first of the new tranche of ILR companies, broadcast a two-hour gala concert performance by the Welsh National Opera. Capital Radio again led the field, with nine concert recordings in its *Great Conductors of the World* series featuring such maestros as Zubin Mehta, Ricardo Muti and Sir Colin Davis. In conjunction with little Radio Orwell in Ipswich, Capital presented a series of concerts at Snape Maltings, including performances by the Royal Philharmonic Orchestra and London Philharmonic Orchestra.

Audiences for Classical Music on ILR

Another measure of the impact of classical music programming on ILR was the level of audiences achieved. Data on this are uneven. Research surveys were conducted generally for individual stations, within their own transmission areas, and many of the smaller stations were unable to fund such research in their early years. Nevertheless, there is enough information from the larger stations—and especially Capital Radio—from which to extrapolate for the network as a whole.

Capital's *The Collection*, a weekly two-hour programme of classical music—often featuring live concert recordings—was a staple element in the station's Sunday evening programming up until the mid-Eighties. At the start of the Eighties, Capital Radio was attracting almost 350,000 listeners to its classical music each week, at a time when the average reach for Radio 3 in Greater London was 1,152,000.[xxvii, xxviii] Extrapolating this ratio across the initial 19 ILR stations can only be a guesstimate, in the absence of any equivalent data, but it is not unreasonable to assume that, in the areas covered by ILR stations, they were achieving an audience for their classical music programmes of around 30% of the total Radio 3 audience.

At the start of the Eighties, the number of ILR stations—still with specialist music programmes and live music obligations—increased swiftly, from 19 in 1979 to 60 by 1989, and their total audiences from 14 million in 1979 to nearly 18 million in 1989. Taking the 30% base, it would be reasonable to posit a classical music audience on ILR across all of the areas served in 1980 of over 750,000 adults, rising to around 1 million by the mid-Eighties.[xxix] This remarkable figure, for what was by no means only popular run-of-the-mill programme output, bears out Jean Seaton's (1997: 319) assertion that there is 'a resilient consensus' in favour of public service broadcasting, which arguably extended to ambitious classical music broadcasting on ILR stations.

Of equal significance to the size of the ILR classical music audiences was their composition. The Wren Orchestra, considered below, was a leading player in providing classical music to ILR audiences, and its conductor Howard Snell was in no doubt that the orchestra had captured a new audience outside the static pool of people interested in concerts, theatre and ballet:

> You can tell by their response. They clap between movements. They look different. They apparently aim to enjoy themselves.[xxx]

Similarly, the IBA noted that:

> one of ILR's strength is in breaking down the sometimes elitist barriers that can intimidate potential new listeners from experiencing different types of music. In Liverpool, research showed that about half the audience attending Radio City's summer series of 'Proms' with the Royal Liverpool Philharmonic Orchestra were attending a classical music concert for the first time. BRMB's series of Saturday family concerts in conjunction with the CBSO were designed to enable parents to enjoy a concert with their children.[xxxi]

The audience data for demographic groups need to be approached with caution. The sample sizes are too small to permit anything other than broad indications to be asserted. Figures are for individual half-hours, and are not aggregated for complete programmes. The raw numbers are likely to fluctuate hugely, given the small sample sizes. Nevertheless, the five surveys into Capital Radio's *The Collection* programme seem on the face of it to support the contention that ILR audiences for classical radio were not made up in the same way as those for BBC programmes.[xxxii]

BBC audiences for Radio 3 (and to a less marked degree for Radio 4) were heavily weighted towards older, male listeners. 61% of the 1980/1981 audience was male; 52% was aged over 55; and 57% was drawn from the ABC1 category.[xxxiii] Capital's audience profile by contrast, was notably more lower class (C2DE) than upper class (ABC1). Unlike the BBC, there were times when more women than men were listening, and the audience was predominantly made up of younger people.[xxxiv] This was surely 'transcendent culture' in Matthew Arnold's construction (1875), meeting also David Hendy's criterion for public service broadcasting of being worthwhile content not 'restricted to the lucky few', but 'spread around, so that all can share in its benefits' (2013: 46). It demonstrated once again that classical music need not be the preserve of the few, provided that there is no empowered elite wishing to exclude the many.

Secondary Rental and Programme Sharing

The statutory and contractual basis for secondary rental has been discussed earlier.[1] Its impact, especially in the field of classical music programmes, was substantial. This was enhanced by the introduction of a scheme, funded by secondary rental money, to encourage and allow individual radio stations to share 'programmes of merit' around the ILR network. From early 1978, a combination of pride in the programmes they made and a wish to get regulatory 'brownie points' meant that a good number of programmes were offered for sharing with such of the other ILR stations as wished to take them. That amounted to as many or more than 25 programmes in a month, once the system was up and running (Stoller 2010: 139–140).

From the beginning of the programme-sharing scheme in 1983, quite a wide range of ILR stations offered classical music programmes for sharing around the network. These were by no means just easy-listening

---

[1] See Chap. 5, pp. 136–137.

options. In 1983 Radio Clyde in Glasgow offered a series of concerts from the Scottish early music consort while the tiny Reading station, Radio 210, recorded the premiere of a modern chamber opera by the local university professor, Peter Wishart. In 1984, when the programme-sharing scheme was fully underway, there was a cornucopia of classical music offerings. Capital Radio offered a concert of Schubert played by the Wren Orchestra from Snape Maltings; a performance of Verdi's *La Traviata* from the London Coliseum; and a National Youth Orchestra performance of works by Richard Strauss. Radio Trent in Nottingham provided a concert by the Allegri String Quartet, a recital of Schumann, Chopin and Brahms by Gervase de Peyer and Gwynneth Pryor; and County Sound in Guildford a recital by the Brodsky String Quartet. Radio Clyde also made available its *Cantilena* classical music programmes, the first example in the programme-sharing scheme of a full series of programmes rather than a single concert promotion, but illustrating what had been the approach in many individual ILR stations from the outset.

1985 saw continued musical promotion through the programme-sharing scheme by Capital Radio and Radio Clyde. They were joined by Radio City in Liverpool with its own *Last Night of the Proms*, concerts by the Royal Liverpool Philharmonic Orchestra. Some of these concerts were popular classics, while others showed real ambition, such as the performance of Walton's *Belshazzar's Feast* by the London Choral Society and the Royal Philharmonic Orchestra under Simon Rattle. More stations joined the process later in the Eighties, with the local nature of much of ILR's classical music promotion demonstrated by Hereward Radio's programme featuring the Peterborough Roth Quartet, while Piccadilly Radio in Manchester broadcast and offered for sharing the Hallé Orchestra's Christmas Concert.

The stations ventured beyond just concert output too. Among the items on the programme-sharing scheme were a documentary from Red Rose Radio in Preston about Kathleen Ferrier who was born in Preston; from BRMB in Birmingham about West Midlands soprano Dame Maggie Teyte; while even the news-and-talk London station LBC was not to be left out with a documentary series celebrating the life of Yehudi Menuhin. Although only a sample of the tapes which were circulated around the ILR network in these years are archived, these programmes show competence and ambition from small local stations which went beyond merely observing the letter of their contractual obligations.

Perhaps foremost among all the ILR initiatives continued to be Capital Radio's support for and ownership of the Wren Orchestra. This was an outstanding example of the use of secondary rental to provide extensive on-air programming, material for programme sharing, promotional activity out and around the community and a significant boost to London classical music as a whole. Founded in 1976, the Wren was swiftly taken up by Capital Radio which effectively ran the board which supervised the orchestra up to and beyond the watershed of 1990. That support for the Wren became a corporate jewel akin to the business sponsorships which sustain so much of classical music and its broadcasts in the USA. The orchestra and its concerts enjoyed the trappings of corporate support. Kevin Appleby, Orchestra Manager of the Wren from 1989 and later General Manager, recalls that fireworks accompanying concerts were a significant attraction: 'I remember an English Heritage representative saying that the Capital Music Festival concert had a budget twice as big for fireworks than on any other night in the season!'[xxxv]

Although the Wren ceased to have any on-air presence on an increasingly commercial Capital Radio in the late Eighties, Appleby is clear that 'nobody at Capital Radio would have dared to close it down while the founding chairman, Richard Attenborough (later Lord Attenborough) was still around'.[xxxvi]

The 'Heathrow Conference'

ILR's commitment to classical music—and indeed to its full public service statutory remit—had continued unabated in 1983. New licensing meant that by the end of 1983 there were 42 stations broadcasting regular classical music programmes as well as undertaking related community activity and concert promotion. The IBA, proud of what was being broadcast and largely oblivious to the gathering storm, enjoyed noting that:

> ILR's confidence and reputation in the provision of high standard classical music programming grew over the year. Metro Radio won the music teachers' discretionary media award for the best musical education project; its classical calendar was designed to alert O and A level students to relevant set works broadcast in the weekly programme in the classical mood; comprehensive background material on the works of their composers

was included in the programme. Neighbouring Radio Tees' *Fine Tuning* focused on a different aspect of local music-making each week.[xxxvii]

Radio Tees put forward the young and then unknown Brodsky Quartet to be the IBA's entry into the EBU *International String Quartet Days* in Cambridge in 1983. Selected from half a dozen similar proposals, the Quartet won the competition. It has become one of the most adventurous UK string quartets, and remains as a surviving example of what was being achieved by ILR stations in the Eighties before they turned their back on public service output.

From 1984 however, the sands began to run out on the IBA's vision of *independent* radio, and with it the steps the stations had taken in respect of classical music output. The programme companies started to come under pressure from city analysts to find ways of growing their businesses exponentially, an inevitable consequence of the decisions taken by the larger companies to seek stock market listings. The majority of the older ILR companies began to consider mounting challenges to their public service obligations, their management and directors hoping to achieve the potential financial returns which many believed greater commercial freedom would provide for their companies and shareholders. They were also anxious at the prospect of national commercial radio competition, and were emboldened by the deregulatory spirit of the middle years of the Thatcher administration. And so ILR began the process of shedding its public service obligations and becoming *commercial* radio—and, along the way, jettisoning classical music output (Stoller 2010: 142–153). That took another half-dozen years, before confirmation in the 1990 Broadcasting Act, but it was in a conference at the Sheraton Skyline Hotel, Heathrow, on 23 June 1984 that the process was set in motion.

That gathering of the Chairmen and Managing Directors of the ILR companies, known as the 'Heathrow Conference', marked the start of the collective move against the IBA and the regime which it was implementing (Stoller and Wray 2010). For those among the ILR executives who had embraced the public service ethos, this event and its aftermath had unintended consequences. Seeking some easement of the financial impositions caused by the nature of the regulatory regime, they found themselves involved with those more commercially driven, and all set off along the road towards commercialism. This also fitted in well with the Thatcher Government's intention for a market-based regime for Independent Television. In response, and without any worthwhile resistance from the Independent Broadcasting Authority, the Broadcasting Act 1990 specifically ended ILR's public service obligations and with that its brave history of classical music broadcasting.

The harsh irony in terms of ILR's classical music involvement was that 1984 represented the highest point which that genre had yet reached in the private sector in the UK. In the Belfast area, for example, Downtown Radio's *Concert Choice* achieved a markedly higher weekly audience than any programme on Radio 3.[xxxviii] The iconic accolade came when Piccadilly Radio's *Mr Hallé's Band* won the prestigious Sony Radio Award for the best radio classical music programme in 1984. All this would be gone by 1990.

Classical Music Radio 1985–1989

Radio 3's output increased in 1985 with the addition of an extra hour up until midnight, with the consequence that for the first time more than 100 hours of classical music programming were broadcast nationwide each week. The BBC's programme approach had moved back to the middle ground—probably partly a defensive pre-emption of the Peacock Committee's deliberations, and the imminent renewal of the BBC Charter. There is no evidence that this was a response to ILR, although Seaton (2015: 106) notes that BBC2 and Radio 3 increased their simulcasts as a response to Channel 4's music initiatives.

Major programmes continued on Radio 3, alongside the staple content of sequence music and music feature materials. In the 1985 sample week, two operas were broadcast on Saturday: Handel's serenata *Parnasso in Festa* and the first of the Wagner *Ring* cycle in a recording from the 1980 Bayreuth Festival. Tippett's *King Priam* was given by Kent Opera on Tuesday evening, completing an impressive triple. With a relay of the St Louis Symphony Orchestra from the Royal Festival Hall on Wednesday, the BBC Welsh Symphony Orchestra from Bangor on Bank Holiday Monday and St David's Hall on Thursday, the BBC Scottish Symphony Orchestra in Stirling on Saturday morning and the BBC Philharmonic across Thursday lunchtime from Hull, there is evidence of renewed vigour. However, routine output did not extend much beyond the centre of the classical canonic repertoire. Despite significantly increased hours, the number of composers featured hardly increased and the list is notable for the absence of almost any modern compositions.

As discussed below, BBC music strategy continued to be dominated by personality issues. Drummond, who had rejoined the BBC in 1985 from running the Edinburgh International Festival was engaged for his first two years in battles over who should be the dominant senior figure in BBC classical music, and with the Proms. Perhaps as a consequence, although Radio 3 continued to be the chief destination for established classical music listeners, during this period it broke rather more new ground in its drama and arts feature output than in music. Drummond's musical initiatives tended to organise themselves into specific projects or festivals: celebrations, for example, of William Glock's 80th birthday in May 1988 and Michael Tippett's 85th in January 1990; and a season of Scandinavian music in 1990. Only by October 1991 was he confident enough to introduce *Mixing It*, which addressed contemporary, cross-genre music.

Despite the infighting over its own future, ILR continued its commitment to classical music output. The IBA could still report that:

> As a curtain raiser to the 1985 International Youth Year, Radio Clyde recorded the National Youth Orchestra of Scotland performing works by Beethoven and Prokofiev. Clyde also became the first ILR station to offer classical music to the European Broadcasting Union programme exchange, with performances by the Scottish Early Music Consort and Catalina.[xxxix]

In the early Eighties, the ILR companies were hit by the general UK recession. As profits fell, only £168,000 in secondary rental was available for distribution in 1985 (Stoller 2010: 137). It is therefore notable that the ILR stations continued with their classical music ambition, rather than reining that back. ILR was steadily building involvement between the metropolitan stations and regionally based symphony orchestras. The smaller stations were not to be left out. Radio 210 presented a series of concerts at the Wilde Theatre in Bracknell, and Chiltern Radio concerts by the Leipzig Gewandhaus. Radio Wyvern produced a documentary on the life of Elgar and Hereward Radio sent the Roth String Quartet of Peterborough to Salzburg as finalists in the EBU's 1986 International String Quartet competition.

Politically, broadcasting reform was in the fast lane. The Peacock Committee reported in March 1986 and recommended—as it had effectively been set up to do—the privatisations of Radio 1 and Radio 2, but proposed leaving Radio 3 largely untouched. It also endorsed all that the

ILR companies might have wished in terms of potential deregulation, although despite this there was no sign yet of any lack of enthusiasm or ambition for classical music output across ILR.

Following the then-traditional route for constitutional reform of broadcasting, the Peacock Report was followed by a Green Paper in 1987 entitled *Broadcasting in the 90s: Choice and Quality*.[xl] That envisaged Radio 3 (and Radios 1 and 2) being virtually a continuous music station. It also foreshadowed the surrender of BBC frequencies for new Independent National Radio services; Radio 3 was to be broadcast only on VHF/FM, and carry 90 minutes each weekday of schools programmes. The BBC was not displeased, and in its five-year strategy later that year paraded the idea of a 'leaner, fitter Radio 3' remaining 'the nation's premier cultural service'.[xli] These changes were not to be implemented until 1990, and their impact is discussed in the following chapter.

When a White Paper was presented to Parliament in 1988, the keyword 'competition' was added to 'choice and quality' from the Green Paper, as a clear statement of the government's intent.[xlii] For ILR, this effectively announced the imminent demise of *independent* radio, and its replacement by *commercial* radio. This was given extra force by the decision of Capital Radio to seek a full listing on the London Stock Exchange. Capital remained at that time the major provider and promoter of classical music among the ILR stations, but this ambition was not to survive into the next decade with a stock market quote to sustain.

However, the effect was not felt immediately and the process of ditching public service output—and classical music programmes along with it—was not completed until 1990. The IBA noted that:

> despite constant pressure on programme budgets, independent radio maintained a strong commitment to serious music. Most stations retained a weekly slot, combining music and performance with reviews of local events ... Programmers are developing, with increasing success, the art of presenting serious music in a style attractive to mainstream audiences.[xliii]

Indeed, the end of the requirement for ILR stations to simulcast on AM and FM provided an opportunity for some to experiment with more rather than less classical music. That they chose to do so is further evidence that ILR was going beyond what was required by statutory or regulatory fiat, even at this late stage. Piccadilly Radio in Manchester, for example, took advantage of the opportunity to split its frequencies and offer prestige classical music concerts with the Hallé.[xliv] GWR ran a separate Brunel Radio service on AM only, which was to be an unexpected harbinger of a national commercial classical music service.[2]

Away from political developments, there were intimations by 1987 of major changes at the BBC which would impact significantly upon listeners and audiences for classical music radio. In June, Drummond won the contest with McIntyre to be Controller of Music, Proms Director and Controller, Radio 3. That was part of the process which saw the BBC Music Division disbanded and replaced by a Radio 3 Music Department, a further break with the founding philosophy of the Third Programme. The BBC Governors sacked Alastair Milne, appointing Michael Checkland in his place. Checkland in turn appointed David Hatch as Managing Director Radio.

BBC classical music output in 1987, now all back on Radio 3, was much in line with previous years in terms of quantity and balance. What if anything stands out? Not obscurity, despite Drummond's claim when he took over later in the year that 'less time shall be devoted to the obscure works of obscure men'.[xlv] Drummond was the 'champion of opening the doors to Europe',[xlvi] but he had misinformed himself about where Radio 3 had got to before he took over as Controller. In the 1987 sample week, a concert by the BBCSO of works by Per Nørgaard from the Brighton Festival on Saturday evening was the only obviously contemporary output over the weekend of the sample week, and listeners had light/light classical music programmes *Baker's Dozen*[3] and *Your Hundred Best Tunes* across on Radio 4 to console them if needed, both presented by BBC news-reader and classical music devotee Richard Baker.

By 1988, the Thatcher government was preparing to change the broadcasting structure. This was a personal issue for the Prime Minister, driven by her suspicion of the BBC. However, that was displaced in the late spring by even greater fury towards ITV and the IBA. Thames Television produced a documentary, *Death on the Rock*, which asserted that an SAS squad had killed three unarmed IRA members in Gibraltar,

---

[2] See Chap. 7, p. 200.

[3] No *Radio Times* listings are available for this series of programmes, which ran between 1977 and 1988. However, an LP compilation issued by BBC Records in 1976 (REB 247) included single movements of works by Delius, Brahms, Mendelssohn and Pascetti, along with songs by Dvořák, Canteloube and Puccini and other light classical works.

and the IBA refused repeated government requests and then demands to prevent its broadcast (Stoller 2010: 177–179). Mindful surely of her near-assassination four years earlier, the broadcast of the documentary on 28 April 1988 swung the PM's aim from the BBC to Independent Television, its cosy commercial closed shop and its regulator, the IBA. The end of *independent* radio in favour of a *commercial* model—along with its ambitious classical music output—was merely collateral damage.

Freed from the risk that the Peacock Report might propose its privatisation, little changed on air for Radio 3 in 1988. Drummond carried through his undertaking the previous year that the Radio 3 audience should rediscover Beethoven, whose works received more plays in 1988 than any composer across all of the sample weeks considered in this history. Along with extensive playing of Mozart, the central canonic repertoire was dominant. Nevertheless, a large number of composers were included, notably in programmes linking relatively unknown composers either by their nationality (for example, American songs, with works by Barber, Copland and Ives in the sample week) or by a sub-genre of classical music such as *Seventeenth Century Chamber Music* on Monday morning featuring Froberger, Schmeltzer and Biber.

Typical of Drummond's time as Controller, bringing together innovations into distinct packages, the sample week included a continuation of Radio 3's Australian Season. If any listener chose to tune in they could hear on Tuesday afternoon, for example, *Figures in a Landscape*, works billed in the *Radio Times* as by 'Antipodean composers and their response to the environment' including Mills, Butterley, Antill, Sculthorpe, Sunderland and Grainger—all but Grainger probably heard for the first time (although Nigel Butterley's String Quartet had been in the BBC Radio 3 repertoire in 1974 (Grimley and Wiegold 1977)). The only two operas of the week featured a rarely heard Australian work, *Fly* by Conyngham, on records, along with Donizetti's comic opera, *La Fille du Regiment*, in a recording from the Sydney Opera House the previous year of the Australian Opera Company.

Even if the threat of privatisation had passed, much of the BBC's programming was still clearly aimed at a popular audience, although by no means all. *Morning Concert* every weekday and *Mainly for Pleasure* each weekday afternoon both offered highly accessible mainstream material; then again, a live relay from the Concertgebouw, Haarlem of an EBU 20th anniversary season concert of works by Messiaen, de Leeuw and Chausson, was the main featured item of the week and broadcast on

6 THE EIGHTIES: KEEPING THE PHILISTINES AT BAY 179

Monday evening. The almost unknown Australians in *Music in Our Time* could be balanced against revivals on record of the piano-playing of the piano virtuoso Solomon on the Saturday afternoon of the sample week. Again, there was a 'hook' for this programme: Solomon Cutner, known simply as 'Solomon' throughout his distinguished professional career, had died in February 1988 aged 86. Following a severe stroke in 1956, he had not played again but remained a revered figure.

The impression given is one which was to last right through until the end of Drummond's time at the BBC in 1992, that a great deal of popular music was offered at a reasonably undemanding level, that there was some ambitious and unusual programming—although away from the avant-garde mainstream—but that little attempt was made to relate one to the other. The only feature output of the sample week which was music related was *Music Weekly*, broadcast in the peak time of Sunday morning and then repeated on Monday afternoon.[xlvii]

In ILR meanwhile, classical music programming continued, but on a downward curve as the end of this type of output came closer. Neither the IBA's *Annual Report* nor its *Handbook* for 1988 make any significant mention of classical music output, a sign of how far the regulator's priorities had shifted.

Capital Radio, however, by this stage a public company, maintained its support of the Wren Orchestra. Its former General Manager Appleby stresses that the Wren was still backing the Bolshoi and Kirov Ballets at the end of the decade.[xlviii] Capital's personality DJs were happy to plug concerts if they thought them accessible, another sign of the extent to which the previously sceptical ILR folk had come to value their classical output:

> When [the Wren] started, it was different, because there was a sense that classical music was still that elite art form that people didn't engage with. However, if the *Collection* programme on a Sunday night offered two hours of classical music, potentially you'd listen to it if Kenny Everett said to you, 'Don't miss the next Wren Orchestra gig' ... Chris Tarrant wouldn't talk about the Mahler Eight at the Royal Albert Hall. What he would talk about is, 'Oh, don't forget, come to Kenwood on Saturday night, it's the Capital Radio Music Festival ...'

In 1989, there were at last some efforts on Radio 3 to link higher brow output with the popular, and to educate an audience attracted by popular output. As well as *Music Weekly* on Sunday morning and Monday afternoon, there was an interesting discussion in *Third Ear* early on Thursday evening between composer Oliver Knussen and music critic Nicholas Kenyon (soon to be elevated to the Controllership of Radio 3) about the place of the modern symphony orchestra. The intervals of several concerts were adorned not by the unrelated talks which had previously been placed there but by features on the music itself. Beyond this, David Owen Norris presented *The Worms* on Friday evening, 'a down-to-earth look at the grassroots of music', while on Tuesday afternoon there was *An Afternoon with Ravel*, billed by *The Guardian* as 'a dramatised conversation'.[xlix]

Not only conventional composers were given airtime. *Composers of the Week* featured 'Mozart's Rivals in Vienna', and extended beyond Salieri to such as Vanhal, Paisiello and Kozeluh. There was even a smattering of women composers: Clara Schumann, Grace Williams, Rebecca Clarke and Elisabeth Lutyens. Add in Radio 3 relative favourites Fanny Mendelssohn and Ethel Smythe, played from time to time on Radio 3 but not during the sample week, and there was a hint of a chance to move the classical music canonic repertoire away from being wholly male.

Across in the private sector, the IBA had acquiesced in the wiping out of most public service obligations for ILR in the new legislation after 1990. That need not have been the case. The Broadcasting Act retained an obligation on the new commercial radio stations to broadcast news, material of local applicability and of high quality. The Authority appears to have made little effort to protect one of the great and unexpected successes of its time of responsibility for public service radio. Part of this reflects a change of personnel at the IBA. In 1987, John Thompson had retired, and John Whitney—who had moved from being Managing Director of Capital Radio to become Director General of the IBA in 1981—returned to the commercial world. There seems thereafter to have been an institutional reluctance to do anything much to protect the achievements of the independent broadcasting system, in the face of what amounted at times to an onslaught from a government fiercely antagonistic to anything connected with ITV and the IBA, following the transmission of *Death on the Rock*, discussed above.

The ILR companies simply took an opportunistic approach to the ending of the old regime, cutting their wider programme output (and costs). Fiona Talkington, then the presenter of Radio 210's *Masterworks*, recalls from 1989:

> I don't remember having a sense of a long run up to it ending, other than one day [the station Managing Director] told me along with all the other specialist presenters that *Masterworks* was to go ... I remember feeling that this wasn't just some whim of 210, but this was general policy that the music world on radio as we knew it was about to change.[l]

Capital's Peter James says that there was:

> no official end to classical music on Capital ... There was a total revamp of weekend programmes...and other programmes like Brian Rust's weekly vintage jazz *Mardi Gras* bit the dust at the same time. Probably drama went then too.[li]

Listeners though have long memories. Talkington again:

> Still to this day postmen knock on my door with parcels and say 'I remember working in the sorting office when you were on 210'. That was the beauty of 210. The loyal audience would happily listen ... morning, noon or night ... whether it happened to be classical music, or the rock show, or the country show.[lii]

It is notable that barely a couple of years after making so much in its published pronouncements of the importance of classical music on ILR, the IBA spurned a chance to establish a classical music station in London as part of the belated extension of ILR through the 'incremental' licences in 1988 (Stoller 2010: 173). The applicant for this licence argued that 'what Capital Radio has done so well for pop we, or people like us, can do for classical music in London'[liii]; but they were not to be given that opportunity. Following the Monopolies and Mergers Commission Report in 1988, which had foreshadowed the end of the restriction of needletime, even copyright arrangements seemed to be conspiring in favour of the broadcasting of commercially recorded pop music. The arrival of Classic FM just three years later appeared at this point to be most unlikely.

Internationally, there were events afoot which appeared to mark the end of the old World Order and held out the prospect of a new one. The late Eighties saw the collapse of the Soviet empire in middle and eastern Europe, the end of the Cold War and the apparent triumph of the liberal capitalist model. This affected so many aspects of Europe and the wider world, having a marked effect also on classical music. The strained dialectic between the Western world and the Eastern Bloc had generated what Richard Taruskin has called the 'utopian thinking' of avant-garde musicians, including the serious composers. With the collapse of Soviet communism in 1989, many of those returned to tonality:

> The loosening of cold-war thinking allowed the reopening of many old and ostensibly settled questions, including the question whether commitment to historical progress was worth the sacrifice of the audience. No longer shadowed by the spectre of totalitarianism, 'accessibility' regained a measure of respectability. (Taruskin 2010: 437)

The opening of the Berlin Wall on 9 November 1989 seemed to complete the period of history which had begun in the Thirties. These were highly symbolic weeks for classical music. On 12 November 1989, the Berlin Philharmonic Orchestra conducted by Daniel Barenboim played a concert for East and West Berliners in the Potsdamer Platz, performing Beethoven's Seventh Symphony. This may have been an accidental programme choice. Barenboim recalls that there was no particular reason for choosing this symphony. It was 'a purely practical decision because we'd been practising it for the recording' they had been rehearsing at that time.[liv] There was no such accident about Leonard Bernstein's involvement. He made haste to get to Berlin, and on Christmas Day he conducted an international orchestra in Beethoven's Ninth Symphony with Schiller's *Ode to Joy* recast as an *Ode to Freedom*, with *An die Freiheit* (freedom) replacing *An die Freude* (joy) in the text for the choral triumphs of the final movement.[4] The performance was broadcast across much of Europe. *Mitteleuropa*, which had given birth to classical music, now reunited in its performance and broadcast, and music began to escape from the dead-end of serialism.

Jürgen Habermas had posited in 1981 'the irreconcilable nature of aesthetic and social worlds',[lv] an approach which had already been required thinking among most classical composers from the end of the war. In 1989, with Beethoven ringing across the now-redundant no-man's-land between East and West Berlin, and around the broadcasting world, it was no longer necessary to observe Habermas' orthodoxy, and

---

[4] Although that was possibly also a restoring of the original wording from Schiller's poem before it was amended for publication.

a way opened for a new approach to the broadcasting of classical music and its composition in the Nineties (Taruskin 2010: 508).

With some classical tunes re-entering the contemporary popular and advertising awareness, there are faint echoes of the mixed concert programmes of the early years of the twentieth century, and the early Prom concerts.[5] When an operatic aria could reach number two in the UK hit singles chart, this offers a modern gloss on the debate about high and popular culture: *Nessun Dorma* from Puccini's opera *Turandot*, sung by Luciano Pavarotti and used by the BBC for its coverage of the 1990 football World Cup in Italy, was in the UK singles chart for eleven weeks in 1990.[lvi]

Classical music thus briefly resumed centre stage internationally in November 1989, as it had not done since the Second World War. The Leonard Bernstein concert was evidently a rather contrived set piece. Not so the concert in Prague the previous month:

> It was 7.36 pm in the opulent art nouveau Smetana Hall in the People's Palace. As the last strains of *My Country* by the Czech composer, Smetana, faded away, the conductor of the Czech Philharmonic Orchestra turned to the audience and raised his hand in a victory sign. The audience of 3000 stood up cheering. A man in a bow tie strode to the podium to read the historic message. The news of the mass resignation of the politburo electrified the hall. People with eyes moist from the emotion of the music wept.[lvii]

The BBC relayed Bernstein's concert on BBC2 television on Christmas Day, but not it seems on the radio. Drummond was to lead a Berlin weekend on Radio 3 the following year, but little about the BBC's radio music set-up tended towards spontaneity. That is arguably symbolic of where classical music output had got to on Radio 3 at the end of the decade. The music was there, both popular and high brow (though still rarely adequately linked) but there was an absence of the sort of passion which could connect with the mass audience. No wonder there was so much space for Classic FM to occupy; and just as well also that a new Controller was to be tasked with recasting the BBC's approach to classical music radio.

---

[5] See Chap. 2, p. 13.

Notes

i. Board of Management minutes, 10 January 1980. BBC WAC R92/40/1.
ii. Memorandum from Controller Music (Ponsonby) to Deputy Managing Director Radio (Muggeridge), 20 February 1980. BBC WAC R 92/40/1.
iii. Orchestral strategy. Memorandum from Managing Director Radio (Singer) to Controller Music (Ponsonby), 21 February 1980. BBC WAC 92/40/1.
iv. Board of Management minutes, 10 January 1980. BBC WAC R92/40/1.
v. Memorandum from Chief Assistant Radio Management (Programmes) (Starks), 29 January 1980. BBC WAR R92/40/1.
vi. Letter from John Morton, Musicians' Union to Anthony Jennings, Legal Adviser, BBC, 30 April 1980. BBC WAC R92/40/1.
vii. Board of Management minutes, 28 April 1980. BBC WAC R92/40/1.
viii. Letter from John Morton, General Secretary Musicians' Union to Sir Michael Swann, Chairman BBC, 18 June 1980. BBC WAC R92/7/1.
ix. Board of Management minutes, 28 April 1980. BBC WAC R92/40/1.
x. The Goodman plan for the Proms. Memorandum from Controller Music (Ponsonby) to Director General (Trethowan), 9 July 1980. BBC WAC R92/7/1.
xi. Managing Director Radio's management minutes, 2 June 1981. BBC WAC R92/7/1.
xii. Board of Management minutes, 4 August 1980. BBC WAC R92/7/1.
xiii. Simpson's essay was quoted in *The Listener*, 10 September 1981, p. 261 and extensively in subsequent issues.
xiv. Carey Blyton. *The Listener*, 29 October 1981, p. 512.
xv. Robert Ponsonby. *The Listener*, 10 September 1981, p. 262.
xvi. Ronald Hayman. Can the radio Philistines be kept at bay? *The Times*, 21 August 1981, p. 12.
xvii. Ibid.
xviii. BBC broadcasting research. *Radio Weekly Bulletin*, week 19, 1981. BBC WAC R9/38/4.
xix. Chris Dunkley. Langham Diary. *The Listener*, 31 December 1981, p. 820.
xx. http://www.theguardian.com/media/2007/may/28/guardianobituaries.broadcasting.
xxi. The BBC's symphony orchestras: strategy and responsibility. Note by Deputy Managing Director Radio (McClelland) covering a note by Controller Music (Ponsonby), 18 March 1982. BBC WAC R92/8/1.
xxii. Radio Joint Audience Research (RAJAR). See Appendix B.
xxiii. Miles Kington. Moreover ... *The Times*, 13 April 1983, p. 9.
xxiv. Jim Lee (BBC), personal communication, 25 April 2014.

6 THE EIGHTIES: KEEPING THE PHILISTINES AT BAY   185

xxv.   *IBA Annual Report 1980/1*, p. 44.
xxvi. *IBA Annual Report 1981/2*, p. 46.
xxvii. JICRAR Radio Network Survey 1979.
xxviii. From the private papers of Tim Blackmore.
xxix. Based on Hallett Arendt special analysis of JICRAR/RSL data, which indicates a weekly reach for Radio 3 in ILR areas of around 2.5 million.
xxx.   Robin Stringer 'Wren takes off'. *Daily Telegraph*, 2 October 1978, p. 10.
xxxi. *IBA Annual Report 1981/2*, p. 47.
xxxii. JICRAR reports, 1980/1. From the private papers of Tim Blackmore.
xxxiii. *BBC Annual Review of Audience Research Findings 1980/1*. BBC WAC R9/1038/1.
xxxiv. JICRAR reports, 1980/1. From the private papers of Tim Blackmore.
xxxv. Kevin Appleby, personal communication, 29 November 2014.
xxxvi. Interview with Kevin Appleby, General Manager of the Wren Orchestra, 24 April 2013.
xxxvii. *IBA Annual Report 1983/4*, p. 52.
xxxviii. *IBA Annual Report 1984/5*, p. 38.
xxxix. *IBA Annual Report 1984/5*, p. 38.
xl.   Home Office. 1987 Green Paper, Cmnd 92.
xli.   Richard Morrison. Leaner, fitter Radio 3? *The Times*, 24 October 1987, p. 18.
xlii. Home Office. 1988 White Paper, Cmnd 517.
xliii. *IBA Annual Report 1985/6*, p. 37.
xliv. *TV & Radio 1987*. London: Independent Broadcasting Authority, p. 144.
xlv.   Nick Higham. How Radio 3 found Beethoven again. *The Times*, 12 August 1987, p. 27.
xlvi. Interview with Gillian Reynolds, 29 October 2014.
xlvii. In the temporary absence of *Talking About Music*.
xlviii. Interview with Kevin Appleby, April 2013.
xlix. *The Guardian*, 20 December 1987 (when the item was first broadcast as part of a BBC mini-season marking the 50th anniversary of the death of Ravel).
l.   Interview with Fiona Talkington, 2 November 2012.
li.   Peter James, personal communication, 28 September 2014.
lii.   Interview with Fiona Talkington, 2 November 2012.
liii. Sir Ian Hunter. Music on radio. *The Times*, 17 August 1989, p. 11.
liv.   https://www.theguardian.com/world/2009/nov/09/fall-of-berlin-wall-1989.
lv.   Jurgen Habermas. Modernity an incomplete project. *New German Critique* Winter 1981 vol. 22, p. 10.
lvi.   G. Betts. *Complete UK Hit Singles 1952–2005*, 2005. London: Collins, p. 606.
lvii. Richard Bassett and John Holland. Anthem of liberation echoes in streets of Prague. *The Times*, 25 November 1989, p. 6.

Bibliographic Sources

Arnold, M. 1875. *Culture and anarchy*, 2009th ed. Oxford: Oxford University Press.
Carpenter, H., and J.R. Doctor. 1996. *The envy of the world: Fifty years of the BBC third programme and Radio 3, 1946–1996*. London: Weidenfeld & Nicolson.
Doctor, J.R., A. Garnham, D.A. Wright, and N. Kenyon. 2007. *The Proms: A new history*. London: Thames & Hudson.
Goodman, D. 2011. *Radio's civic ambition: American broadcasting and democracy in the 1930s*. Oxford: Oxford University Press.
Grimley, M., and M. Wiegold. 1977. *Catalogue of music broadcast on Radio 3 and Radio 4 in 1974*. London: British Broadcasting Corporation.
Hendy, D. 2013. *Public Service Broadcasting*. London: Palgrave Macmillan.
Kenyon, N. 1981. *The BBC symphony orchestra: The first fifty years 1930–1989*. London: British Broadcasting Corporation.
Ponsonby, R. 2009. *Musical heroes: A personal view of music and the musical world over sixty years*. London: DLM.
Seaton, J. 1997. *Power without responsibility: The press and broadcasting in Britain*, 5th ed. London: Routledge.
Seaton, J. 2015. *Pinkoes and Traitors. The BBC and the nation 1974–1987*. London: Profile Books.
Stoller, T. 2010. *Sounds of your life: The history of independent radio in the UK*. New Barnet: John Libbey.
Stoller, T. and E. Wray. 2010. 1984 and all that. The impact of political change on independent radio in the UK. *Communication Journal of New Zealand* vol. 11 no. 1. New Zealand Communications Association.
Taruskin, R. 2010. *Music in the late 20th century*. Oxford: Oxford University Press.
Turner, A.W. 2010. *Rejoice, rejoice! Britain in the 1980s*. London: Aurum.

CHAPTER 7

The Nineties: Saga Louts and Dumbing Down

Classical music radio in the early Nineties—the recasting of Radio 3—the arrival of Classic FM—classical music radio 1993–1995—comparing Radio 3 and Classic FM—engaging the potential audience—towards the Unknown Region.

The mid-Nineties reintroduced inclusive and accessible classical music radio. The 1990 Broadcasting Act broke the final BBC broadcasting monopoly by sanctioning national commercial radio—and thus, indirectly, Classic FM—while permitting the abandonment by ILR of its public service activities, including the broadcasting of classical music. Almost simultaneously, concerned at the lack of wider appeal of Radio 3, the BBC took advantage of the departure of John Drummond as Controller, Radio 3 in 1992 to appoint Nicholas Kenyon, whom they hoped would be a moderniser and populariser. The station was reinvigorated by a combination of accessible popular output, high ambition in the presentation of serious music—culminating for the parameters of this book in the *Fairest Isle* programme series across 1995—and cheerful iconoclasm, allowing innovations such as the *Blue Peter Prom* from 1999. The positive symbiosis between a recast Radio 3 and an initially culturally aspirational Classic FM represented the third high point of post-war UK classical music broadcasting.

These were years when classical music briefly re-entered the mainstream of popular culture, enjoying but coming to the end of the great CD boom. That success was bracketed by *Nessun Dorma* at the football

© The Author(s) 2018
T. Stoller, *Classical Music Radio in the United Kingdom, 1945–1995*,
https://doi.org/10.1007/978-3-319-64710-4_7

World Cup in 1990, and the hugely successful *Three Tenors* concerts four years later. As a result of it being taken up by Classic FM during that station's first weeks on air, Gorecki's contemporary *Symphony of Sorrowful Songs* remarkably reached number six in the UK overall album chart.[i] The commodification of classical music had become ubiquitous and inescapable, and radio providers could not ignore it.

The Nineties produced a new flowering of multi-channel classical music radio, just when it had seemed to be at a low ebb with a restricted BBC output and ILR quitting the field. At the instigation of new Director General Michael Checkland, Radio 3 was recast to address itself to a much broader audience and seized the opportunity of popularising some of the output while retaining excellence in high-brow programmes. Meanwhile, in the commercial sector a brand new national radio competitor began broadcasting in September 1992, Classic FM. In direct lineage from the earlier Music Programme on the BBC in the Sixties, this service more than doubled the amount of classical music radio on offer to listeners and, alongside the recast Radio 3, produced a multi-channel offer which would regain the mass audience for classical music radio. Both innovations served to reawaken the continuing debate about valid popularising as against 'dumbing down'. Classic FM might be dubbed 'an instant classic' by the Sunday papers or its listeners derided as 'Saga louts' by Alan Bennett. Either way, the reactions illustrate the broader relationship between culture and society in Britain.

UK politics and economics in the Nineties and beyond constituted the continuation of Thatcherism by other means. Almost the last effective legislation passed by the troubled Major administration in 1996 was to provide the legislative framework for the introduction of digital television and digital radio (Stoller in Mollgard, ed., 2012). Into the new century, successive New Labour Governments under Blair continued advancing the primacy of 'the market', not least in broadcasting.[ii] National economic discomfiture at the start of the Nineties soon gave way to increasing prosperity and a prolonged credit-fuelled boom which was to last until 2008.

CLASSICAL MUSIC RADIO IN THE EARLY NINETIES

As the Nineties began, composer Michael Tippett, now far from his antagonistic days within the Third Programme Defence Society, reached his 85th birthday and Radio 3 'cleared its schedules' in celebration.[iii]

Otherwise, John Drummond's schedules were by then well established. The weekdays were built around the daily *Morning Concert* and two *Composers of the Week* (one on weekdays in the morning and an evening repeat of the previous week's composer). *Morning Sequence* was mostly sequence programming or grouped by rather contrived attempts to provide a linking theme for a range of usually fairly popular works: *Inspired by Israel* on 7 May 1990, the *Georgian Music Room* on 15 May and *Always It's Spring* on 18 May. *Mainly for Pleasure*, on weekday late afternoons was another staple, as was Friday afternoon's *The Works*.

The 1990 sample week in May saw the first performance of Hans Werner Henze's *Das Verratene Meer*, based on Yukio Mishima's novel *The Sailor Who Fell from Grace with The Sea*, and a production in Russian of a lesser known opera by Tchaikovsky, *Vakula the Smith*. Typical of Drummond's approach was the Berlin Weekend earlier in May, which involved extensive relays of live or specially recorded concerts, together with feature material. Drummond regarded this—along with a similar weekend the following year from Minneapolis and St Paul—'as peaks in his achievement for Radio 3' (Ponsonby 2009: 110).

While the broad output and the pattern of listening seemed stable, debate was stirring as the prospect of a commercial alternative became more than merely a chimera. A leader in *The Times* on 28 January 1990 spoke of Radio 3 as being 'so long sunk in musicological elitism'.[iv] The possible arrival of competition—though at this stage by no means certain—also prompted discussion about the impact of monopoly. Janet Daley wrote that the debate was:

> not between those who wish to replace Mozart with Mantovani. To the extent that one could call the defender's attitude elitist, it is elitism based not on quality but on esoterica ... there are those who frankly regard Radio 3 as the official outlet for the musical establishment: as a promoter of British composers, to protect the British orchestral players and a noticeboard for what those on the inside like to call 'the living tradition' of British music.[v]

It is wholly possible that many in Radio 3 regarded the second part of this catalogue as compliments rather than criticisms. Nevertheless, those who felt aggrieved attacked Daley in turn, framing the debate in terms of likely new commercial competition. Yehudi Menuhin, for example, responded that:

it is this offering of an essential background to informed and sophisticated opinion and taste in all realms, from the political to the musical, that has created the very hallmark of British leadership and its standards, both broad and high, in so many spheres. The new commercial classical music radio channel will no doubt profitably provide a favourite fare of most beloved works, on which, incidentally, no royalties will be owing and no musicians costs incurred ... We will need Radio 3 as it is now more than ever.[vi]

Menuhin's assertions about royalties misunderstood British copyright arrangements. Classic FM paid the record companies represented by PPL and PRS on behalf of all composers, performers and arrangers handsomely for its use of commercially recorded music.[1] Unlike the BBC, though, it funded individual elite musicians only when it paid to broadcast their own concerts. Arguably, both sides overstated their case to make their general points about mass and popular culture in UK society; equally, few spotted in advance the symbiosis that was to emerge.

1992 was the year when everything changed. Drummond, embracing journalist Tim Gardam's ironic description of him as having been 'tainted by [the] experience' of BBC internal politics,[vii] left Radio 3 to be replaced by Nicholas Kenyon. Radio 3 ceased broadcasting on AM (on 29 February 1992), with the frequency being transferred to the Radio Authority for eventual use by Virgin Radio. John Birt moved from being Deputy Director General to become BBC Director General, although not until after his predecessor Michael Checkland had appointed Kenyon, and Classic FM began broadcasting on 7 September 1992. That same year, Peter Ackroyd published his novel *English Music*. His youthful protagonist, Timothy, comes finally to understand the power of the composer over what is heard, and himself to hear the 'English music'. With the changes in Radio 3 that year, that may be thought to apply also to the BBC; and, by extension, to Classic FM as well.

The imminence of Classic FM now had the BBC's full attention. A research study in May 1992 addressed audience responses to what it called Classic FM's 'test transmissions', which are discussed below. It noted that people had reacted positively to Classic FM, with 50% saying they liked it a lot and hardly anyone disliking the station. There was little gender differentiation in the response, nor any significant class variation, although

---

[1] See Chap. 5, p. 136n.

unsurprisingly older people were more likely to respond positively. The research conclusion was that Classic FM would be a significant challenge to the BBC:

> Radio 3 listeners may be 'closet' listeners. They are more hesitant about praising Classic FM, but nevertheless, many were attracted to their repertoire. As such, Radio 3's share is more vulnerable than its weekly reach. Radio 2 has more of a potential problem. Radio 2 listeners who like Classic FM may desert Radio 2, and hence share and reach are vulnerable. And although Classic FM is unlikely to damage the strong parts of Radio 4's schedule, it may represent an alternative when listeners do not want speech radio.[viii]

Radio 3's output during the week that Classic FM launched at the end of September 1992 shows that it had firmly embraced sequence programming. *On Air*, *Morning Sequence* and *In Tune* dominated the weekday daytime schedule. The whole of Sunday morning was covered by two such programmes, *Morning Concert* and *Brian Kay's Sunday Morning*, and Saturday by *Morning Concert* and *Record Review*. Radio 3's *Composer of the Week* during Classic's launch was the canonically uncontroversial Tchaikovsky. Radio 3 broadcast the Proms throughout that September week, but had to devote Saturday from 10.25 am to 7.30 pm to live commentary of cricket's NatWest Trophy final from Lord's.

THE RECASTING OF RADIO 3

Thirteen years earlier, Kenyon had chided the then outgoing Controller, Radio 3, Stephen Hearst, for judging:

> the acceptability of the BBC's programmes to the public by the listening figures they attract. The consequences, clearly, were dire. How can the BBC preserve its role of 'public service broadcasting' ... if the beastly competitor is turning out programmes which are fun?[ix]

Now Director General Checkland and Managing Director of Radio David Hatch brought him in as Controller, Radio 3 in March 1992 to cope with precisely that conundrum, and it is they, along with Kenyon, who should be seen as the true instigators of change at Radio 3. Checkland is clear about the nature of the task:

> We told Nick what we wanted to do – it wasn't so much content, it was more about style and accessibility, in terms of the tone of the presentation and the way programmes were organised, and generally loosening the way that music had been presented.[x]

For Kenyon himself, the situation he inherited was strikingly high minded:

> John Drummond, though he would fiercely say he had made many changes to Radio 3, and many of them for the better, was still on a very high intellectual level, and was considered by BBC management to be off-putting. I think there was a mood shared within the musical world that the announcers were a bit stuffy, and the programming was a bit set in its ways.[xi]

Belatedly, the BBC was remembering that there was a substantial underserved potential market for classical music radio, which it termed 'Radio 3's missing listeners'. A research survey conducted in June 1992 identified far more people who actively consumed classical music than listened to Radio 3, representing:

> a large potential audience for Radio 3, [but] Classic FM will of course target these people, and has the advantage of being a new station with a blast of novelty about it, that may make people try it rather than Radio 3.[xii]

A report on the listening patterns in the first four weeks of Classic FM broadcasts noted that in achieving a substantial early audience:

> Classic FM has probably gained a small proportion of its audience from Radio 3, but has also gained a new listening *by appropriating some of the potential audience that Radio 3 has been trying to attract* [my emphasis].[xiii]

There are echoes here of BBC attitudes in earlier years. The size of potential audience posited in 1992 is broadly equivalent with that identified by Robert Silvey back in 1946.[xiv] Just as before, the BBC was taking a proprietorial attitude towards them; they *ought* to be listening, and steps need to be taken to *make* them listen. That an upstart commercial competitor might attract them instead was unthinkable, almost *lèse-majesté*.

One reaction to the arrival of Classic FM was a Radio 3 poster campaign during September 1992, designed by Saatchi & Saatchi and concentrated in London. One series of posters focused on drivetime, seeking to promote Radio 3's late afternoon programming but without specifically naming *On Air* or *In Tune*. The other, a *Great Composers* series, aimed to communicate the station's role in live music. Neither campaign was a success. Research showed that 'awareness of the posters was low'. In the London area only 16% had noticed any of them. Even where they saw them, 'people tended to take away fairly general messages about Radio 3 playing classical music, rather than the specific messages'. Worse still, 'the adjective used most often to describe the *Great Composers* series was "boring"'.[xv]

Once installed at the BBC, Kenyon urgently set about recasting Radio 3. He faced not only the natural inertia of the organisation, but the stifling tradition of how it was presented to audiences and positioned in the perception of high-brow supporters. This evokes echoes of the battles of the Fifties and late Sixties, discussed in earlier chapters. While Kenyon observes that 'the producers were entirely focussed on internal battles, which they ran with consummate enthusiasm',[xvi] for the listener it was simply the programmes which counted.

Equally it is a mistake to assume that the changes were only a competitive response. As Checkland makes clear, competition was really just a catalyst for overdue change:

> the BBC would probably have been happy to have carried on, and it needed something really to jog it. It was rather like ITV arriving in the Fifties.[xvii]

In that sense, the arrival of Classic FM was an opportunity not to be missed. Given that 'some Radio 3 devotees undoubtedly think that Kenyon is knocking the last nail in the coffin of civilisation',[xviii] he would have been hard pressed to make as many changes as he did without the opportunity and the excuse of competition.

Kenyon was able to drop the 17-year-old discussion show *Music Weekly*, reduce the amount of drama and end the documentary programme, *Soundings*. He introduced a new late night live arts programme, and a three-hour show presented by Brian Kay on Sunday mornings. There were also two new music shows on weekday early mornings and evenings, confirming the place of sequence output: *On Air* in the mornings and *In Tune* every weekday evening. They annoyed the elitists no end. Senior Labour politician Gerald Kaufman claimed that the station was 'plunging down market' and would 'degenerate into junk radio'.[xix]

Kenyon's personal mission was clear:

> I always regarded myself as an enthusiast and a communicator on behalf of classical music, and that was what underlaid how we should be broadcasting; a knowledgeable, informed companion. And so it's worth saying that we did invent quite a few programmes then which survive to this day, Michael Berkeley on *Private Passions*, and *In Tune* which eventually settled down with a single lead presenter, Sean Rafferty.[xx]

He concentrated on presentation styles and personnel initially, rather than major changes to the content (although these would come later). But he was concerned to acknowledge, accelerate and implement change, even if he set about that with what he now considers might have been a little too much haste:

> I wanted a much more integrated system where people who talked on Radio 3, talked from a position of knowledge and enthusiasm, and I would say, looking back at it, that we probably changed too much, too soon ... [but, as] de Tocqueville says about the French Government in the 18th century, the worst thing about change is when you leave it too late.

The actual content did not change hugely. Looking at the output data for the equivalent sample weeks from May 1990 until May 1996—therefore starting even before Classic FM was more than an unlikely possibility—what stands out is the consistency of output allied to a steady growth in sequence programming, suggesting that what Kenyon altered initially was indeed style and approach rather than musical content (Tables 7.1 and 7.2).

Consistency in the actual output is evident also in the number of composers whose works were featured in programme listings in those sample weeks.

Challenging the old-school approach to presentation on Radio 3, inherited and largely unchanged from the days of the Third Programme, Kenyon brought in a slightly more demotic approach with presenters who might demystify both the music and the platform on which it was

7 THE NINETIES: SAGA LOUTS AND DUMBING DOWN

Table 7.1 Radio 3 classical music content 1990–1995 in sample weeks

Radio 3	Total classical music output	Record-based programmes	Sequence programmes	Feature programmes
	(hours:minutes)			
1990	92:30	32:40	22:00	–
1991	96:25	41:50	28:40	4:35
1992	97:20	36:35	26:30	2:30
1993	95:50	43:35	34:30	1:40
1994	99:45	35:00	39:30	3:00
1995	101:05	31:00	38:15	3:50

Table 7.2 Radio 3 classical music composers featured 1990–1995 in sample weeks

Radio 3	Number of composers	Most frequently played (number of plays)
1990	112	Beethoven (13), Bach (10), Debussy (7), Mozart (7)
1991	115	Beethoven (12), Mozart (10), Chopin (8), Brahms (6), Dvořák (6)
1992	111	Beethoven (20), Mozart (10), Haydn (6), Stravinsky (6), Bach (6), Maxwell Davies (6)
1993	114	Mozart (10), Schubert (9), Brahms (8), Haydn (7)
1994	109	Dvořák (9), Beethoven (8), Bach (8)
1995	107	Brahms (8), Britten (6), Debussy (6), Ravel (6)

being broadcast. That involved dispensing with the services of a number of those 'announcers' who as the *Daily Telegraph* reported 'seem to have been there since Marconi's days'.[xxi]

This was akin to the desacralisation of music in the concert hall, and equally if not more disconcerting to conservative listeners. It provoked a milder public version of the elitist storms which had periodically greeted changes to the Third Programme, characterised this time by a protest letter from Bamber Gascoigne and Viscount Norwich.[xxii] The language is highly reminiscent of the reactions to the curtailing of the Third Programme hours in the mid-Fifties and then to the arrival of Radio 3 in the late Sixties, as discussed in preceding chapters:

> The old Third Programme, in particular, was conceived as provider of serious music for discerning listeners; ratings were a secondary consideration.

Is this basic philosophy – which has made its successor admired and envied across the world – now to be cast aside ...? In short, as the time approaches for the renewal of the BBC's charter in 1996, we are faced with yet another symptom of the desperate identity crisis which the Corporation is obviously suffering and which, if allowed to continue, threatens to destroy it altogether.

John Julius Norwich had a well-developed sense of the value of culture made popular, and was later to present *Evening Concert* on Classic FM for three years, while Gascoigne similarly had popularised learning as the founding host of *University Challenge* on BBC television, from 1962 to 1987. But the response of others of those who were effectively heirs of the Third Programme Defence Society of the mid-Fifties, and of the Campaign for Better Broadcasting in the late Sixties, may be thought to reveal that continuing strand in British cultural society which demands high-brow provision notwithstanding the needs of a wideraudience. It is a mark of the effectiveness of the efforts of Nicholas Kenyon at the BBC that he was better able than his predecessors to resist—mostly—the pressures of the cultural elite. Nor was it the impact of Classic FM's output which somehow 'drove' Radio 3 in the Nineties towards the centre of the canonic repertoire. This was ground which it had usually assertively occupied.

It was the manner of presentation rather than the matter which needed to be addressed first, if Radio 3 was to achieve the optimum fusion of ambitious output with accessibility of listening, linking the high brow with the broader middle brow in output and audience appeal. And that Kenyon tackled purposively, although not—as will be seen—without incident.

THE ARRIVAL OF CLASSIC FM

The Independent Broadcasting Authority had been responsible for introducing Independent *Local* Radio, the first challenge to the BBC's monopoly of classical music radio. In the Broadcasting Act 1990, the IBA's responsibilities were split between three separate institutions: a privatised transmission company, National Telecommunications Ltd; and two regulatory statutory corporations, the Independent Television Commission and the Radio Authority. It therefore fell to the Radio Authority to introduce Independent *National* Radio. Classic FM was the first of the three national commercial radio stations to be licensed, and the only one on FM.

A transitional body, the Shadow Radio Authority (SRA), took on the initial task of planning how the three new INR channels should be deployed. There was extensive regulatory, governmental and parliamentary discussion and uncertainty before the eventual decision to make the only FM frequency a non-pop service—but by no means necessarily a classical music one (Stoller 2010: 202–204). Even as late as 22 February 1992, when the Broadcasting Bill had already reached the radio sections at Committee stage, SRA Chair Alun Chalfont was writing to the then-Culture Minister, David Mellor, asking for the power to say which services each INR station should provide.[xxiii]

Chalfont had already gone on record as personally favouring using the FM frequencies for a classical music service. In one of the last initiatives by any contemporary government to protect the concept of genuine diversity in programme output on commercial radio, Mellor acknowledged the risk that 'the economics of radio are such that this on its own might result in the emergence of three essentially pop-based stations with the minimum necessary diversity mixed in'.[xxiv] The Bill was therefore to be amended to make sure each service was different from the other, and that 'one of the new stations ... must include a substantial proportion of music other than pop music',[xxv] but without specifying a classical music channel. Speaking in the House of Lords in June, Minister of State Earl Ferrers revealed the government's less than subtle understanding of different pop music genres. Referring to the service which was to be 'devoted to music other than pop music' he opined that 'I am sure that that will please some of your lordships. It will not all be "Thump, thump, thump"!'[xxvi]

However, a classical music service was never prescribed by Government or regulator, and came within a whisker of not happening. The licence, advertised on 11 January 1991, was required by statute to be awarded to the highest cash bidder, irrespective of programme format (so long as it was not pop music). After the original Classic FM consortium announced that it was withdrawing from the race, a group which had been brought together by the GWR local radio group linked with some of the original Classic FM team to put in a last-minute application under that name. The driving force behind the new consortium, Ralph Bernard, who was at that time Managing Director of GWR, recalls that 'everyone thought we had deliberately put our application in late to shock. The reality is we got it in so late because we cocked it up'.[xxvii]

The reason for the eleventh-hour delay? The group's Chairman, Henry Meakin, had become trapped without his keys in the corridor between his flat door and the front door to the building. In the end, he had to shout for help through a letter box for someone to let him out of the building, so that he could get to the crucial meeting at merchant bankers Hambros in time to approve the figure which Classic FM would bid for the licence.[xxviii] On such threads do seminal events at times depend.

And initially, Classic FM's application failed. A higher bid had come from First National Radio (FNR) with £1.75 million. It proposed 'Showtime', a service of light music linked by a showbusiness theme, and with an assurance that 'music defined as "not pop music" will form at least 75% of all music broadcast'.[xxix] Classic FM had only bid £670,000, and INR1 was duly awarded to Showtime on 4 July 1991. However, FNR was unable to raise sufficient capital by the deadline of Friday 16 August 1991. Consequently, the Radio Authority turned to Classic FM, offering it the INR1 licence subject to the consortium demonstrating that it could raise the necessary funds. Classic FM delivered the necessary documents to the Authority at 11.40 am on 30 September 1991, this time beating the deadline by just 20 minutes.[xxx] The UK got a commercially funded national classical music radio station after an almost comedic sequence of events and by the skin of its teeth. Ironically, the Showtime proposal had needed to raise £12 million, given an ambitious business plan. Had FNR been more prudent in its proposals, it is wholly possible that the almost £10 million they actually raised would have been enough to gain the licence, forestalling Classic FM.

Given the role of Margaret Thatcher's personal animus in bringing about the end of the old ITV system in 1990, it has been argued that Classic FM came about as a result of government action driven by the 'Conservative anti-establishment' who were hostile to Drummond's embrace of new rather than traditional music on Radio 3, and 'demanded dismemberment of Radio 3 in recompense for Glock and Drummond's confirmation of their prejudices' (Blake 1997: 64). That is not what happened. As this history demonstrates, Classic FM came about as much through a series of accidents as a result of deliberate policy by either government or the regulator. The eventual contractual obligation was solely to provide programming which comprised at least 75% 'predominantly classical and light classical music, but may include some film and stage music', with up to 25% of the music programming permitted to be pop music.[xxxi] Within those limits, Classic FM's music choice was a matter solely for the station itself.

7 THE NINETIES: SAGA LOUTS AND DUMBING DOWN

How much linkage was there between ILR's classical music lineage and the arrival of Classic FM? In some ways, less than might have been expected, given ILR's achievements in this field between 1973 and 1990. There had been an unconventional application in 1972 for the London General and Entertainment franchise—subsequently awarded to Capital Radio—proposing a light classical music station, but that had come to nothing.[xxxii] A consortium under the name of Classic FM had applied, unsuccessfully, for one of the so-called 'incremental' local licences offered by the Radio Authority in December 1988.[2]

In another sense, the ILR inheritance was definitive. As discussed above,[3] the GWR group's Brunel Radio in Bristol and Wiltshire was one of those stations which had expanded its classical music output when it split its AM and FM frequencies in 1988. It had broadcast on AM only a daily, three-hour afternoon show of classical and light classical music, devised by Michael Bukht, who was to design the Classic FM schedules four years later. Bernard recalls that:

> we put together a schedule of popular classical music, and it sounded fantastic. People started talking about it in Wiltshire and in Bristol. It was a sea-change, because you had … people in their thousands listening to local commercial radio and hearing classical music.[xxxiii]

Although the GWR board initially declined to apply for a national classical station, it was persuaded by Bernard and the Brunel experience to put together a consortium, and it was that which eventually linked up with the original Classic FM—when the latter's supporters began to fall away—to make the application a practical proposition, and from which the new station arose.[xxxiv]

Classic FM began broadcasting at 6 am on Monday 7 September 1992. It had been able in advance to 'play around with the programming in live time'.[xxxv] The Radio Authority granted it six short-term licences for three weeks from 24 February 1992 in Bath, Coventry, Durham, Edinburgh, southwest Manchester and Teddington, 'to test the reaction to [Classic FM's] classical music programme format prior to the station's national launch'.[xxxvi] A BBC report on research into these trials, entitled *Will Classic FM Threaten the BBC?*, concluded that:

---

[2] See Chap. 6, p. 181.
[3] See Chap. 6, p. 177.

> Classic FM is making classical music digestible. It is therefore much more attractive to most classical music listeners than Radio 3, which is believed to play long and heavy pieces. And perhaps ironically – Classic FM is seen to offer more choice than Radio 3, because it hardly counts as a choice if you do not like any of it.[xxxvii]

The station at its launch divided the commentariat. Steven Pettitt thought that it was 'saccharine' and that culturally it would 'contribute to the relegation of the status of serious music from high art to low entertainment'.[xxxviii] Richard Ingrams, on the other hand, observed that:

> There will be people – many of them, I imagine, working for Radio 3 – who will sneer at ... an 'undemanding' diet; I see nothing wrong with it. Personally I would rather listen to a single movement of a Mozart symphony then to a whole batch of bassoon concertos by C.P.E. Bach.[xxxix]

Brian McMaster, a former director of the Edinburgh Festival, believed that 'it is wonderful to have a classical music station, and ... fuddy-duddies like me will have to adjust to the style'.[xl] Nicholas Payne, Director designate of the Royal Opera, summed up the dichotomy:

> My radio is permanently tuned to Radio 3, but my PA really believes that classical music in bite sized chunks is going to be the trend.[xli]

So it was to prove, with many more young people and women listening to the commercial station than to Radio 3. However, BBC Audience Research's warning also stands up, that plenty of the great and the good were 'closet' Classic FM listeners as well.[xlii]

By December, it was clear that Classic FM was at least a *succès d'estime*. It won a remarkable 4.3 million listeners in just a few months,[xliii] when the station itself expected to reach fewer than 3 million by that stage.[xliv] It was dubbed 'an instant classic, the sound of middle England, the voice of the heartland'.[xlv] When 'George calling from his car along the M4' won a magnum of champagne in a competition to find the link between Beethoven, Haydn and Strauss,[xlvi] the caller turned out to be the Housing Minister, Sir George Young.[4]

---

[4] The answer, of course, was 'Emperor'.

The station was on air for 24 hours a day, an innovation which Radio 3 was to copy in 1996. It was partly the highly commodified product which its critics had anticipated, but it also aspired to a place within the longer tradition of classical music broadcasting in the UK. Most of the daytime output comprised sequence programmes built around personality presenters, but the station showed more ambition at lunchtimes and especially in evening programmes, and before long included some live relays of concerts and operas.

Classic FM's first programme controller was Michael Bukht, who had been the original and highly successful Programme Director of London's Capital Radio. Bukht—who enjoyed a parallel career with a separate television persona as Michael Barry, the 'Crafty Cook', on BBC's *Food and Drink* programme[xlvii]—deliberately approached planning Classic FM's schedules along the same lines as his creation of Capital Radio in 1973. He liked to claim that 'Classic FM was Capital come again but with slightly smarter clothes',[xlviii] which included the presence of some established BBC voices, such as Susannah Simons and Margaret Howard. Simons remembers that:

> when Classic came along, [Bukht] did most, or an awful lot of the same things, with memorably, an awful lot of the same people [as at Capital] … The mixture of programming at the very beginning reflected his view that you could make classical music accessible if you placed it in the same context as pop music and you treated it in exactly the same way.[xlix]

Paul Gambaccini's verdict is even simpler: 'Bukht was a programming genius', while adding that Classic FM in those first years, 'was one of the great rides of my life'.[l]

The station tried to make a virtue of both its informality and of mistakes in presentation. When Classic breakfast presenter Nick Bailey announced *Jesu Joy of Man's Desiring* and played instead the prelude from Previn's *Invisible Drummer*, the station's managers just laughed.[li] Had that happened on the BBC, Radio 3's Continuity Department would have been apoplectic.

Simons stresses that the station's presenters felt that they were participating with their listeners in a shared learning experience:

> The bulk of us … were all on the same learning journey, so in a way what we were doing was taking the audience with us on this voyage of

discovery ... always treating it with respect and love, but a spirit of curiosity, and making absolutely no assumptions about how much or how little they knew – and that was the secret.[lii]

The sequence programmes, which accounted for at least 20 of the 24 hours of daily broadcasts, generally included short pieces of music, just as if this was a popular music station, together with commercial radio staples of interviews, recipes and guests. Bernard, who was the launch Chief Executive as well as the begetter of the station, is forthright about this:

> We discovered ... that people did not reject the notion of classical music or classical music as such, but ... they knew what they liked and they liked what they knew. They weren't terribly adventurous, because the outlets for classical music were so few and forbidding and somewhat elitist, so Radio 3 would not have been [suitable] for the vast majority of the UK listening public. Attending a concert at the Albert Hall they might do once in their lifetime, or attend a live classical music concert, but if they heard it on a commercial on ITV, or they had experience of it in a regular format so that they could become used to it and familiar with it ... if it was wrapped up ... and styled and presented in a way which was acceptable, then it became admired and enjoyed.[liii]

Alan Bennett dubbed listeners to Classic FM 'Saga louts', going on to say:

> I loathe Classic FM more and more for its cosiness, its safety and its wholehearted endorsement of the post-Thatcher world, with medical insurance and Saga Holidays rammed down your throat between every item. Nor does the music get much respect; I'm frequently outraged when they play without acknowledgement or apology a sliced up version of Beethoven's Ninth, filleted of all but the most tuneful bits.[liv]

Bernard however feels not so much unapologetic as vindicated:

> There was never, ever any doubt in our minds. There was no debate about whether we would play movements or whole symphonies. It was a complete no-brainer to us. We would be programming the station like a pop station, so we would no more play a full symphony then we would play a full album. However we did say that we would play full symphonies in the evening.[lv]

The debate about playing extracts from works 'intended' to be an integral whole is a continuing one, and has a long history. Many classical composers were a good deal less 'pure' than their latter-day apologists; themes, movements were redeployed, moved around, added into or removed from supposedly complete works. Schubert was particularly prone to do this, and his *Quartetsatz* is a jewel of the classical repertoire, despite finding itself standing alone without its intended surrounding movements. Beethoven's *Grosse Fugue* was formerly the concluding movement of his Op. 130 String Quartet.

Nevertheless, those hostile to Classic FM—and to some of Kenyon's innovations on Radio 3—were most critical of all about Classic FM's decision to broadcast single movements of symphonies, the so-called 'bleeding chunks', although, as noted above, this was hardly a complete innovation.[5] Jonathan Miller condemned Classic FM for what it said— he supposed—about something wholly contemporary; the station was 'a symptom of global decline where all thought is reduced to soundbites'.[lvi]

Classic FM's music choice was based on the expectation of Bukht and Bernard, drawn from their experience of popular music radio, and supported by pre-launch research, that the station should:

> adhere systematically to a core repertoire of popular classical music … Given the tendency to narrow segmentation elsewhere in UK radio, it was reasonable to expect many listeners of Classic FM would not willingly accept too broad a definition of the classical repertoire.[lvii]

Its initial music catalogue, compiled by programme consultant Robin Ray, listed virtually every work in the established canonic repertoire of recorded classical music, providing timings for single movements and complete works for over 50,000 items. Only one recording of each work was included (although presenters were given scope to select their own favoured recordings for programmes such as *Classic Countdown*[lviii]). Tracks were identified as either 'essential repertoire', 'standard repertoire', 'widely popular' or 'universally popular'. Each track was labelled as either 'clean' (having a positive end or beginning) or 'fade' (where the end or beginning requires fading in or out). This provided the Classic FM repertoire, which the Selector computer programme would

---

[5] See Chap. 5, p. 138n.

then choose from according to guidelines established by the Programme Committee of Bernard, Bukht, Ray, Nicolas Tresilian and others from time to time.

Ray's seriousness of approach is indicated by a note on the draft catalogue: 'apologies are offered for the fact that this word processor cannot provide accents for capital letters'. Evidently, he remained strongly influenced by the expectations and aspirations of the BBC, for whom he had broadcast on classical music since 1965. Ray had been part of the abortive consortium which had applied in the name of Classic FM for a local London licence in the late Eighties. Relations between him and the radio station soured over time, leading eventually to an action in the Chancery Division of the High Court of Justice challenging 'the entitlement of [Classic FM] to the intellectual property rights in five documents containing proposals how the tracks on music recording should be categorised'. The High Court eventually upheld Ray's claim that his copyright had been infringed, shortly before his death in November 1998.[lix]

It is not fanciful to conclude that the catalogue Ray produced represents the ultimate fulfilment of Theodor Adorno and others' concern about the commodification of culture and especially of classical music. However, as one part of a duopoly of output, with Radio 3 offering alternative recordings and works not listed in Ray's catalogue, it is equally possible to argue that it was part of a necessary balance which served to open up the entire canonic repertoire—50,000 works of art—to listeners who did not and would not wish to identify with the elite.

CLASSICAL MUSIC RADIO 1993–1995

By 1993, Radio 3 was blending popular and high brow, and an easy listening style with more traditional formal presentation. The weekdays held to a steady pattern. *On Air* between 7 am and 9 am, *Morning Sequence* between 10 am and noon and *In Tune* from 5 pm to 7.30 pm were the cornerstones of the sequence output. However, although their presentation was relaxed, not all of the music was wholly middle-brow. *Record Review*, broadcast on Saturday morning and then repeated on Wednesday afternoon of the sample week, ranged from Handel and Vivaldi to Stravinsky and Heinichen. *Morning Sequence* attracted criticism from the stalwarts, but its contents seem unexceptional. Monday had a Strauss *Concertino*, Tuesday a Suk *Fantasy*, Wednesday a Goetz *Piano Trio*, Thursday a Schmidt *Concertante* and Friday Alwyn's

Overture to a Masque. There was no 'dumbing down' here, despite the accusations that were made. However, by positioning the station as newly accessible, the BBC maintained its audiences in the face of a highly successful competitor, and drew complaints from the guardians of the high brow, even where those were not justified.

The number of composers featured was close to that earlier in the decade, with Mozart, Brahms, Schubert and Haydn maintaining the First Viennese School's preponderance, and the amount of music was similar. It was the presentation of the musical offering which was greatly changed. The proportion of records to live or original recordings was also much higher, and the amount of sequence programmes much increased, comprising over one third of the total Radio 3 output of classical music.

The *Saturday Opera* continued to be a feature of the early evening on Radio 3, in the sample week with the performance of *Falstaff* from the Vienna State Opera. By contrast, the channel programmed Hindemith's contemporary opera *Neues vom Tage (Today's News)* on Thursday afternoon, highlighting again the balance between mainstream popular and challenging avant-garde. A major programme on Wednesday evening, running for over three hours, explored European music in the context of the rebellions of 1968; the featured modernist composers were Berio, Pousseur, Stockhausen, NoNo and Xenakis. Taken together, the clear impression is of a diverse network, soundly based in the classical canonic repertoire, unafraid to test the margins of that repertoire or to blend the comfortably popular with potentially uncomfortable modern or early music, while providing consistent linkages between the two in a way which made the whole accessible to a wide audience. If this outcome was a consequence of commercial competition (and that was by no means the only cause), then it seems a pretty benign one.

Classic FM's output of hours of classical music was almost double that of Radio 3. By direct contrast, only 21 hours of its weekly total of 161 hours were not sequence programmes, while there were five hours of music features. The database shows that in the non-sequence programmes Beethoven was the most often featured composer, although listings in the *Radio Times* were confined to a quarter of a page so that there are scant data about the detailed programme content—and, indeed, there was little detail provided for listeners, who seemed not to be too worried about that. Daytimes were built around personality presenters: Nick Bailey, Henry Kelly, Susanna Simons, Petroc Trelawny and Margaret Howard on weekdays; and Paul Gambaccini, Petroc Trelawny,

Adrian Love, Sarah Lucas and Nicky Horne at weekends. Along with short pieces of music, there were features unrelated to the music: interviews, recipes and guests. The two programmes vying for the highest rating, Gambaccini's *Classical Countdown* and Bailey's *Classic Romance*, were both effectively copies of shows scheduled by Bukht on Capital Radio, but with classical music in place of pop music.

The station's ambition to be taken seriously is shown in the sample week by its weekday *Lunchtime Concerto*—an hour of, respectively, Kabalevsky, Haydn, Kodály, Beethoven and Bach—the broadcasting of Bellini's *Norma* in the classic recording with Maria Callas on Saturday night, and of Fauré's *Requiem* on Sunday. In its own way, Classic FM was trying to do what Radio 3 was trying to do—find the right blend of the popular and the serious for its own audience. There was a two-hour concert every weekday evening, with complete major works on records, preceded by an hour-long feature. These differed in style of presentation from Radio 3, but not in ambition nor in erudition. In the sample week, they covered early Verdi operas in *Authentic Performance*, Humphrey Burton's *Life of Leonard Bernstein* and Hugh MacPherson's *Opera Guide*. At 6 pm each weekday Margaret Howard, a former BBC stalwart, introduced a news programme, *Classic Reports*.

Commentators remained divided. Celebrating—that is not too strong a word—the first set of official audience figures for Classic FM in January 1993, *The Times* thought that more than 4 million listeners was 'happy news for everyone who cares about serious music and about the standards of popular taste'. It argued that:

> For those who believe that exposure to high art – of which great music is one of the most approachable forms – can benefit everyone, the popularity of Classic FM must be immensely cheery. Even in small, easily digested doses, the enjoyment of fine music is a civilising pastime. If the presentation of it can be divested of the intimidating, class-bound order with which it has tended to be surrounded in Britain, then a great many lives will be enriched.[lx]

In case anyone had missed the point, *The Times* leader continued:

> Those who defended the monopoly of classical music broadcasting by Radio 3 argued that any infiltration by commercial interests would mean the death of standards. But in a country in which more people attend

concerts than attend football matches (and in which the sale of classical recordings has risen dramatically) it could scarcely be acceptable to have only one radio station broadcasting classical music. Pluralism has added more choice and subtracted nothing. Instead of the barbarians sacking the temple, all that has happened is that far more people are hearing and appreciating the music which is rightfully part of their own cultural heritage.

This was not a universally held view. Composer Harrison Birtwistle felt that British music was suffering from 'a crisis of misplaced populism. Its currency is being devalued by things like Classic FM'.[lxi] Birtwistle's argument was that having the radio on was not the same as listening, and that the effort of a composer to produce complex structures needed to be differentiated from 'aural wallpaper'. The BBC's Music Programme in the Sixties had also been accused of providing 'musical wallpaper', another indication of the legacy which Classic had inherited from the earlier BBC channel.[6] Columnist and BBC presenter Libby Purves, on the other hand, opined that in 70 years of British radio history it was 'Classic FM which came closest to a real popularisation of classical music'.[lxii]

Both stations were evolving by 1994. The amount of sequence programming on Radio 3 had increased slightly. Classic FM, on the other hand, was even more music-based than before, having dropped its regular news magazine programmes. In the 1994 sample week, the weekend pattern is the most interesting. Radio 3 was completely record-dominated through Saturday morning, with *Record Review* followed by *Building a Library*, *Record Release* and then *Reissues*. Over on Classic FM, the morning was entirely sequence programming (also of records), with *Classic Countdown* between 9 am and noon, a top-of-the-classical-pops, but the station then detoured into what might be thought BBC territory, with a 2-hour programme hosted by Margaret Howard investigating English folk song and dance, followed by *Gardening Forum*. Early Saturday evening on Classic FM included the rather strange *Classic America* programme, which blended records with in-studio performance in an attempt to do something with sound that resembled BBC ambition, but without the BBC's level of accomplishment. *Independent* critic Adrian Jack wrote that 'production values were rather low'.[lxiii]

---

[6] See Chap. 4, p. 107n.

The same pattern of an ambitious but relatively more accessible BBC and a popular but still aspirational Classic FM was evident again on the Sunday. Radio 3's first morning programme, *Sacred and Profane*, was effectively a sequence programme. *Brian Kay's Sunday Morning* sequence offered unashamedly popular works, concluding with Beethoven's *Pastoral Symphony*. By contrast, *Music in Our Time* on Radio 3 that evening had a piano recital of works by Conlon, Nancarrow, James Wood and Xenakis, followed by an entire performance of *The Seasons* by Haydn. On Classic FM, the standard sequence programmes were balanced by an hour-long *Master Class* in the afternoon exploring string instruments, *Authentic Performance* in the early evening discussing early Verdi operas, an *Evening Concert* and then *Contemporary Classics*.

Both stations were also making audience progress, with research stressing the symbiosis between them.[lxiv] There was a similar increase in weekly reach year on year for both stations: Radio 3 gained an extra 400,000 adult listeners (to 2.9 million), and Classic FM gained 500,000 (to 4.8 million). The two stations shared a significant overlap audience of around 1 million, with a third of Radio 3's listeners also tuned into Classic FM, and a fifth of Classic FM's listeners also tuned into Radio 3.[7]

Kenyon[lxv] and Bernard[lxvi] both indicate that the stations had in effect worked out a *modus vivendi*, at least in the middle ground, but the public debate between the elitists and the popularisers continued. Former Controller of the Third Programme Ian McIntyre berated the new BBC Radio Managing Director, Liz Forgan, for saying that 'Radio 3 must adopt a new tone that reflects the sound of the nation'.[lxvii] Critic Peter Barnard announced that he had decided to desert the 'Classic FM fan club' because of its 'banal ... gimmicky' programming.[lxviii] His fellow *Times* writer Brenda Maddox confirmed the stereotype, but from an approving stance, seeing their combination as 'a classic duet of British success':

> Classic FM's main achievement lies in its unashamed appeal to the uninitiated. It will provide the name of any piece of music played on air if listeners ring up and say when they heard it. And for those starting a collection, its new magazine ... recommends Beethoven's Fifth: the one that begins 'da da da dah'. How very different from Radio 3, which recognises a serious listener as one who buys more than one version of the same piece of music and who is willing to weigh 30 different performances of Sibelius' Second

---

[7] Classic FM's total audience was much larger, hence the variation.

Symphony before settling on von Karajan and the Berlin Philharmonic because 'nothing is overstated, there is an abundant sense of atmosphere and the temptation to build up excessive climaxes is held in check' ... Radio 3 is a success story too. In the face of competition it has held its audience fairly steady [and] has survived the cost-conscious and yoof-oriented BBC management.[lxix]

Each station attempted to move its tanks onto the others' lawn at times. In February 1994, Classic FM 'poached' the entire team from one of Radio 4's most popular programmes, *Gardeners Question Time*. Nevertheless, it is reasonable to conclude that each was doing its rather considerable if separate best. Radio 3 had managed by recasting its approach to hang on to most of its middle-brow, middle class audience, despite the attraction of Classic FM. Classic FM remained true to at least some of the heritage of the long tradition of UK classical music radio. The stations can convincingly be seen as different but complementary responses to the increasing modernisation of society as a whole, and the commercialisation and commodification of culture. Each in their different ways was offering a means of preserving an important aspect of heritage for a broad audience.

Taken together, they represented the third comprehensive fusion of the high brow and the middle brow, the elite and the popular, with—crucially—effective links between those within the stations themselves and de facto between the stations as well. The amount of dual listening bears out this last point. When this symbiosis is achieved, it serves to set aside the restrictions of class, to offer the opportunity to expand the horizons of taste for a mass audience, and to allow high culture to enter with comfort into the popular sphere, echoing Said's view expressed that same year of classical music as a universal heritage, that 'Beethoven belongs as much to West Indians as he does to Germans, since his music is now part of the human heritage' (1994: 28).

On Radio 3 in 1995, the influence of a year-long festival of British music—*Fairest Isle*—was felt across the whole programme range. For Kenyon, this was a central initiative and also a reaffirmation of the vigorous health of Radio 3:

> As well as all the changes that we were making, to make Radio 3 more available and accessible and welcoming, I was looking for a big statement that proved that it was still a really important cultural patron that could

do major things with a major impact, because I felt that that was so often taken for granted. All the live music; all the orchestras; all the new commissions; all those things were somehow under the radar of how Radio 3 was perceived.[lxx]

In the 1995 sample week, *Fairest Isle* provided a running thread for music features, and the context for a major Thursday afternoon and evening broadcast from Birmingham featuring the composer Mark-Anthony Turnage, plus music by Bantock, Elgar and Britten. British composers were much more prominent in the sample week, led by Britten who in numbers of plays is followed by Elgar, Purcell (all of whose surviving music was broadcast during this 300th anniversary year) and Tippett.[8] Classic FM paid much attention in the sample week to the 50th anniversary of VE day, broadcasting a sequence programme of wartime romance on Sunday morning and giving over its Monday evening concert to a Bank Holiday celebration live from Blenheim Palace.

John Birt had become Director General of the BBC in 1992, after an apprenticeship alongside Michael Checkland. His modernising zeal had left Radio 3 untouched in his early years. He was not even on the interview panel which was to appoint Kenyon, and his major reorganisation of radio structures did not take place until 1996. However, in 1995 he began to challenge the station. Kenyon believes that Birt did not sign up to 'the difference between Classic FM and Radio 3 … his approach was, "these are both classical services, and why is Classic FM getting a much bigger audience?"'[lxxi]

Birt (2002: 386–387) largely confirms this in his autobiography:

> Radio 3 … was like a stuffy private club, out of tune with meritocratic modern Britain, in which love of serious music was growing, as the extraordinary success of Classic FM – with many times Radio 3's audience – demonstrated. Radio 3's defenders in the 1980s had acted like old cultural buffaloes, snorting and charging at any invader threatening change. Controllers Nicholas Kenyon and later Roger Wright worked valiantly to build a bridge to new audiences while maintaining the cultural and intellectual authority and integrity of the station – but the bridge was never quite completed in my time as Director General.

---

[8] Handel was ahead of all three, even if he was strictly only a 'British composer' by adoption.

Pressure from Birt gave rise to the highly symbolic Paul Gambaccini issue. Gambaccini is a respected author, film critic and popular music radio presenter, and was also one of the most popular and prominent presenters on Classic FM when it launched. With audience research showing that Radio 4 listeners switched to Classic FM at the end of the *Today Programme*, Kenyon was pressed to provide a more populist programme to attract them to Radio 3 instead. The result was unfortunate, as Kenyon recalls:

> It was also a time when independent production was growing ... and so the idea [arose] of giving another section of the daytime to an independent producer, in this case Mentorn Radio ... They offered us Paul Gambaccini, who I still believe, to this day, is an extremely professional ...very good broadcaster ... We persevered and we defended it, but at the end of the day it just didn't work, and so we agreed to take it off.[lxxii]

For Kenyon, Gambaccini's arrival from Classic FM in 1995 was not merely the BBC rushing after popularity, but also taking the opportunity to experiment:

> It was taking risks with a well-known name in the hope that he might draw people in who would not have otherwise thought of even tuning into Radio 3. But the balance between that well-known name and whether they could actually do what you were asking them to do proved to be a mismatch.[lxxiii]

The battle lines resembled the previous confrontations between the elitists and the popularisers. The Chairman of the House of Commons National Heritage Select Committee, Gerald Kaufman, announced that as a consequence of the deteriorating intellectual quality on Radio 3, he regretted endorsing the renewal of the BBC's charter. He would not vote for it again unless clauses were inserted obliging the BBC to safeguard standards. Giles Coren reported that fellow-journalist Anne Karpf 'railed to all who will listen, in the Guardian and on Radio 4's Today programme, that Mr. Gambaccini signals the arrival of "Radio 2½"'.[lxxiv]

In vain might Coren point out that Gambaccini was an Oxford graduate and an accomplished classical pianist. The point was that he symbolised everything which the defenders of the elite aspects of Radio 3 felt was under threat, as Coren's ironic tone captures:

Gambaccini's crimes are manifold, it seems. First of all he is American, which is not suitable at all. Then he is a purrer, not an announcer. His voice is too treacly and smooth for the serious business of introducing music played on wood, string and brass. And then, of course, he is a defector from Classic FM, the channel for people who do not already know their Bach from their Berio.[lxxv]

Simons notes that Classic FM presenters such as Nick Bailey, Petroc Trelawney, Robert Cowan and Paul Gambaccini—for all their skill and knowledge—had voices that at that time 'wouldn't have fitted on Radio 3 ... Gambaccini could get away with it on Classic FM. He didn't get away with it when he went to Radio 3'.[lxxvi]

Gambaccini himself saw his role as breaking open the Radio 3 mould, to allow that greater accessibility to follow which Kenyon was seeking to bring about:

> I understood my job, I remember saying that I was the equivalent of the Sex Pistols, someone else was going to be the Clash. Meaning that the Sex Pistols are going to open the door but the Clash are going to go through it ... That's what happened. Petroc Trelawny was the Clash.[lxxvii]

Nevertheless, for Gambaccini himself, it was a tough time:

> I was astonished, I have to admit it was one of the rare moments in my career when I was really astonished by the ignorance of the press, at the outpouring of hatred.[lxxviii]

In institutional terms, the Gambaccini incident exemplified the tensions created within the BBC by aggressive popularising. In terms of broadcasting and culture, it illustrates how the perceptions of the producer and consumer of classical music radio had been distorted by the dominance of elite assumptions right through the Seventies and Eighties, and how difficult it was to put that right.

After a gap on leaving Radio 3, Gambaccini returned to Classic FM in 1997, but that did not invalidate the basic hypothesis, the determination of Radio 3 to be open to new styles of presentation even more than of content. Kenyon again:

> It got the debate going about how people wanted to have classical music presented to them. And I don't think you would have had Petroc

Trelawny, the excellent Sara Mohr-Pietsch and a few others who are now around on Radio 3, had we not, as it were, opened Pandora's box.[lxxix]

In a sign of how far along the popularising route Radio 3 was to travel, at the time this book is being written, 20 years after those events, Petroc Trelawney is the main presenter of Radio 3's breakfast show and a mainstay of the BBC's concert presentation team. Rob Cowan's shows are also central to Radio 3's current approach, while Paul Gambaccini presents the regular BBC musical quiz, *Counterpoint*, as well as *Pick of the Pops*.

COMPARING RADIO 3 AND CLASSIC FM

Detailed comparisons of the two stations' output—usually limited by the lack of listings information for sequence programmes—are made possible by three BBC research studies 1995. The first survey was based on two days in December 1992.[lxxx] It shows Classic FM to have had at least twice as much speech during music programmes as Radio 3, comprising chiefly news, travel and weather, interviews and advertisements, with speech about music, competitions and events listing less prominent. Radio 3 broadcast speech about music primarily, with some news, travel and weather, music-related interviews and events listing. The average length of a piece of music on Radio 3 was twice as long as on Classic FM, 12 minutes compared with around 6 minutes.

However, although Classic FM was offering shorter pieces of music, the average length of piece in the BBC sequence programmes was also quite short: *On Air* averaged 8 minutes, *In Tune* just 4 minutes. This indicates a different but analogous approach by the two stations to providing accessible listening for quite a wide range of listeners. There was a similar two-edged conclusion to the analysis of how many complete works were played. Radio 3 played over twice as many complete works as Classic FM: four fifths of pieces on Radio 3, compared with only two fifths on Classic FM. Yet between 37 and 41% of the works broadcast on Classic FM were complete works, which accounted for nearly half of the total hours of Classic FM output.

The research found that the most heavily featured composers on Radio 3 were Sibelius, Mozart and Stravinsky; on Classic FM they were Mozart, Puccini and Dvořák. More 'modern' music was played on Radio 3 but, once again, the figures for Classic FM although lower are still creditable. Both stations played more romantic music than any other and—again, possibly counter-intuitively—that the percentage of baroque music was broadly the same on each. The researchers had expected that Classic FM might play more orchestral music, but the same research shows that the balance of orchestral, chamber, keyboard and vocal music across the two stations was broadly similar.

Add in the audience composition discussed below and it is shown that the two stations were achieving surprisingly similar results from surprisingly similar output. In many ways what is common between them outweighed what was different. Essentially, both were based in the middle-brow mainstream, but had different aspirations for how they extended beyond that. Radio 3 struck 'upwards', in demographic terms, Classic FM mostly 'downwards'. Radio 3 was more exclusive in its appeal, Classic FM more inclusive. Radio 3 listeners tuned into Classic FM in notably significant numbers; Classic FM listeners were much less likely to find in the differences of Radio 3 something to attract them.

This squares with qualitative research carried out for the Radio 3 Strategy Group early in 1993, which questioned people who listened to classical music but not on Radio 3. It speculated that:

> the very things that make Radio 3 distinctive will be too challenging for many classical music listeners: serious conversation about music (and the arts), complete works (i.e. long), a wide range of music, not all of which is designed to be accessible, and a higher proportion of contemporary music [on Radio 3] than Classic FM.[lxxxi]

Even if this was not necessarily the case, those assumptions reflect the BBC's own preconceptions (and has echoes of that revealing phrase 'unable to engage on equal terms' from the Forties). Most striking were the key aspects of each station accorded to them by those interviewed by the researchers (Table 7.3):

Two content analyses in 1995, when both stations had settled to the competitive reality, came to similar conclusions, analysing output in January[lxxxii] and during the fourth quarter of the year.[lxxxiii] Radio 3 comes out of this research as the 'worthier' and the broadcaster of more substantial pieces. Classic FM is more popular, caring less for the traditional shibboleths of classical music radio. But the counter-intuitive findings are again striking: Radio 3's average length of piece was just 8.4 minutes, albeit longer than Classic FM's 5.6 minutes but still rather short; as much

7 THE NINETIES: SAGA LOUTS AND DUMBING DOWN 215

Table 7.3   Key attributes of Radio 3 and Classic FM

Classic FM	Radio 3
For ordinary people	For serious music buffs
Plays popular classics	Obscure, difficult music
Short pieces (good)	Long pieces (bad)
Easy to listen to	Demands concentration
Could get boring for some	Some nice surprises, but probably not worth the effort

as 45% of Classic FM's broadcasts in terms of time were accounted for by complete works; and Classic FM continued to play a respectable amount of music from the modern period.

In terms of audiences, Classic FM very quickly achieved the audience levels which it was to sustain throughout the decade, between 4 and 5 million listeners, compared with 2.5 million for Radio 3. As well as their much larger numbers, Classic FM listeners tuned in for nearly twice as long each week as those to Radio 3. It also won more loyalty: Radio 3 took 12.6% of its listeners' weekly radio patronage, with 9.3% of that going to Classic FM; Classic FM, on the other hand, took 24.3% of its listeners' patronage, with only 3.4% of that going to Radio 3.[lxxxiv] The effect of removing the high-brow presumptions in presentation lend further support to the argument that it was the perceived elitism of Radio 3 as much as its content which kept those 'missing' listeners away.

Classic FM was wholly if pleasantly taken aback by its initial audience figures. Gambaccini recalls that:

> towards the end of the first quarter John Spearman [Managing Director of Classic FM at that time] said, 'We're going to have ratings and the best case scenario is 2.9 million'. So we're all prepared for something less than 2.9 million, RAJAR comes out and it's 4.3 million. I remember everyone just going, 'What did we do right?'[lxxxv]

Once Classic FM was available for comparison, the lack of listener loyalty to Radio 3 was thrown into sharper relief. Hours listened each week to Radio 3 were very low, averaging just over 3 hours per listener compared with the 10 hours or more which were typical of Radio 2 and Radio 4. Well over half of 'Radio 3 listeners' only tuned into the station on one day of an average week. At most times, more 'Radio 3 listeners' would be tuned into Radio 4 or Radio 2 than to Radio 3 itself (Table 7.4).[lxxxvi]

Table 7.4 Weekly audiences for Classic FM and Radio 3, 1991–1996[lxxxvii]

Year	Classic FM weekly audience (adults 15 +)	Radio 3 weekly audience (adults 15 +)
1991	–	2,800,000
1992	4,255,000	2,500,000
1993	4,494,000	2,736,000
1994	4,587,000	2,380,000
1995	4,751,000	2,397,000
1996	4,586,000	2,407,000

This is not to denigrate the audience impact of Kenyon's recasting of the network. Radio 3 stood up well to the initial onslaught from Classic FM. Its audiences for 1991, the year before it faced direct competition, had averaged around 2.8 million, and fell only to 2.7 million in 1993 before settling at around 2.4 million. There was room and demand for both, as the reach figures above illustrate. Both stations enjoyed their largest audiences for programmes on Sunday morning. Moreover, at that time Radio 3's single programme audience was its highest for any sample week since 1979, despite the competition with Classic FM.

Taking the 1993 figures for the first quarter, Classic FM's largest audience of the week was 441,000 adults between 11 and 11.30 am. It exceeded 400,000 listeners for the entire period between 10 am and noon. Radio 3's largest audience was 290,000 adults between 10 am and 10.30 am, and Radio 3 exceeded 200,000 listeners between 9 am and 11 am. The following year they shared exactly the same peak time, 10 am to 10.30 am on Sunday, with Classic FM having an audience of 435,000 adults and Radio 3 an audience of 170,000 adults. By 1995, Classic FM kept the same peak half-hour with virtually the same audience, but that of Radio 3 had gone back to between 9 am and 9.30 am, with only 154,000 adults listening. There is continuing evidence therefore of room existing for both services, even when head-to-head in their peak listening times.

Across the week as a whole, all the conventional demographics are surprisingly similar. Classic FM's audience is slightly younger, slightly less ABC1 and slightly less male; but if any of the demographic data were to be viewed casually, on their own and unlabelled, the audience patterns might be allocated to either station. The audience demographic for classical music in the Nineties was remarkably consistent, on whichever of the two stations, and different from the demographic for Independent Local Radio in the Seventies and Eighties, which had been notably younger, lower class and less male dominated.

ENGAGING THE POTENTIAL AUDIENCE

The position by the mid-Nineties illustrates the extent of missed opportunities in long periods during the preceding fifty years. The revival of listening to classical music on radio from 1992 onwards demonstrates once again that the *potential* radio audience was substantial right through the years after the Second World War. When there was adequate middle-brow provision, the middle market listened. For long periods, the BBC's stereotyping of the classical audience, blinded by its own class assumptions, had meant that it had failed to engage and involve the broader middle-brow consumer. As the influence of class diminished, the multi-channel combination of a recast, accessible Radio 3 and a popular Classic FM reawakened the demand for classical music radio.

By the mid-Nineties, more people listened, and for longer. Once the BBC station had become more accessible, it attracted a similar type of audience to that of its commercial rival, albeit in rather lower numbers and a bit older. The total audience figures indicate that there was a consistent, coherent but certainly not wholly homogeneous audience available for a classical music station which provided properly for it.

By the end of 1995, therefore, thanks to the binary nature of its provision, classical music radio in the UK provided for the whole range of potential listeners. That was happening because both stations centred their output in the established canonic repertoire, departing from it in different directions to provide for both high-brow and more popular taste. The effect was two complementary audiences, with a reassuringly significant overlap. This represented an important return to the position which had applied in those earlier years when the audiences were best served: in the late Forties, by the range of output on the Home Service, Third Programme and Light Programme; and in the late Sixties, on a comparable multi-channel platform. It is reasonable to conclude that the situation at the end of 1995, within the context of UK society in the Nineties, came close to being optimum.

Not everyone would have agreed. Harrison Birtwistle, Yehudi Menuhin, Richard Rodney Bennett and others regarded Classic FM as the antithesis of valid music radio, and detrimental to culture in society as a whole. Yet Classic FM firmly belonged in that part of the tradition of classical music radio broadcasting in the UK since the Second World War which was concerned to widen the audience franchise beyond the higher educated elite, who were often the producers of such services. As such, it has a clear place in the continuing tradition. Moreover, Classic FM took the form it did because of the cultural character of the society into which it emerged. Britain in the Nineties was a fluid, packaged and market-driven society, in which the old limitations of class were for a while less significant. Successive Conservative Prime Ministers were first a grocer's daughter, and then the son of a circus performer, rather than old Etonians.[9] Classical music radio was regarded as a proper entitlement of those in an aspirational society: the new classless consumers, the new owner-occupiers, the new mass shareholders. Just as the BBC threw open the doors of Radio 3, so Classic FM demonstrated that everyone could enjoy at least some of the cultural luxuries previously reserved for the few.

As discussed above, 1995 is the year when this history concludes its detailed analysis. The danger of confusing history with journalism becomes ever more acute as the years narrow between the past being considered and the present acting as a distorting lens. Not least, the arrival of digital and internet radio—with Digital Audio Broadcasting being launched in 1995—deserves much fuller consideration with the proper benefit of scholarly perspective at a later date. It is appropriate therefore to consider 1995 as the culmination of the main part of this narrative, and the final section of this chapter will offer just a sketch of subsequent and further anticipated developments.

Towards the Unknown Region

In Leeds in 1907, a choral work composed by the young, then largely unknown Ralph Vaughan Williams heralded a sea change in British music. Setting words by the American poet, Walt Whitman, it took as its title a line from one of Whitman's poems: 'darest thou now,

---

[9] Although an evolutionary reversal was to occur 15 years after the end of this history, with the election of Old Etonian David Cameron as Prime Minister in 2010.

O Soul/walk with me towards the Unknown Region'.[lxxxviii] Classical music on radio a century later looks into an equally unmapped future.

The period examined in detail by this history ends in 1995, with a recast Radio 3 and an ambitious Classic FM operating at their most effective and inclusive. They may be seen to be exemplars of the two great traditions: preserving and making available through radio the high art of classical music; and addressing, serving and encouraging popular appetite for this genre. In that, they confound the assumptions of Bourdieu, LeMahieu and others, that the competence and willingness to embark on the appreciation of classical music requires innate, class-based preconditioning of the consumer and service from the producer on that same rarefied basis only.

Just as happened with the two previous high points—in the late Forties and the late Sixties—the fortunate multi-channel conjunction of elite and popular output in the mid-Nineties did not survive undamaged much beyond the end of the period reviewed in this history. Radio 3 continued along the path set for it by Kenyon under his successor, Roger Wright, from 1998. Kenyon's valedictory, *Sounding the Century*, a two-year long festival running from February 1997 which presented a retrospective account of twentieth-century music, showed once again what Radio 3 could do in making high-brow material broadly accessible, despite continuing shifts in daytime programming towards more accessible content and a more demotic presentation style. However, continued internal and external pressures about the comparative audience levels between Radio 3 and Classic FM drove the BBC further towards the popular.

Demands to deliver high audiences became steadily more insistent. In serving the broadly 6 million people who might listen to classical music radio, Radio 3 in the years up to 1995 consistently appealed to around 2.5 million, and Classic FM to between 4.5 and 5 million. By 2000, however, Radio 3's audience had fallen to below 2 million and that of Classic FM was close to 6 million. The balance was much the same in 2005, and it was only after some rather desperate searching for a popular audience that Radio 3 climbed above 2 million listeners in 2010, although it has been a struggle to sustain that level thereafter, and Classic FM has also slipped back in audience terms (Table 7.5).

By the second decade of the new century, digital transmissions of radio services raised extensive questions about accessibility; more reliable reception was offered, but only to the still minority of those who had

Table 7.5 Weekly audiences for Classic FM and Radio 3 from 1995 onwards[lxxxix]

Year	Radio 3	Classic FM
1995	2,397,000	4,751,000
2000	1,980,000	6,041,000
2005	1,973,000	5,910,000
2010	2,216,000	5,790,000
2015	2,051,000	5,520,000

digital radio sets which could use the new technology. More significant as it turned out, digital and internet technologies were changing the way in which radio was accessed, especially what may be dubbed 'destination programmes'. Although sequence programming continued as a usually synchronous activity with daily life, more specialist output might as readily be accessed through a podcast, or simply by the BBC and Classic FM's Listen Again services, at any time of the listener's choosing.

Even as soon as the late Nineties, however, Classic FM had stepped aside from some of its aspirational output. That was partly influenced by a change in the legislative environment. The 1996 Broadcasting Act allowed a much greater concentration of ownership than hitherto within the commercial radio industry. One consequence of that was that the GWR group—which had been a leading figure in the setting up of Classic FM, but had not been allowed to operate the station in its own way, having only a minority stake—took over full control of the station. GWR had built much of its success on a concentrated approach to radio formatting, influenced in particular by Australian commercial radio. That involved getting rid of what it considered 'distractions', such as Classic FM's regular opera programme, just as the group had done in the Eighties with its ILR stations.

When Bukht ceased to be Programme Controller at Classic FM in 1997, the station shifted towards the more focussed music formats deployed by the GWR group across its by now extensive range of local commercial stations, which were themselves increasingly networked according to music genre and brand. Classic FM's subsequent ownership by first GCap and then Global has confirmed this approach. The increased audience levels benefitted the station's commercial prospects, and as a consequence the stock market valuation of its parent companies. However, by abandoning some—though not all—of its aspirational output, Classic FM risked weakening the multi-channel symbiosis which had served the total classical music radio audience so well.

7 THE NINETIES: SAGA LOUTS AND DUMBING DOWN   221

This was not a circumstance unique to classical music radio. A very similar pattern of the abandonment of public service elements by the BBC's commercial competitors was worked through in Channel 4 and then with ITV as a whole, while in commercial radio the 'brand' became an all-consuming focus for new owners. The shift in the focus of the commercial television companies is often seen as a consequence of the arrival of satellite television. That was certainly a proximate cause, although the advent of BSkyB was almost as accidental as the arrival of Classic FM, and even more precarious at the start (Horsman 1997). Technological determinism only operated so far: the eventual form of the new services and their social impact was very much at the mercy of chance. There is also a sense towards the end of this period of 'class overtaken by age'.[xc] Although the UK is by no means a classless society, its cultural preconceptions as the new century began were arguably much more segmented by age, a process hastened by the consumer implications of technological change.

The facilitation of UK digital radio transmissions was the other major impact of the 1996 Broadcasting Act. That permitted the introduction of digital radio into the UK, both for the BBC and in the form of commercially operated multiplexes, all using Digital Audio Broadcasting (DAB) technology. It was another almost accidental consequence; since the legislation was intended to introduce digital television in the UK, it seemed to the legislators almost as an afterthought that they might as well include digital radio, although there was no settled view at the time how that might be done, and no idea at all whether there was any public appetite for it (Stoller in Mollgard, ed., 2012). The BBC had launched its first experimental DAB services, including Radio 3, only in September 1995, and receivers did not become generally available even in small quantities until 1999. The first full-scale national commercial services came on air in November 1999, including—as the legislation enabled—a simulcast of Classic FM. The regional commercial services began coming on air from 2001. Notably, there was no effort to extend the number of classical music-playing radio stations, amid the plethora of—often indistinguishable—popular music services.

The first DAB transmissions in September 1995 attempted a rather slow-motion radio revolution, which may come to be seen in hindsight as constituting a technological wrong turning. Institutional factors played their part in these arrangements. By committing to DAB, Classic FM avoided having to re-tender for its licence and the Government avoided what it saw as the electoral disadvantage of being seen to jeopardise the future of a station so popular with its likely voters. A similar inducement was offered to the other commercial radio services (Stoller in Mollgard, ed., 2012). Nevertheless, as podcasting, time-shifting and internet-streaming prosper, DAB in its 1990 form now appears to be approaching a technological dead-end, and needs to be superseded by newer and better digital transmission technologies. Digital listening across multiple platforms is steadily increasing, but still only some 32% of all radio listening is to DAB transmissions, despite extensive promotion and Government support for over 20 years. The 2016 *Communications Market Report* from Ofcom showed that digital listening increased by *less* than analogue listening to radio.[xci]

Wider aspects of digital technology present a challenge to basic assumptions about radio. The internet gives listeners access to classical music radio stations across the world, and also allows the streaming of classical music. The pattern identified in this history as 'multi-channel', referring only to conventional radio, has now become 'multi-platform'. The recent portability of the internet, especially using 4G technology, has overcome the initial restrictions of such access being only on a wired basis. The use of MP3 to play music portably and personally, and the near-ubiquity of Apple's iPods and iPads—together with file-sharing options through Spotify, Napster and others—is having at least as much effect as the original arrival of gramophone records in making classical music the ultimate cultural commodity.

For radio, the BBC's use of iPlayer since its initial public trial in October 2005, and podcasts from both Radio 3 and Classic FM, potentially mark the beginning of the end of linear radio as we have known it since 1922—although to date reports of its likely death have been premature and exaggerated. Wright, Controller, Radio 3 from 1998 to 2004, regards the option to 'listen again' to concerts as being 'incredibly important', because 'the audience naturally expects to take its consumption of material when it wants it and how it wants'.[xcii] There is growing evidence of a continued shading down in listening figures to conventional radio services in the present decade,[xciii] although the research needs to be treated with caution, given the methodological challenge in measuring time-shifted listening. It is also far too soon to assume specific cause and effect, but the data are at the least indicative of a gradual change in listening behaviour.

7 THE NINETIES: SAGA LOUTS AND DUMBING DOWN 223

The story of classical music radio did not end in 1995, but it began to change fundamentally around that time or quite soon thereafter. The period when radio stood alone as the provider of this genre of broadcast output did indeed cease soon after 1995, with the intrusion of the internet, and the arrival of MP3 players in 2000, BBC iPlayer in 2005 and Classic FM's Listen Again service too. The fifty years when the postwar medium provided unique access to broadcast classical music in 'real time' were a remarkable cultural and social entity. When the programmes were at their best, open to all, free from class-based preconceptions, they made a significant positive contribution to the overall cultural health of UK society. When they fell short, the loss and lack were palpable. Whether any of the new offering of narrowcast music output will ever replicate the intense affection felt by listeners towards what they enjoyed in the second half of the twentieth century seems improbable, and that in itself may delay the supposed demise of free-to-air, broadcast classical music radio well into the new century.

Notes

i. http://www.nonesuch.com/artists/henryk-gorecki.
ii. *A New Future for Communications.* 2002 White Paper, Cmnd 5010.
iii. Richard Morrison. Quartet joins the celebrations. *The Times*, 4 January 1990, p. 18.
iv. Mozart Immortal. *The Times*, 28 January 1991, p. 11.
v. Janet Daley. Radio 3: a classic case of conspiracy. *The Times*, 11 January 1991, p. 10.
vi. Yehudi Menuhin. Radio 3 discord. *The Times*, 25 January 1991, p. 13.
vii. Interview with Gillian Reynolds, 29 October 2014. Drummond's (2000) autobiography is entitled *Tainted by Experience*.
viii. *Will Classic FM threaten the BBC?* May 1992. BBC WAC R9/1267/1.
ix. *The Listener*, 23 August 1979, p. 239.
x. Interview with Michael Checkland, 20 September 2013.
xi. Interview with Nicholas Kenyon, 15 July 2013.
xii. *Radio 3's missing listeners*, August 1992. BBC WAC R9/1286/1.
xiii. *Classic FM: listening patterns in the first four weeks*, October 1992. BBC WAC R9/1235/1.
xiv. *A year of the Third Programme.* BBC Audience Research Special Report, 6 November 1947. BBC WAC R9/9/11.
xv. *The Radio 3 poster campaign*, October 1992. BBC WAC R9/1304/1.
xvi. Interview with Nicholas Kenyon, 15 July 2013.

xvii. Interview with Michael Checkland, 20 September 2013.
xviii. Richard Morrison. Speak easy on the new Radio 3. *The Times*, 4 May 1992.
xix. Gerald Kaufman. A musical turn-off. *The Times*, 17 August 1992, p. 10.
xx. Interview with Nicholas Kenyon, 15 July 2013.
xxi. *Daily Telegraph*, 26 March 1992. Quoted in Carpenter (1996: 339).
xxii. 'Free market' fears for Radio 3 future. *The Times*, 5 May 1992, p. 11.
xxiii. Letter from Alun Chalfont IBA to David Mellor, Home Office, 26 January 1990.
xxiv. David Mellor speaking in London at a Campaign for Quality Television [*sic*] Forum, 18 April 1990.
xxv. Shadow Radio Authority minutes, 15/16 September 1990.
xxvi. *Hansard* (1991) House of Lords, 23 May 1991. Vol. 529, Col. 423.
xxvii. Interview with Ralph Bernard, 19 November 2007.
xxviii. Ralph Bernard, personal communication, 27 March 2017.
xxix. First National Radio application. *Radio Authority Archive*, May 1991.
xxx. *Financial Times*, 1 October 1991, p. 8.
xxxi. Classic FM licence. *Radio Authority Archive*, September 1992.
xxxii. Interview with John Thompson, 16 December 2013.
xxxiii. Interview with Ralph Bernard, 13 June 2013.
xxxiv. Ralph Bernard, personal communication, 2 December 2014.
xxxv. Interview with Ralph Bernard, 13 June 2013.
xxxvi. Press release. *Radio Authority Archive*, 24 February 1992.
xxxvii. *Will Classic FM threaten the BBC?* May 1990. BBC WAC R9/1267/1.
xxxviii. Stephen Pettit. *The Times*, 3 September 1992 (page not specified in digital archive).
xxxix. Richard Ingrams. Beethoven jumps into the bathtub. *The Times*, 9 September 1992, p. 1[S].
xl. Brian McMaster. *The Times*, 9 September 1992, p. 1[S].
xli. Nicholas Payne. *The Times*, 9 September 1992, p. 1[S].
xlii. *Will Classic FM threaten the BBC?* May 1992. BBC WAC R9/1267/1.
xliii. Radio Audiences Joint Audience Research: Source RAJAR/RSL. Quarter 1 1993.
xliv. Interview with Paul Gambaccini, 10 May 2017.
xlv. *Sunday Telegraph*, 7 February 1973, Review, p. 1.
xlvi. News. *The Times*, 30 December 1992.
xlvii. https://www.theguardian.com/tv-and-radio/2011/aug/07/michael-bukht-obituary.
xlviii. Interview with Michael Bukht, 2 February 2009. Quoted in Stoller (2010: 215n).
xlix. Interview with Susannah Simons, 19 August 2013.
l. Interview with Paul Gambaccini, 10 May 2017.

7 THE NINETIES: SAGA LOUTS AND DUMBING DOWN   225

li. *Observer*, 20 September 1992, p. 65.
lii. Interview with Susannah Simons, 19 August 2013.
liii. Interview with Ralph Bernard, 13 June 2013.
liv. Alan Bennett. What I did in 1996. *London Review of Books*, 2 January 1997. The reviewer attributes the phrase 'Saga louts' to Hugh Stalker, but it has attached itself firmly to Bennett.
lv. Interview with Ralph Bernard, 13 June 2013.
lvi. Ivan Hewett. Smoothly does it for Classic FM. *Daily Telegraph*, 23 August 2002, p. 22.
lvii. Interview with Ralph Bernard, 13 June 2013, quoting research undertaken by Lauren Benedict and by Deanna Hallett.
lviii. Interview with Paul Gambaccini, 10 May 2017.
lix. *Fleet Street Reports FSR 622 1998, PatC*, 18 March 1998.
lx. High Culture for the People. *The Times*, 30 January 1993, p. 15.
lxi. Richard Morrison. Sir Harry rides into the fray. *The Times*, 1 December 1993 (page not specified in digital archive).
lxii. Libby Purves. Tune into my dream. *The Times*, 22 September 1993.
lxiii. *Independent*, 29 December 2013.
lxiv. *Radio 3's new listeners: where have they come from?* BBC Broadcasting Research, March 1994. BBC WAC R9/1491/1.
lxv. Interview with Nicholas Kenyon, 15 July 2013.
lxvi. Interview with Ralph Bernard, 13 June 2013.
lxvii. Ian McIntyre. I'm sorry I'll read that again. *The Times*, 28 January 1994, p. 14.
lxviii. Peter Barnard. Capital idea, but not yet OK. *The Times*, 21 September 1994, p. 39.
lxix. Brenda Maddox. A fish called Haydn? I care not. *The Times*, 18 October 1995, p. 23.
lxx. Interview with Sir Nicholas Kenyon, 24 April 2014.
lxxi. Interview with Nicholas Kenyon, 15 July 2013.
lxxii. *Ibid.*
lxxiii. *Ibid.*
lxxiv. Giles Coren. Classic rock 'n' roller. *The Times*, 12 October 1995, p. 19.
lxxv. *Ibid.*
lxxvi. Interview with Susannah Simons, 19 August 2013.
lxxvii. Interview with Paul Gambaccini, 10 May 2017.
lxxviii. *Ibid.*
lxxix. Interview with Nicholas Kenyon, 15 July 2013.
lxxx. *Radio 3 and Classic FM: Content Analysis of Output*, BBC Audience Research, April 1993. BBC WAC R9/1370/1.
lxxxi. *Reactions to Radio 3 and Classic FM*, February 1993. BBC WAC 9/1360/1.

lxxxii. *A content analysis of Radio 3 and Classic FM (January 1995)*. BBC Broadcasting Research, 10 March 1995. BBC WAC R9/1545/1.
lxxxiii. *Content Analysis of Radio 3 and Classic FM (Q4 95)*. BBC Broadcasting Research, 22 February 1996. BBC WAC R9/1599/1.
lxxxiv. *Broadcasting Research Report 95/108C—Radio 3 Audibility*, May 1995. BBC WAC R9/2163/1.
lxxxv. Interview with Paul Gambaccini, 10 May 2017.
lxxxvi. *Broadcasting Research Report 95/108C—Radio 3 Audibility*, May 1995. BBC WAC R9/2163/1.
lxxxvii. Radio Audiences Joint Audience Research. Based on 4th quarter of each year, so not necessarily the same as quoted elsewhere. http://www.RAJAR.co.uk/listening/quarterly_listening.php. The 1991 figure derives from an average of JICRAR data.
lxxxviii. Walt Whitman. Darest Thou Now, O Soul. *Leaves of Grass*, 1900.
lxxxix. RAJAR/RSL quarter 4 for each year. http://www.RAJAR.co.uk/listening/quarterly_listening.php.
xc. Interview with Gillian Reynolds, 29 October 2014.
xci. www.ofcom.org.uk/_data/assets/pdf_file/0032/94838/The-Communications-Market-Digital-Radio-Report-2016.pdf. But note Ofcom's reservation that 'in 2016, RAJAR implemented a new methodology which essentially reallocated unspecified listening which had previously been categorised as "analogue/digital not stated" and "digital not stated". This change in methodology means that new data are not entirely comparable with historical data'.
xcii. Interview with Roger Wright, 10 October 2014.
xciii. http://www.rajar.co.uk/listening/quarterly_listening.php.

Bibliographic Sources

Ackroyd, P. 1992. *English music*. London: Hamish Hamilton.
Birt, J. 2002. *The harder path: The autobiography*. London: Time Warner.
Blake, A. 1997. *The land without music: Music, culture and society in 20th-century Britain*. Manchester University Press.
Drummond, J. 2000. *Tainted by experience: A life in the arts*. London: Faber.
Horsman, M. 1997. *Sky high: The inside story of BSkyB*. London: Orion Business.
Mollgard, M. (ed.). 2012. *Radio and society: New thinking for an old medium*. Newcastle upon Tyne: Cambridge Scholars.
Ponsonby, R. 2009. *Musical heroes: A personal view of music and the musical world over sixty years*. London: DLM.
Said, E.W. 1994. *Culture & imperialism*. London: Vintage.
Stoller, T. 2010. *Sounds of your life: The history of independent radio in the UK*. New Barnet: John Libbey.

CHAPTER 8

Conclusions: Engaging on Equal Terms?

The pattern of classical music radio provision 1945–1995: content; audiences–elite and mass culture–the nature of listening to classical music radio–presentation–the relevance of biography–the changing nature of public service radio broadcasting–a story worth the telling.

Having begun before the launch of the Third Programme, the detailed account of this book closes with the aftermath of the arrival of Classic FM, at a new high point for multi-channel classical music radio in the UK. At the end of 50 post-war years, that was also the time when the completeness of free-to-air provision of sound broadcasting began to fracture in the face of alternative platforms and delivery systems.

At that point, radio as it had been understood throughout the twentieth century was starting to be significantly challenged by digital media deploying the internet and audio streaming, as well as launching its own digital radio transmission systems. The speed of technological change is unprecedented, and the implications of new technologies for the production and consumption of audio classical music continue to evolve, turning current affairs into almost-history. Nevertheless, the continuity provided by the established radio services into the digital age, and the continued mass audience for terrestrially transmitted traditional classical music radio, suggests that this process will be evolutionary rather than revolutionary.

The history of classical music radio in the UK is worth attention in its own right: it also illuminates many aspects of culture, class and society

© The Author(s) 2018
T. Stoller, *Classical Music Radio in the United Kingdom, 1945–1995*,
https://doi.org/10.1007/978-3-319-64710-4_8

227

in the UK in the years after the Second World War to the end of the last century. Running through the entire story, as an almost operatic *leitmotif*, is the tension between the demands of the elite and the too often unacknowledged needs and entitlements of the mass audience. In 1953, the BBC was doubting whether it welcomed the patronage of listeners who were unable to 'engage on equal terms' with its cultural output. By the Nineties, that class-driven assumption had been well and truly exploded, although not until it had enjoyed far too long a run.

The historical narrative is characterised by a series of attempts to achieve a symbiosis between those two provisions, followed by a series of retreats from it; and just as for this genre of broadcasting, so also for the UK in other respects. Each instance of reformation and then counter-reformation in the provision of classical music radio reflects the same institutional—and class-based—defensiveness which ensured that successive bouts of political and social radicalism in the UK as a whole would be rapidly followed by resistance and reaction. Just as the radical achievements of the Attlee Government were diminished and partly reversed in the years which followed them, so Haley's efforts to establish a class-mobile pattern of radio broadcasting were in their turn set aside in the Fifties. The British cultural revolution of the Sixties partly ran into the sand in the following decade, just as happened to the BBC's innovation of the Music Programme. And in the same way as Thatcher's 'revolution of the right' fundamentally undermined long-established British institutions, facilitating the triumph of market liberalism, so the initial success of ILR and the eventual failure of such commercially funded public service radio—together with the unsustainability of elite output from public sector broadcasting—produced a market-led response from a recast Radio 3 and a culturally aspirational Classic FM.

THE PATTERN OF CLASSICAL MUSIC RADIO PROVISION 1945-1995

There were four periods between 1945 and 1995 when the producers of classical music radio successfully challenged the defensive and self-sustaining elite (as Fig. 8.1 illustrates). Three of those had an inclusive impact on national radio, setting aside hidebound restrictions on culture and providing classical music radio to a wider audience, and can be regarded as fundamental shifts. The fourth instance—that of

8 CONCLUSIONS: ENGAGING ON EQUAL TERMS? 229

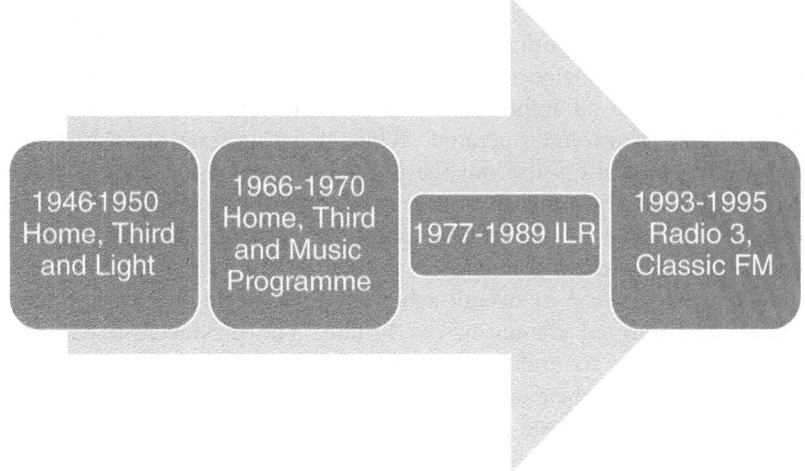

Fig. 8.1 Highpoints for inclusive classical music radio

Independent Local Radio (ILR)—achieved much but only in particular localities.

The first high-water mark was in the late Forties, when there was a wide range of music provided on multiple channels, with clear links between the high-brow and the middle-brow. Director General William Haley's introduction of the Third Programme as one part of a pyramid of classical music radio provision meant that music from the most recondite to the most recognisable was offered across the BBC's radio output. More than that, there was a conscious intention (on Haley's part at least) to provide an escalator between the different levels of the pyramid; to repeat his compelling image—the listener might enter at ground level to hear the waltz from *Der Rosenkavalier*, and progress over time to enjoying the full opera at the apex.

There were strong grounds for believing this to be possible. Research in 1946 had indicated that around a third of enthusiasts for the Third Programme were 'working class', a legacy not least of that wartime 'cultural renaissance' in Britain which had been a driving force in establishing the channel in the first place. However, although the elite provision of the Third Programme continued pretty largely unchanged, the conscious and swift abandonment by the BBC of its once-vaunted efforts to bring a wider public to an appreciation of higher culture shows how the interests of class continued to dominate UK society at that time. The Third Programme Defence Society (and later the Campaign for Better Broadcasting) was an archetypal manifestation of the ways in which the British *haute bourgeoisie* operated. While their interests flourished, the removal of classical music from the Light Programme in daytime disenfranchised a weekly audience of at least a million listeners, who were no longer going to be able to find this output serendipitously in an environment where they felt welcome.

The second period of overall achievement came in the Sixties, amid societal and cultural change across Britain. The producers of classical music radio came to understand that serving only the elite was unacceptable, although their approach to the demotic was more measured than their popular music contemporaries. By providing in the Music Programme 'an almost continuous service of good music' during the daytime, as part of a multi-channel approach with the Home Service and the Third Programme, the BBC reached the second high-water mark of classical music radio in the UK. For the first time, a listener could tune into this genre of radio at almost any time across the week, and be exposed to a wide range of composers in an accessible format. Further, this freed up the Third Programme to advance its high-brow efforts while maintaining the links between the multiple channels of output, enabling listeners if they so wished to progress from one to the other. With almost triple the output, and double the number of composers featured, this represented a true cornucopia, and is a key time in this narrative history. The significance of the Music Programme lay not only in what it provided: it was the precursor of the way in which classical music radio was to develop as the century progressed; and foreshadowed genre radio across the BBC as a whole, although in this instance without immuring classical music within a cultural ghetto.

An unwelcome precedent set by the first high-water mark of the late Forties was that the tide did not stay in for long. The second set of 'good years' ended just the same. As a consequence of the BBC's decision to reorganise all of its national services following *Broadcasting in the Seventies*—and not least in response to the counter-insurgency of the elite led by the Campaign for Better Broadcasting—Radio 3 corralled the elements of classical music broadcasting which had been more widely spread before 1970. Those were confined within a citadel which could be defended against mass intrusion by the approach and tone of its presentation, even more than by the selection of music. Radio 3 seemed often to exist in a parallel universe to the rest of UK society, except when a wider audience was glimpsed, as when economies obliged the BBC to simulcast classical music with Radio 4.

Following the breaking of the radio monopoly in 1973, the ILR stations gradually provided a significant opening-up of classical music radio, although geographically limited. That these mixed service stations—while essentially pop music based—could provide and draw substantial audiences to classical music output reinforces the more general observation that a wide potential audience existed for this genre of output, which did not need to be reserved by and preserved for the elite. It is notable that the composition of the ILR audiences differed not only from that of the BBC services but also of the later Classic FM, though sharing with the latter a remarkably immediate impact in building audiences (Stoller 2010: 88). These were different listeners, younger people unconditioned by the sacralisation of classical music which the BBC hitherto endorsed.

The two earlier widenings of the classical music radio franchise had fallen foul of the entrenched elite. ILR's offering was undone by the new overwhelming force in British society, the triumph of market liberalism. In pursuit of commercial opportunity, ILR had by 1990 shucked off its public service obligations, and in doing so discarded what in the Eighties had been a time of real achievement in the provision of classical music radio.

There were new forces ascendant in the UK in the Eighties, and their confrontational attitudes also encouraged the BBC to challenge the Musicians' Union over the issue of BBC house orchestras, making the decade an uncomfortable time for classical music radio on the BBC. Yet one of the side-effects of the Thatcherite assault on British institutions was that the old elite was progressively disempowered. Arguably, international developments in Europe following the fall of the Berlin Wall, which ended the pre-eminence of extreme modernism in classical music composition, undermined the elitists also in the UK.

At the start of the Nineties, the BBC set in motion the recasting of Radio 3, ensuring that blend of popular and high-brow programming which represents the medium at its best. Simultaneously, the conscious dismantling of the old structures of Independent Broadcasting made possible the arrival of Classic FM. As this book has made clear, the new institutional dispensation did not dictate that, and to a degree it was accidental. Yet it is difficult to escape the conclusion that the social dialectic of the early Nineties strongly indicated—even if it did not require—such an outcome. Since Classic FM arrived amid a resurgence within the BBC, it began with a significant sense of the heritage of UK classical music broadcasting and retained public service-type aspirations for some years.

In practice, neither station was wholly fish or fowl during these later years: Radio 3 avowedly wanted to be more popular than it had been, not least to head off threats to its continued existence; Classic FM—in the period considered by this history and arguably thereafter—sought the respectability of some intellectual aspiration. Together, they represented the logical culmination of classical music radio, and are paradigmatic of how that genre illustrates the changing relationship between class, taste, culture and society in the UK between 1945 and 1995.

As a consequence of the conjunction between a recast of Radio 3 and an aspirational Classic FM, the UK enjoyed its ultimate high-water mark of classical music radio—multi-channel, serving both high-brow and middle-brow tastes and with educative intent. There was competition of course, often intense. Yet Radio 3 and Classic FM, taken together, represented for traditional linear radio probably the final benign fusion of the high brow and the middle brow, the elite and the popular, with—crucially—effective links between those within the stations themselves and de facto between the stations as well. The amount of dual listening bears out this last point. When this symbiosis is achieved, it serves to set aside the damaging effects of class, offering the opportunity to expand the horizons of taste for a mass audience, while allowing high culture to thrive in itself and also to enter with comfort into the popular sphere.

Content

Probably the most notable element of the longitudinal analysis of classical music radio is how its quantity expanded across the second half of the twentieth century. This was remarkable for a supposedly minority genre, although in line with the expansion of radio broadcasting services generally. As Fig. 8.2 summarises, from just under 20 hours in the sample week in 1945, the provision had grown to 258 hours in the sample week in 1995.

Equally striking is the consistency of that content over 50 years and across almost a dozen channels at different times. The number

8 CONCLUSIONS: ENGAGING ON EQUAL TERMS? 233

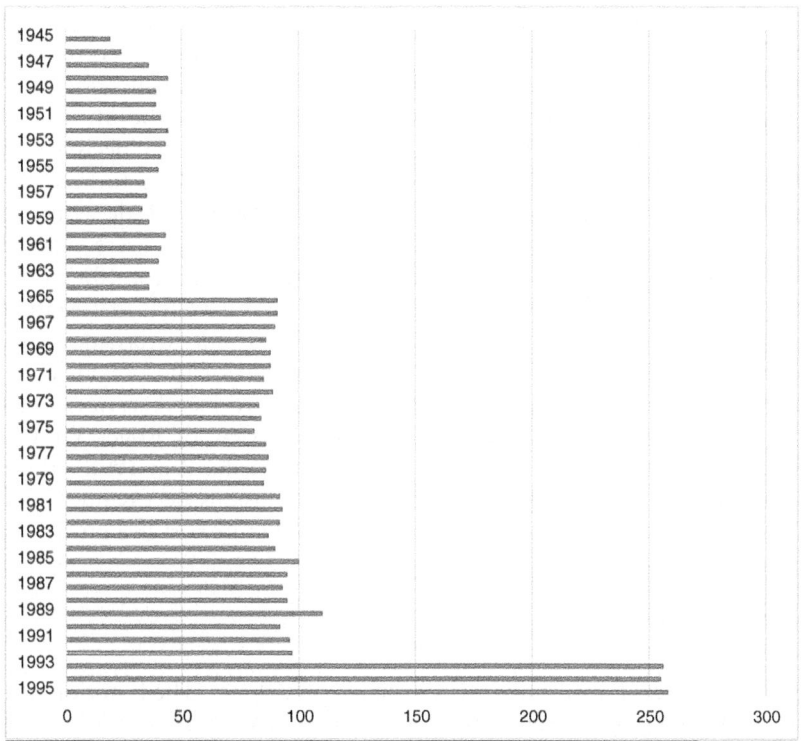

Fig. 8.2 Total hours of classical music radio in sample weeks 1945–1995

of composers featured increased from 39 in 1945 to as high as 133 in 1983, settling at around 110.[1] Yet the output was consistently dominated by the centre of the radio canonic repertoire. Beethoven was the most played composer in the sample weeks during 22 of the 50 years, Mozart for 18, spread evenly across the period. Between 1945 and 1950, the two most played composers in the sample weeks were Beethoven on five occasions, Mozart and Haydn on two. Between 1990 and 1995, they were Beethoven on four occasions, Mozart on two. The classical music repertoire expanded, certainly, but its centre of gravity remained unchanged.

---

[1] See Appendix A4, p. 253–254.

The huge expansion in output was made possible to a large degree by increasing use of commercially recorded gramophone records. For most of this period the BBC's Gramophone Department was confined to producing light music programmes, but when the Music and Gramophone Departments came together in 1982, the decision to appoint the Gramophone Department's Christine Hardwick to head the new arrangement reflected a sea change in approach. As little as 5% of the musical content of BBC classical music programmes were derived from records in the early Fifties. That rose to getting on for 40% in the Nineties. Cultural theorist Walter Benjamin would have felt that music's auratic quality adhered only to live performances, not to broadcasting, let alone mechanical reproduction. Yet at the end of the period, commercial radio demonstrated the potency of a record-based service, while the BBC had come to appreciate that—in the view of Roger Wright, who succeeded Nicholas Kenyon as Controller, Radio 3 in 1998—there should be no valid value judgement that live music is necessarily better than a recording, even though on occasions and at its best live music can provide something unique.[i]

Audiences

Radio audiences for existing services change only slowly. The historical narrative and longitudinal analysis demonstrate a remarkable consistency of potential audience for this genre of radio throughout the second half of the twentieth century. Across the whole period, a surprisingly diverse audience of 5 to 6 million people was available to listen to accessible classical music radio if that was offered to them in an accessible way, and if it was present on channels which they felt they were allowed to approach. That does not mean that programmes which failed to achieve measurable audiences were axiomatically not worth broadcasting; on the contrary, almost all the radio services reviewed in this book understood an obligation to broadcast at times challenging and untried content. But just becuase a composition is obscure is not a sufficient rationale for including it a radio programme.

During the periods when classical music radio was multi-channel and offered a fusion of high-brow and middle-brow output, the number of people listening was much greater, and the composition of those audiences more diverse, than elitist assumptions would allow. Just as in the late Forties the BBC admitted [*sic*] that one third of the listeners to the Third Programme were working class, so during those years when the

Music Programme was operating, for ILR in its public service years and in the early Nineties, the make-up of the audience was much more gender neutral, less hidebound by class and at times younger than might be expected. BBC and former ILR presenter Fiona Talkington points out that even for the smallest of ILR stations:

> the existence of classical music programmes pervaded the whole output. Because the daytime programmes would trail the specialist programmes, listeners would pick up on things; there was a sense of dialogue between the programmes.[ii]

The history of UK classical music radio—echoing David Goodman's view of commercial radio in America (2011)—demonstrates that it is wholly possible for producers and consumers to regard the presence of classical music on radio as normative, when its provision and tone of voice are not hidebound by elitist practice and assumptions. Far more people were prepared to listen to this genre of radio than were able to engage with it on what high-brow producers believed to be 'equal terms'.

ELITE AND MASS CULTURE

Classical music is not in itself elitist, although as Wright acknowledges 'there are social and historical circumstances which have led some to regard the consumption of it to be elitist or only for a certain part of society'.[iii] Nevertheless, self-conscious elitism persisted in classical music radio throughout much of this period, demanding protection of the supposed purity of that high culture of which classical music was the outstanding instance. Its influence diminished to a degree, as social class became less rigid and popular taste had the opportunity to become better developed. Equally, the breakdown of the old hierarchies was hastened by the imposition of market liberalism, although to a degree that simply inserted a new elite, with their own similar if slightly different sensitivities.

From Karl Marx onwards, academics have lined up to condemn the increasing commodification and mechanisation of culture—especially, for Benjamin, Theodor Adorno and others, of classical music—and to protect its supposed 'purity' from contamination by that mass appreciation which they suppose only happens in a largely worthless, uneducated way.

Like Pierre Bourdieu, they have asserted that class and education are revealed by consumption and taste. Yet this history demonstrates that the most worthwhile manifestation of classical music radio happens when the high-brow and the middle-brow are offered in parallel and in synthesis; a wide range of output, readily accessible, to be consumed variously at a cerebral and a visceral level, with a clear link between the elite and popular offerings and escalators running up and down between the two. That conclusion recalls agreeably the earliest reaching-out by J.S. Bach into the coffee houses of Leipzig.

There are plenty of people today who fret about 'dumbing down', the commodification of culture amid a retreat from eclectic output in classical music radio in modern times. As this history shows, that is not a recent phenomenon, and in any event is a reflexive process driven chiefly by audience response—or the lack of it. In effect, it was those who set out to stereotype the potential audience for classical music radio, and to cast them in their own image, who have done the genre the greater disservice. Seeking to protect an elite view of, and access to, a particular 'high culture' has meant that its democratisation has been rebuffed consistently throughout this period. It was only when that self-defining elite was side-lined, along with so many other national institutions in the Eighties, that its influence diminished. If the old Establishment continues to reassert itself in the changing UK political dispensation of the new century, there can be no certainty that such accessibility will be maintained. If such a new reversion to type occurs, it will serve to confirm classical music radio as a remarkably precise signifier of the wider cultural, social and political development of UK society as a whole. That will be conditioned in the twenty-first century, however, by the impact of podcasting, streaming and time-shifting of radio services, and the digital availability of music—just as will apply in other, wider, cultural and social areas.

In one respect, though, the history of classical music radio does not quite fit the accepted cultural pattern between 1945 and 1995. The notion of a continuing canon was never challenged in classical music in the way that it was in the literary and visual arts. Equally, the 'shock of the new',[2] which so changed popular music, was for consumers of

---

[2] This was the title of art critic and historian Robert Hughes' (1980) examination of the impact of radical innovation in 20th-century visual arts, but it serves equally well for other cultural forms.

classical music merely a side channel running alongside the main stream. *Popular* music was never the same after Elvis, and nor was popular music radio; but *classical* music continued and continues to be dominated by Beethoven and his contemporaries—Messiaen, Boulez and Reich notwithstanding—and classical music radio similarly. In that way, it is a signifier of a more slowly evolving *zeitgeist*, where heritage and tradition maintain a significant place—just as they do in British society throughout this period.

That *leitmotif* of tension between the elite and the accessible, the high-brow and the middle-brow, dominates this history. There is repeated evidence across the half-century that when both aspects of the genre were properly represented in radio output, the medium was at its strongest and most relevant, even though sustaining the delicate balance was difficult and rarely long-lasting. UK media scholarship has tended to place an undue focus on the Third Programme and Radio 3, ignoring the many other channels which offered classical music broadcasts and thus obscuring some of the broader social and cultural significance of the genre, when 'ordinary people' are able to tune into accessible classical music. Yet it is the approach of Edward Said which wins out: to paraphrase his observation (1994: 28): 'Beethoven belongs as much to the mass as he does to the elite, since his music is now part of the human heritage'. It is germane that Beethoven is the most played composer of all on radio between 1945 and 1995. Not that it is safe to fall into the trap of treating Beethoven—or any other classical master who is also popular with large audiences—as middle-brow; such work is at the highest brow, and it has been the singular achievement of radio producers and consumers to make that high culture popularly accessible.

The Nature of Listening to Classical Music Radio

Few aspects of this high-brow anxiety have been sharper than the debate over whether it is permissible for classical music to be broadcast with the awareness that it would be for background not foreground listening; being, as Benjamin Britten (1964: 16) put it, 'at the mercy of any loud roomful of cocktail drinkers'. Harrison Birtwistle in 2013 dubbed such music 'aural wallpaper',[iv] while Jean Cocteau likened it to the furnishings in a room, calling it 'musique d'ameublement'.[v] A series of self-appointed defenders of the Third Programme and Radio 3 argued that using classical music as a background accompaniment to daily tasks devalued a supreme art. That approach received ready adherence from many elements within the BBC, who regretted that classical music programmes were being broadcast to those 'unlikely to be able to meet them on equal terms'.[vi]

Class and educational snobbery was at its most extreme in this elevation of music to the status of liturgy. When Bach took his sublime music into those Leipzig coffee houses, it was not in some way a diminished art; what changed was its accessibility. We need to acknowledge that the same person listens to classical music in different ways—foreground or background—according to their immediate wishes and circumstances. Classical music radio is at its best when it provides for both purposes, when it is referenced either to individuals or to groups (but not classes) of listener. That squares with David Hendy's (2010) notion of a 'hierarchy' of listening, so long as it is qualified by Kate Lacey's (2013) concept of listening as a *cultural* practice which can change over time. 'Listening in' to classical music radio as a normative, quotidian activity is enhanced by periodic 'listening out' for greater intellectual engagement. Neither need be the separate preserve of an individual listener. Anyone can do both. Equally, classical music radio producers need to offer content which 'sounds in' amid routine programming, and also that which 'sounds out' to enhance the intellectual potential of the medium.

Transmission technology has conditioned the listening experience to classical music on radio throughout the period under review. Medium wave (AM) transmissions were probably acceptable in the years before the war, when the frequency bands were not so crowded. However, they are very open to interference, as well as offering a much less satisfactory auditory experience in the evening and after dark as transmissions become distorted by the impact of sky waves. Given that until the arrival of television this was prime time for radio listening, Adorno's reservations about the quality of classical music provided through radio are understandable. There was a particular problem for the Third Programme, as it was planned to come on air using a frequency which was likely to be interfered with by high-power transmissions from Riga. As the broadcasters' attention turned towards VHF (FM) transmission technology from immediately after the war, the situation improved markedly. FM is an attractive transmission technology for the listener, although the range of reception from individual transmitters is geographically limited.

Since 1996, radio services in the UK have increasingly been broadcast using digital transmission technology, adopting the standard of Digital Audio Broadcasting (DAB). The BBC, the commercial radio companies and latterly the UK Government seem to have bet their shirts on DAB as the most appropriate digital transmission technology. Unfortunately, while it was attractive in the immediate years when it was launched, now—more than 20 years later—it appears increasingly as outdated and unsatisfactory. It remains to be seen whether there is any opportunity to row back from the heavy commitment made to it by the UK Government in alliance with commercial interests. The listening experience on DAB is also in some ways less satisfactory than on FM; tuning is much easier, but the standards adopted for DAB provide a less robust signal than might be optimum. FM listening with a good external aerial is probably more attractive for the purists. Repeated suggestions that analogue technology—that is to say, AM and FM transmissions—was to be shut down have always seemed premature and unrealistic. Unless Government is prepared to exercise *force majeure* to deny millions or even tens of millions of listeners access to their radio sets, that is likely to remain the case for some years yet, by which time DAB will be more than ever the previous century's technology.

Shifting technology for the personal consumption of classical music is also starting to change the nature of listening. From the Sony Walkman, to MP3, to Napster and to iPlayer (and, no doubt, beyond), consumers are now able to select to a very substantial degree what they listen to and when they listen to it. In Wright's words:

> there is no dress code, there is no pass, there is no limit on where you do it, how much you do it, who is with you.[vii]

Outside the concert halls—and increasingly within them as well—sacralisation of classical music is a concept of a past world. As a consequence, the nature of listening to classical music radio is likely to alter fundamentally; arguably, it has done so already. Once again, the genre is a signifier of past cultural practice, current change and future possibilities.

Presentation

It is evident from this history that it is not just the actual music played which defines a radio service, and determines who does or does not listen. Indeed, the range of classical music compositions played on UK radio stations between 1945 and 1995 was notably similar, based on an acknowledged and largely consistent canonic repertoire. What made the difference was the way in which it was offered to potential listeners. That put a premium upon the styles of presentation and the tone of voice adopted by each station and its presenters/announcers, as that varied over time.

Two of the most recent examples make the seminal importance of presentation very clear. When Kenyon came to recast Radio 3, his brief was as much to change the presentation (and therefore, those who were presenting) as to alter the musical choice. For Classic FM, its very distinctiveness arose from a more demotic voice, where the occasional mistakes or infelicities if anything added to the appeal of the station. Ever since the BBC had started broadcasting classical music, for rather a lot of what should have been its potential audience it had been a bit like listening to one's betters or one's teachers, talking together about matters and in a style from which one could not help but feel excluded. If a presenter on Classic FM fluffed pronouncing a composer's name—not that they actually did that very often—or when Paul Gambaccini brought the timbre of popular radio presentation into the very heart of Radio 3, it was as if a curtain had been drawn back, allowing listeners who had previously been kept on the outside to enter the gilded rooms of classical music.

The heralded position of the 'continuity announcer' within the BBC in the immediate post-war years was only partly a harking-back to the earlier, Reithian BBC. It was also evidence of a continuing sense of *de haut en bas* within the Corporation. That was by no means unwelcome to many of its listeners: indeed, the move away from it in the Nineties provoked agitation and some anger. Nevertheless, it was a throwback to what was only an imagined 'golden age', and as such served as a hindrance to the development of Radio 3 certainly, and earlier output to a degree.

The ILR stations had solved this problem by locating themselves within the vernacular, in terms of both vocabulary and style of speaking, including in presenting their classical music output. It was harder for the BBC, with its long tradition, and its unwillingness to let go entirely of the sacralisation of classical music on air lest that should damage also the element of 'mystery'—as Walter Bagehot would have understood it—protecting the Corporation. That is one of the reasons why Classic FM sounded such an upstart in the ears of those who were used to the tone of voice of the Third Programme and then Radio 3. But voice and language reflect the times and change with the times, and the successful interchange of presenters and voices between the BBC and Classic FM in very recent years shows how much had changed for the better by the end of the century.

The Relevance of Biography

David Hendy (2013) has stressed the place of individual biography in broadcasting history. Its importance is evident in the history of classical music radio, with its often-quoted names of William Haley, William Glock, Hans Keller, Aubrey Singer, John Drummond, Nicholas Kenyon, Michael Bukht and Ralph Bernard. However, it is open to debate whether the nature of classical music radio would have changed fundamentally in the absence of any one of them. Each encapsulated the mood of their era and implemented what the wider social dialectic indicated.

Of all the seminal figures in classical music radio, Glock is arguably the most instructive in considering the relevance of individual biography to media history. Under his stewardship of BBC music, listeners were given the opportunity to move from the fusty atmosphere of late Fifties Britain into the more open, freer but unpredictable climate of the Sixties. Yet that was no more than was happening in society and culture at large, and the narrative and content analysis makes clear that his impact on radio output—as distinct from concert output—was less pronounced than his reputation suggests. Similarly, Singer, for all the *ad personam* attention he generated at the time and subsequently, was arguably just another manifestation of the polarising forces which generated Thatcherism. An equal case for seminal influence could be made for Richard Marriott at the BBC and John Thompson at the IBA, behind the scenes. These and the other men (for it was almost always men) were a product of the society in which they lived, just as were the different manifestations of classical music radio. Where they have enhanced importance for the media historian is as signifiers for the times they characterise.

The Changing Nature of Public Service Radio Broadcasting

Classical music may be characterised as an archetypal element of public service radio broadcasting (PSRB).[3] It is widely regarded as a highly worthwhile art and cultural form, so its provision on radio may be

---

[3] 'Public service radio broadcasting' is abbreviated here to 'PSRB' to distinguish it from the common usage of 'PSB', which also covers television.

considered a significant public good. Hitherto, the Third Programme and Radio 3 have been regarded as the most conspicuous producers of this aspect of PSRB. However, the narrative history demonstrates a wider provision. While much of that has been done within the institution of the BBC, a significant amount since 1973 has been provided by the small ILR companies; and then by the overtly commercial Classic FM. This challenges the view that PSRB can only be provided by 'broadcasting run neither by the state nor by private commercial interests, but by large public bodies working in what they have thought of as the public interest' (Hendy 2013: 2). It suggests instead that alongside an institutional conception of PSRB there needs to be an acceptance that aspirational production can engage a wide range of consumers with material which—picking up on the definition of classical music established for this book—offers 'the opportunity for intellectual engagement with the music as well as sensory enjoyment'.[4] Where prior assumptions of class, intelligence and educational attainment can be set aside, different broadcasting aesthetics can be equally authentic and equally valid in offering access to a transcendent culture.

But might the output of ILR and to an extent Classic FM be regarded merely as regulatory artefacts? Certainly, classical music was effectively mandated on the local independent stations, but this book has shown that the enthusiasm with which those obligations were embraced and expanded upon demonstrated genuine public service inclination. Equally, Classic FM was a self-generating phenomenon, not a regulatory imposition, and the aspirational nature of its broadcasting during its early years came about without any formal contractual requirement. Those involved with classical music (and no doubt with all art forms) possess an enthusiasm for it to be heard in its best manifestations by as many and as diverse people as can be found. The popularisers of classical music radio in those years—William Haley, John Manduell and Nicholas Kenyon for the BBC, Michael Bukht, Ralph Bernard and Robin Ray in private radio—wanted to reach out to the audience they knew was there, without cheapening what they wished to offer.

Jean Seaton (2015: 89) argues that music 'was part of the BBC's unstated duty to sustaining a "common culture"', in which high culture

---

[4] See Chap. 1, p. 20.

and the everyday 'were interrelated positively'. This history demonstrates similarly that such a symbiosis represented classical music radio at its best. That also illuminates the nature of PSRB, as a quality which is not exclusive to the BBC. For a time at least, that inter-relationship was achieved by ILR and Classic FM, which were better at reaching the everyday than Radio 3 could ever hope to do. Similarly, the pedagogic role of radio has changed. It is no longer about formalised education, but about providing opportunities for learning. As a consequence, even if the triptych of information, education and entertainment is still the defining role of PSRB, radio stations no longer need a great institutional panoply to be able to fulfil the educative function.

Demonstrably then, there are multiple institutional options for providing PSRB. These can be funded in a variety of ways—by the state, commercially or through philanthropy—and exist independent of the scale of their providers. They are validated, once again, by a reflexive complicity between the producers and consumers of radio around a particular content and style of provision. This history of classical music radio repeatedly bears out that assertion, at least during those periods when elitist educational and class assumptions were set aside.

A Story Worth the Telling

The book has set out the first comprehensive, longitudinal, narrative history of classical music broadcast on UK radio in the second half of the twentieth century, relating that to the changing political, social and economic circumstances of those decades. Beginning before the launch of the BBC Third Programme, and continuing until after the launch of the commercial station Classic FM and to the end of free-to-air radio broadcasting as an unchallenged entity, it describes and analyses the wide range of services which offered this style of music, describing a far broader spectrum than previous discourse had identified.

These 50 years were characterised by a series of high points, when classical music services were broadcast across a number of different channels, offered high-brow and middle-brow content, provided links between elite and popular output, and were accessible to a broad range of potential listeners. Each of those then provoked a reaction from the self-appointed intellectual elite, concerned at the diminishing of what they regarded as 'high art' in the interest of mass appeal, and reflecting the class-based assumptions of British society during these years.

This account broadens out from the previous narrow preconception of what this genre of broadcasting comprised, which itself reflected educational and class assumptions. Almost all previous academic and popular discourse has addressed classical music on UK radio as comprising merely the output of the Third Programme, and subsequently of Radio 3, and has therefore assumed it to be the preserve of the well-educated, higher class elite. As this book has demonstrated, for much of this period there was a richer, multi-channel offering of surprisingly broad appeal. In the years before 1970, the Third Programme was never the majority provider of this type of radio; the Home Service, the Light Programme and then the Music Programme were much more significant in terms of quantity of output and audiences. In the last quarter of the twentieth century, the Radio 3 offering was added to by classical music provision on ILR; and eventually radically augmented—even, in some ways, surpassed—by the success of Classic FM from 1992 onwards.

The story of classical music radio is a powerful paradigm for the nature and development of the UK in the second half of the twentieth century. It has a different significance from the pop music radio revolution, being at once more subtle and less linear. While popular music was about the impact of an invasive and classless youth culture, the varied lines of development of classical music radio speak to the shifting nature of tradition and institutions in Britain—mediated by the influence of class—and how culture was only periodically opened up to a broader audience. But it is not just an academic signifier; it is primarily a compelling story, adding to the understanding of broadcasting history in the UK, and of post-war British society as a whole.

NOTES

i. Interview with Roger Wright, 10 October 2014.
ii. Interview with Fiona Talkington, 8 October 2014.
iii. Interview with Roger Wright, 10 October 2014.
iv. Richard Morrison. Sir Harry rides into the fray. *The Times*, 1 December 1993 (page not specified in digital archive).
v. *The Times*, 15 April 1966, p. 60.
vi. *The Third Programme, the size and character of its public.* Listener Research Report, May 1953. BBC WAC R9/13/99.
vii. Interview with Roger Wright, 10 October 2014.

BIBLIOGRAPHIC SOURCES

Britten, B. 1964. *On receiving the first Aspen award: A speech.* London: Faber & Faber.
Hendy, D. 2010. Listening in the dark. *Media History* 16 (2): 215–232.
Hendy, D. 2013. *Public service broadcasting.* London: Palgrave Macmillan.
Lacey, K. 2013. *Listening publics: The politics and experience of listening in the media age.* Cambridge: Polity.
Said, E.W. 1994. *Culture & imperialism.* London: Vintage.
Seaton, J. 2015. *Pinkoes and traitors. The BBC and the nation 1974–1987.* London: Profile Books.
Stoller, T. 2010. *Sounds of your life: The history of independent radio in the UK.* New Barnet: John Libbey.

Appendix A: Content Database

Introduction
This history deploys an original database of programme content, on a sample week basis derived from *Radio Times* listings. That provides a snapshot of the daily output across each week of the 50 years covered by this narrative. While illustrative rather than definitive, this enables qualitative assertions to be tested against objective data.

The volume of the *Radio Times* listings data is daunting, but pilot analysis has clearly shown consistency across most weeks of each year, and that neither the hours of output nor the audience level chopped and changed with any rapidity. The programme content database therefore addresses radio output in week 19 (either the first or second week in May) every year from 1945 until 1995. This week was chosen after the pilot testing, being outside main holiday periods, major music festivals or significant variations from the norm. Such 'variations' are sometimes important for the narrative, but they can be reviewed on a qualitative basis—which has been done where that is appropriate. Both the *Radio Times* listings and the audience data in the BBC's Daily Listening Barometer (see below) initially began the broadcast week on a Sunday, changing in 1961 to a Saturday. The content database, and the audience database summarised in Appendix B, follow that approach.

The content database identifies and aggregates the total duration of programmes which contain classical music broadcast on BBC Radio and Classic FM. From 1970 onwards, the total hours of 'sequence programming' is separated out, where 'sequence programming' is understood as a series of works without any conscious link between them and not within a concert setting. Where possible, a quantitative measure of 'features' is also shown, comprising programmes of mainly speech content which cover topics relevant to classical music

In listing the number of 'plays' which each composer receives, multiple songs included in a single recital are scored as one single play. Major works—notably operas and oratorios—are also scored as single plays, and therefore in this sense at least have equivalence with a single movement of a sonata. However, they are usually identified separately in the narrative text.

Four summaries of the full database are set out in this Appendix, in each instance for the sample week:

1. A longitudinal summary of total hours of classical music radio broadcast and the use of commercially recorded music by the BBC (Table A.1).
2. A summary of the output classical music radio on each national station (Table A.2).
3. BBC featured composers, such as *This Week's Composer* or *Composer of the Week*, by decades (Table A.3).
4. A longitudinal summary of composers most featured in BBC output (Table A.4).

For ILR station output between 1975 and 1990, the main source is descriptive: the programmes identified in the IBA's Television and Radio Handbook, and in its Annual Reports. This means that ILR content data are less detailed and robust than for the BBC or even Classic FM, and that no quantitative check can be done. The totals therefore do not include ILR station output, which was in separate and limited localities.

The final table (Table A.4) requires a minimum of 4 plays for inclusion. The symbol = indicates an equal number of plays with the composer in the next column. One further caution is needed in considering these data. The source of them is the *Radio Times*, and some of the sequence programmes—notably *In Tune*—do not have any listings. The information is therefore more valid as comparative than as absolute figures.

APPENDIX A: CONTENT DATABASE   249

Table A.1 Total classical music programmes broadcast 1945–1995

	BBC radio			All radio
	Total hours	Records	Records as % of total hours	Total hours
1945	19'40	4'40	22.9	19'40
1946	24'10	5'30	22.7	24'10
1947	36'00	5'05	15.2	36'00
1948	44'40	3'45	8.4	44'40
1949	39'45	1'30	3.8	39'45
1950	39'05	3'20	8.4	39'50
1951	41'25	1'55	4.6	41'25
1952	44'15	2'05	4.7	44'15
1953	43'05	2'30	5.8	43'05
1954	41'15	3'05	7.5	41'25
1955	40'25	6'00	14.8	40'25
1956	34'25	3'40	10.6	34'25
1957	35'20	3'25	9.8	35'20
1958	33'10	3'10	9.5	33'10
1959	36'15	7'00	19.3	36'15
1960	43'45	3'05	7.1	43'45
1961	41'50	7'20	17.5	41'50
1962	40'40	3'55	9.7	40'40
1963	36'30	4'00	10.9	36'30
1964	36'10	4'40	12.9	36'10
1965	91'50	31'05	33.9	91'50
1966	91'30	31'25	34.4	91'30
1967	90'10	31'20	34.8	90'10
1968	86'35	25'50	29.8	86'35
1969	88'40	24'55	28.1	88'40
1970	88'50	30'15	34.0	88'50
1971	85'35	21'15	24.8	85'35
1972	89'20	27'00	30.2	89'20
1973	83'50	22'35	26.9	83'50
1974	84'45	27'50	32.8	84'45
1975	81'05	27'30	33.9	81'05
1976	86'55	24'35	28.2	86'55
1977	87'45	31'10	35.5	87'45
1978	86'10	24'10	28.0	86'10
1979	85'40	34'05	39.8	85'40
1980	92'55	38'35	41.5	92'55
1981	93'10	37'10	39.9	93'10
1982	92'00	34'50	37.9	92'00
1983	87'40	27'25	31.3	87'40
1984	90'40	35'55	39.7	90'40

(continued)

Table A.1 (continued)

	BBC radio			All radio
	Total hours	Records	Records as % of total hours	Total hours
1985	100'40	31'00	30.9	100'40
1986	95'10	31'15	32.8	95'10
1987	93'35	34'45	37.1	93'35
1988	95'40	40'30	42.3	95'40
1989	110'40	29'05	26.3	110'40
1990	92'30	32'40	35.3	92'30
1991	96'25	41'05	42.6	96'25
1992	97'20	36'35	37.5	97'20

				Classic FM	
				Total hours	
1993	95'50	45'35	47.5	161'00	256'50
1994	99'45	35'00	35.1	166'00	255'45
1995	101'05	31'00	30.7	157'00	258'05

Total hours and minutes of classical music in programmes in each sample week

Table A.2 Summary of each station's output 1945–1995

	Home	Records	Third	Records	General forces	Records
1945	13'25	4'10			5'00	6'15
					Light	
1946	17'30	5'30			6'40	–
1947	16'20	5'05	13'10	–	6'30	–
1948	16'50	3'15	20'35	0'30	7'15	–
1949	15'30	1'10	17'00	0'20	7'15	–
1950	13'10	1'55	20'55	1'25	5'00	–
1951	18'00	1'15	18'30	0'40	6'55	–
1952	17'30	1'15	19'00	0'50	8'45	–
1953	16'00	1'00	21'20	0'30	5'45	0'30
1954	15'42	1'50	19.45	1'45	5'45	–
1955	18'30	4'15	16'40	1'45	5'15	–
1956	15'15	1'40	16'00	2'00	3'10	–
1957	15'00	2'00	16'30	1'25	3'50	–

(continued)

APPENDIX A: CONTENT DATABASE 251

Table A.2 Continued

							Network 3	Features
1958	18'47	1'55	13'35	0'30	–	–	0'45	
1959	17'25	3'55	17'25	1'30	–	–	1'35	0'30
1960	22'45	3'05	16'35	–	–	–	2'40	0'45
1961	21'10	5'05	16'55	0'15	2'00	–	1'00	0'30
1962	23'35	2'40	14'00	1'15	1'00	–	1'45	1'00
1963	21'15	3'20	13'00	0'40	–		2'15	1'15
1964	20'30	2'50	12'45	1'50	1'40		1'30	1'00

	Radio 4				Music programme	Records	Study session
1965	13'00	2'30	15'35	0'30	63'25	28'05	–
1966	11'45	2'20	13'30	–	65'45	29'05	0'30
1967	10'55	–	16'55	3'20	60'50	28'00	0'30
1968	14'35	3'05	12'20	0'40	59'40	22'05	
1969	12'00	2'55	16'35	–	60'05	22'00	

	Radio 3	Records	Features	Seq. progs	Radio 4	Features
1970	88'50	30'15	4'45	12'25		
1971	85'35	21'15	3'00	9'00		
1972	89'20	27'00	6'05	12'45		
1973	83'50	22'35	3'10	13'50		
1974	84'45	27'50	2'45	14'50		
1975	81'05	27'30	2'50	18'10		
1976	80'45	24'35	3'50	16'15		
1977	84'35	31'10	2'25	15'45		
1978	82'10	24'10	2'25	14'45	4'00	
1979	85'40	34'05	2'00	14'35		
1980	86'05	31'45	2'50	19'05	6'50	0'45
1981	90'05	37'10	3'20	22'35	2'50	
1982	89'40	34'50	1'40	22'00	2'20	
1983	87'40	27'25	2'00	17'55		
1984	90'40	35'55	1'40	16'30		
1985	100'40	31'00	2'30	17'30		
1986	95'10	31'15	3'40	20'10		
1987	93'35	34'45	3'00	17'35		
1988	95'40	40'30	1'30	18'25		
1989	110'40	29'05	5'00	17'30		
1990	92'30	32'40	–	22'00		
1991	96'25	41'50	4'35	28'40		
1992	97'20	36'35	2'30	26'30		

(continued)

252   APPENDIX A: CONTENT DATABASE

Table A.2   Continued

					Classic FM	Features	Non-sequence
1993	95'50	43'35	1'40	34'30	161'00	5'00	21'00
1994	99'45	35'00	3'00	39'30	166'00	7'00	22'00
1995	101'05	31'00	3'50	38'15	157'00	7'00	20'00

Total hours and minutes of classical music in programmes in each sample week

Table A.3   Composers selected as either *This Week's Composer* or *Composer of the Week* in each sample week 1945–1995

	This week's composer/Composer of the week
1945	Fauré
1946	Vaughan Williams, Bax
1947	Elgar
1948	Tchaikovsky
1949–1960	None
1961	Berlioz
1962–1964	None
1965	Fauré
1966	Handel
1967	Handel
1968	Rawsthorne and Warlock
1969	Holst and Tippett
1970	Liszt
1971	Rawsthorne, Walton
1972	Vaughan Williams
1973	Nielsen
1974	Tchaikovsky
1975	Domenico Scarlatti, Boccherini
1976	Josquin des Prez
1977	Chopin
1978	Purcell
1979	Brahms
1980	Greig
1981	Monteverdi
1982	Greig
1983	Lennox Berkeley
1984	Smetana
1985	Dvořák
1986	Ockeghem
1987	Rachmaninov
1988	Goldmark
1989	'Mozart's rivals', Ravel
1990	Tchaikovsky, Mendelssohn

(continued)

APPENDIX A: CONTENT DATABASE   253

Table A.3   Continued

	This week's composer/Composer of the week
1991	Poulenc, Gesualdo, Victoria
1992	Beethoven, Barber
1993	Handel
1994	Dvořák, Fauré
1995	Fauré, Brahms

Table A.4   Most played composers in BBC output in each sample week 1945–1995

Year sampled	Total composers	Most	2nd	3rd	4th
1945	39	Beethoven	Tchaikovsky	Mozart	Bach
1946	47	Beethoven	Mozart	Brahms	Tchaikovsky/ Handel/Purcell
1947	52	Bach	Mozart	Schubert	Tchaikovsky
1948	55	Beethoven	Haydn	Liszt	Chopin
1949	66	Dvořák	Beethoven	Debussy =	Chopin/ Stanford
1950	62	Beethoven	Haydn	Mozart =	Schumann/ Schubert
1951	56	Haydn	Brahms	Beethoven	Mozart
1952	72	Mozart	Haydn	Schubert	Teleman
1953	67	Beethoven	Mozart	Haydn =	Liszt/Handel/ Mendelssohn/ Stravinsky
1954	69	Beethoven	Mozart	Haydn =	Bach
1955	57	Beethoven	Bach	Brahms	
1956	58	Mozart	Handel	Debussy =	Beethoven
1957	81	Bach	Beethoven	Schubert	Schumann
1958	66	Bach	Mozart	Sibelius	Haydn
1959	75	Beethoven	Mozart =	Elgar =	Bach/ Rachmaninov
1960	62	Mozart	Haydn	Bach =	Schumann/ Brahms
1961	66	Beethoven	Mozart	Tchaikovsky	
1962	70	Bach	Beethoven	Bach	Haydn/ Schumann
1963	55	Beethoven	Mozart	Stravinsky	Britten
1964	65	Beethoven	Mozart	Debussy	Dvořák
1965	124	Beethoven	Bach	Haydn	Mozart/ Brahms/ Tchaikovsky

(continued)

Table A.3 Continued

Year sampled	Total composers	Most	2nd	3rd	4th
1966	100	Mozart	Beethoven	Bach	Brahms/ Schubert
1967	112	Bach	Mozart	Beethoven	Schubert
1968	109	Mozart	Beethoven	Bach	Haydn/Dvořák
1969	98	Beethoven	Brahms =	Mozart =	Schubert
1970	88	Beethoven	Mozart	Bach	Haydn
1971	84	Beethoven	Mozart	Schubert	Haydn
1972	110	Beethoven	Mozart	Brahms	Haydn
1973	89	Mozart	Schubert	Beethoven	Brahms
1974	96	Haydn	Mozart	Brahms	Beethoven
1975	101	Mozart	Bach	Haydn	Beethoven
1976	98	Mozart	Brahms	Beethoven	Bach
1977	98	Beethoven	Mozart	Haydn	Schubert
1978	101	Mozart =	Schubert	Haydn	Brahms
1979	91	Mozart	Bach	Debussy	Mendelssohn
1980	99	Brahms	Beethoven	Mozart =	Schumann
1981	112	Mozart	Haydn =	Beethoven	Schubert
1982	83	Beethoven	Mozart	Dvořák =	Schubert
1983	133	Mozart	Brahms	Beethoven	Handel
1984	92	Mozart	Haydn =	Beethoven	Brahms
1985	100	Beethoven	Schumann	Mozart	Haydn
1986	117	Mozart	Schubert	Beethoven	Fauré
1987	131	Mozart	Mendelssohn	Haydn	Ravel/Brahms/ Schubert/ Britten/ Schumann
1988	125	Beethoven	Mozart	Schubert =	Dvořák
1989	112	Mozart	Beethoven	Schubert =	Mendelssohn
1990	112	Beethoven	Bach	Mozart =	Debussy
1991	115	Beethoven	Chopin	Brahms	Dvořák
1992	111	Mozart	Beethoven	Haydn	Bach/ Stravinsky/ Maxwell Davies
1993	114	Mozart	Schubert	Haydn	Brahms
1994	109	Dvořák	Beethoven	Bach	
1995	107	Brahms	Britten	Debussy	Ravel

Appendix B: Audience Database

Introduction

Actual audience levels—like actual programme content—can help to underpin qualitative observations wherever available. The audience databases involved two separate, sequential cohorts of data. From 1946 until around 1977, that comprised chiefly audience averages for individual programmes, produced by and for BBC Audience Research and reported *inter alia* in the Daily Listening Barometer. From 1977 onwards, there were broader quantitative data sets produced for the independent stations, advertising agencies and advertisers, under the auspices of the Joint Industry Committee for Radio Audience Research (JICRAR); and from 1992 there is radio-wide research conducted jointly for the BBC and the commercial radio companies to the Radio Joint Audience Research (RAJAR) specification.

As discussed in the narrative chapters,[1] for the earlier period there is a further difficulty. BBC audience research analysis and special reports are very largely concerned with the Third Programme, thus starting from an assumption that the classical music audience is somehow 'higher brow' than the radio audience as a whole, which became a self-fulfilling hypothesis. Yet the size of audiences for classical music

---

[1]See Chap. 1, pp. 23–24.

programmes on the Home Service and the Light Programme measured by the BBC's own Daily Listening Barometer suggest that it is inconceivable these could be as predominantly upper class as those for the Third Programme.

In an approach similar to the programme content analysis, this history deploys two original databases of listening to this genre of output:

1. A comprehensive data set of maximum and median audiences for individual programmes across the entire period from 1945 until 1995 (Table B.1).
2. A longitudinal series of patronage and reach data (Table B.2).

Maximum and Median Audiences

A complete set of maximum and median audience data for the sample week of each year in the period for every station which broadcast classical music has been compiled by analysing the BBC's Daily Audience Barometer reports, and subsequently independent JICRAR and RAJAR data. The value of the maximum figure is obvious; the median figure provides an indication of the overall success of each station in audience terms. In the absence of reach data for the years before 1977 (as discussed below) it provides a comparative indicator of patronage over time.

Table B.1 Maximum and median audiences ('000s) for individual classical music programmes in each sample week

			Home service		General forces	
	Maximum '000s	Median '000s	Maximum '000s	Median '000s	Maximum '000s	Median '000s
1945 (i)			1900	1100	1350	570
					Light programme	
1946			2800	700	2800	1400
	Third programme					
1947	1050	700	2100	1250	3850	1750
1948	360	180	2160	1080	3240	900
1949	210	108	1080	540	1080	720

(continued)

APPENDIX B: AUDIENCE DATABASE 257

Table B.1 (continued)

	Third programme					
1950	146	73	1460	365	5475	365
1951	292	109	4745	730	5110	730
1952	182	109	1095	730	1095	730
1953	146	73	730	365	730	365
1954	150	75	1128	376	376	376
1955	112	75	752	376	752	564
1956	225	75	752	376	752	376
1957	75	37	756	378	378	378

							Network 3	
							Maximum '000s	Median '000s
1958	151	75	756	378			37	37
1959	151	75	567	264			75	37
1960	94	47	429	190			94	47
1961	95	47	524	238	286	286	*(ii)	*
1962	195	97	438	243	341	341	48	48
1963	98	49	588	196			98	49
1964	98	49	441	196	490	490	49	*

	Third programme		Home service		Music programme		Study programme	
					Maximum '000s	Median '000s	Maximum '000s	Median '000s
1965	129	49	297	139	232	139	*	*
1966	200	100	450	200	300	150	*	*
1967	200	100	400	200	150	100	*	*
1968	200	100	450	250	250	150		
1969	150	50	300	150	200	100		

	Radio 3		Radio 4	
	Maximum '000s	Median '000s	Maximum '000s	Median '000s
1970	353	151		
1971	202	101		
1972	303	151		
1973	303	151		
1974	252	101		
1975	404	202		
1976	454	151	353	202

(continued)

Table B.1 (continued)

	Radio 3		Radio 4	
	Maximum '000s	Median '000s	Maximum '000s	Median '000s
1977	555	151	555	(iii)
1978	353	151	151	101
1979	313	156		
1980	261	130	313	208
1981	250	100	150	100
1982	200	100	(iv)	(iv)
1983	150	75		
1984	200	100		
1985–1991	Data not recorded			

	Radio 3		Classic FM	
	(v)		Maximum '000s	Median '000s (v)
1992	214	80	428	120
1993	232	69	467	108
1994	168	56	510	95
1995	200	62	485	122

Sources
1945–1991, BBC Daily Barometer, week 19
1992–1995, RAJAR, quarter 4
Notes
(i) Excluding the unscheduled VE Day concert, simulcast on the Home and General Forces Services to an audience of 3.3 million
(ii) *Audience too small to measure
(iii) Median inappropriate for just two programmes attracting respectively 1.1 and 0.1% of total audience
(iv) Data not available
(v) Based on Sunday listening

Reach/Patronage of Classical Music Radio

BBC audience research across most of this period reported only the average audience for individual programmes. It is customary in radio audience research world-wide to establish a 'weekly reach' figure: i.e. the total number of adults tuning into a station at some time during a given week. 'Reach' roughly equates to 'patronage', a term which BBC Audience Research deployed consistently if casually up until the late Seventies, but which did not have the same measured precision as a 'reach' figure. From that point onwards, proper 'reach' data are available from independent research conducted for JICRAR.

Table B.2 Weekly reach for classical music radio stations 1977–1995

	Weekly reach for Radio 3 (JICRAR/ RAJAR)	Weekly reach for Radio 3 (BBC data)	Weekly reach for ILR (est. from JICRAR)	Weekly reach for Classic FM (RAJAR)
	Radio 3		ILR combined	
1977	2,702,000		750,000	
1978	2,613,000		750,000	
1979	2,350,000		750,000	
1980	2,210,000		750,000	
1981	2,590,000		750,000	
1982	2,684,000		1,000,000	
1983	n/a		1,000,000	
1984	2,695,000		1,000,000	
1985	n/a		1,000,000	
1986	3,109,000		1,000,000	
1987	3,653,000		1,000,000	
1988	3,410,000		1,000,000	
1989	2,750,000	2,690,000*	1,000,000	
1990	3,943,000		Broadcasts ceased	
1991	2,695,000			
				Classic FM
1992	2,500,000			4,255,000
1993	2,736,000			4,494,000
1994	2,380,000			4,587,000
1995	2,397,000			4,751,000

Sources
JICRAR until 1992
RAJAR from quarter 4 1992
*BBC Audience Report 1989

Until the establishment of joint audience research in 1992, under the RAJAR specification, as discussed above, listening figures produced by two rival systems were often contested. For the purpose of this summary, however, JICRAR data can be benchmarked against a number of BBC studies which broadly validate their figures.[2] The total market for classical music radio can be established for the early years from specific BBC

---

[2] Continuous Service Report—radio listening trends 1972–1984, July 1985. BBC WAC R9/979/1.

research and in the later years from reliable independent RAJAR data. BBC research in 1952 suggested a total market of 6.2 million listeners, which indicates the broad level of classical music radio listening in the early Fifties. Reliable data for Radio 3 and Classic FM from 1992 show that between those two stations there was an overlap of around 1 million listeners, which therefore meant an audience for classical music radio in the Nineties of somewhere around 5.5 million listeners a week.[3] It is reasonable to conclude therefore that an audience of between 5 and 6 million listeners was available for this genre of radio throughout the second half of the 20th century (Table B.2).

---

[3]Robert Silvey. The Third Programme and its market. *BBC Quarterly* Autumn 1953 vol. VIII, no 3.

Appendix C: Timeline

1920
Nellie Melba broadcasts on Marconi's Chelmsford station (15 June).

1922
British Broadcasting Company formed (18 October).

1923
First opera outside broadcast: *Magic Flute* from Covent Garden (January).

1927
British Broadcasting Corporation comes into existence (1 January); BBC takes over the running of the Henry Wood Prom series.

1930
BBC Symphony Orchestra (BBCSO) formed; J.C. Stobart, Head of BBC Education Department, floats the idea of a cultural network, the 'Minerva' programme.

1931
Adrian Boult appointed Chief Conductor of BBCSO (until 1950).

1937
Theodor Adorno sails to New York (June).

1939
Outbreak of war (1 September); BBCSO evacuated to Bristol (September).

1940
Royal Philharmonic Society takes over the running of the Proms; German troops overrun Northern Europe, silencing the UK-aimed commercial radio stations apart from Radio Luxembourg (May); Walter Benjamin commits suicide in Portbou, Catalonia (26 September).

1941
Messiaen's *Quartet for the End of Time* performed in Stalag VIIIA prisoner-of-war camp, starting the avant-garde era for classical music (15 January); Queen's Hall destroyed by bombing (10 May); Operation Barbarossa, Germany invades USSR (June); BBCSO moves to Bedford (July, until September 1945); Japan attacks USA naval base at Pearl Harbor (December).

1942
Proms move to the Royal Albert Hall and the BBC resumes running the series; Arthur Bliss becomes Director of Music (until 1944); Royal Liverpool Philharmonic becomes a full-time permanent orchestra; Shostakovich Seventh Symphony premiere (March), performed amid the siege of Leningrad (9 August).

1943
Hallé Orchestra becomes a full-time permanent orchestra; Sibelius burns the completed manuscript of his Eighth Symphony.

1944
Henry Wood dies; Butler Education Act; William Haley becomes BBC Director General (until 1952); Basil Nicholls becomes Senior Controller then Director of Sound Broadcasting (until 1952); Victor Hely-Hutchinson becomes Director of Music (until 1946); *Music Magazine* begins on the Home Service (24 May); Krasa's opera *Brundibar* performed in Theresienstadt for the Red Cross visit, then all those involved deported to Auschwitz (16 October); Haley makes first public announcement of a new cultural network (24 November); City of Birmingham Symphony Orchestra reforms.

1945

George Barnes appointed as Head of Third Network (3 May, until 1948); VE day (8 May); Britten's *Peter Grimes* premiered at Sadler's Wells (June); UK General Election returns Labour Government (July); Home Service and Light Programme begin broadcasting in post-war formats (29 July); atomic bombs dropped on Hiroshima (6 August) and Nagasaki (9 August); VJ Day (15 August); Anton Webern shot in Mittersill, Austria (September); Sadler's Wells Opera reopens, Sadler's Wells Ballet goes to Royal Opera House, Covent Garden, opening with *Sleeping Beauty*.

1946

Cabinet approval given for 'the institution of the third programme' (January); official terms of reference approved (14 January); Bank of England nationalised (March) and coal industry (July); *BBC Quarterly* first published (16 April); BBC television transmissions resume (7 June); first *Darmstadt Ferienspiele* (June); Arts Council founded (August); New Towns Act (August); launch of the Third Programme (6 pm, Sunday 26 September); National Health Service Act (November); Royal Philharmonic, London Symphony, London Philharmonic and Philharmonia Orchestra re-established as self-governing institutions.

1947

BBC Charter and Licence renewed for 5 years (1 January); Covent Garden Opera gives first post-war performance, *Carmen* (January); 'big freeze' hits Britain; fuel crisis—Third Programme and Light Programme closed at 11 pm, Home Service at 11.03 pm (9 February); Third Programme and television service suspended (10 February); Third Programme resumed (26 February); Exeter transmitter opened to improve medium wave reception of the Third Programme (26 February); Indian independence announced (February); first Edinburgh International Festival; BBC Director of Music Victor Hely-Hutchinson dies suddenly, Kenneth Wright becomes Acting Director of Music; US announces Marshall Plan (June); *Last Night of the Proms* first televised (13 September); transistor devised by Bardeen, Brattain and Shockley presented to Bell Laboratories (December).

1948

Railways nationalised (January); Light and Third Programmes resume broadcasting until midnight (11 April); Marshall Plan funds to Britain

(April); *Empire Windrush* arrives at Tilbury (22 June); bread rationing ends (July); British Nationality Act (July); Harman Grisewood becomes Controller of the Third Programme (until 1952); Steuart Wilson becomes BBC Head of Music (until 1950); first Aldeburgh and Bath Festivals; T.S. Eliot, *Notes Towards the Definition of Culture*, F.R. Leavis, *The Great Tradition* and Norbert Wiener's *Cybernetics* published; first long-playing record; Haley commissions reports into music on the Home Service, Third Programme and Light Programme (November).

1949
Clothes rationing ends (March); Cultural and Scientific Conference for World Peace at Waldorf-Astoria attended by Shostakovich and Copland (March); NATO established (April); sterling devalued against US dollar (19 September); Prix Italia inaugurated (25 September); Billy Cotton band show begins on Light Programme; George Orwell's *1984* published; music reports completed (summer/autumn).

1950
European Broadcasting Union formed (12 February); Copenhagen Frequency Plan implemented (15 March); Herbert Murrill becomes BBC Head of Music (until 1952); Malcolm Sargent becomes Chief Conductor BBCSO (until 1957); Third Programme moves to new AM frequencies (15 March); Korean War begins (June); BBC Music Division becomes the Music Department, headed by Herbert Murrill (August); Scottish Orchestra reorganised into the permanent Scottish National Orchestra; Heinrich Strobel, Music Director of Südwestrundfunk, relaunches the Donaueschingen Festival in West Germany.

1951
BBC experiments with VHF (January); European Coal and Steel Community founded (April); new Conservative Government under Churchill (October); Festival of Britain; BBC stages *Festival of Britain Proms*; Hallé Orchestra returns to the Free Trade Hall, Manchester.

1952
Accession of Elizabeth II (February); funeral of George VI (15 February); BBC Charter and Licence renewed for 10 years (1 July); Cage's work *4'33"* first performed (29 August); Haley resigns as BBC Director General to become Editor of *The Times* (30 September); Ian Jacob becomes Director General (1 December); Lindsay Wellington becomes Director of Sound Broadcasting (until 1963); Richard Howgill

becomes Controller of Music (until 1959); first production of the contraceptive pill; first British atomic bomb test (3 October); first 45-rpm single released; *New Musical Express* begins a hit singles chart.

1953
John Morris becomes Controller of the Third Programme (until 1958); sugar and sweet rationing ends (5 February); death of Stalin (5 March); Copland appears before the House Un-American Activities Committee (25 May); Coronation of Queen Elizabeth II (2 June); armistice in Korea (July); Sunday broadcasting starts on Third Programme (27 September); Messiaen's *Réveil des Oiseaux* first performed at the Donaueschingen Festival; Press Council established.

1954
Talking about Music with Anthony Hopkins begins (13 January); *Under Milk Wood* broadcast premiere (January); Toscanini's last concert (5 April); Proms Diamond Jubilee; Bournemouth Symphony Orchestra under Charles Groves expands to become full time; Independent Television Authority established; food rationing ends (July); J.R.R. Tolkien, *Lord of the Rings* published in three volumes (July-October).

1955
Samuel Beckett, *Waiting for Godot* first performed in UK (January); first VHF transmitter opened at Wrotham supplying BBC Home, Light and Third to London and the South East (2 May); ITV transmissions begin for London (21 September); Network 3 begins (30 September); Eden succeeds Churchill (April) winning General Election (26 May).

1956
John Osborne, *Look Back in Anger* opens (8 May); Third Programme's 10th birthday marked by Otto Klemperer conducting Beethoven's *Missa Solemnis* at Royal Festival Hall (29 September); Stockhausen's *Gesange der Jüngelinge* given its premiere in Cologne; Suez crisis (July-December); USSR suppresses Hungarian revolution (November); UK loan from IMF (December); first Marriott Working Party established (early November); ITV extends beyond London; Bill Haley and the Comets, *Rock Around the Clock* and Elvis Presley, *Heartbreak Hotel* issued.

1957
Working Party reports to BBC Governors (January); Macmillan becomes Prime Minister (10 January); Peter Laslett and others launch the Third

Programme Defence Society (24 March); Rudolph Schwarz becomes Chief Conductor BBCSO (until 1962); Common Market established (March); first UK hydrogen bomb test (15 May); Third Programme's frequencies carry test match commentary during daytime for the first time (June); La Monte Young ushers in minimalism with *For Brass* (June); new pattern of broadcasting on the Third Programme frequencies commences (30 September); Third Programme's nightly broadcasting hours reduced by one third (1 October); skiffle craze peaks; Richard Hoggart, *The Uses of Literacy* and John Braine, *Room at the Top* published.

1958
Combined TV and radio licences (8 million) exceed radio-only licences (6.5 million); ITV broadcast nationwide; Committee for Nuclear Disarmament (CND) established (February); first Aldermaston march (April); Howard Newby becomes Controller of the Third Programme (until 1971); Home Service begins *Music at Night* programme, with *Market Trends* moving to the Third Programme (Autumn); Notting Hill race riots (August/September); stereophonic gramophone records first available.

1959
William Glock becomes Controller of Music (until 1972); Glock replaces the Proms Committee with concerts being planned by the BBC Music Division; Vaughan Williams dies (26 August); report under Marriott urges using the three national networks 'to their full capacity'; Keller's series *Functional Analysis* broadcast; UK's first motorway, M1; Macmillan wins 'never had it so good' election (8 October); Colin MacInnes, *Absolute Beginners* and Vladimir Nabokov, *Lolita* published in UK.

1960
Hugh Carleton-Greene becomes Director General (1 January); Pilkington Committee on Broadcasting established (13 July); *Beyond the Fringe* first performed in Edinburgh (conceived by Robert Ponsonby); Glock's first Prom season; first commissioned BBC work at a Prom; Shostakovich and Britten meet for the first time (September); Saturday afternoon music broadcasts begin on Network 3 (8 October); *Lady Chatterley* trial (October/November); 20 BBC VHF stations in operation, covering 97% of the population (31 December).

1961

Glock floats the idea of what was to become the Music Programme to the Pilkington Committee (February); first *Sunday Times* colour supplement published (4 February); Yuri Gagarin completes first manned space flight (12 April); *Private Eye* begins; Establishment Club opens (October); Glyndebourne Festival Opera brings *Don Giovanni* to the Proms for the first time.

1962

Britten's *War Requiem* given its first performance in the rebuilt Coventry Cathedral (30 May); Pilkington Committee reports (June); BBC dispute with Musicians' Union over Music Programme begins; BBC Charter and Licence extended to July 1964 (1 July); BBC starts experimental stereo broadcasts (28 July); Cuban missile crisis (October); first Beatles' hit single issued *Love Me Do* (October); television debut of *That Was The Week That Was* (24 November).

1963

Frank Gillard becomes Director of Sound Broadcasting, then Managing Director Radio (until 1970); National Theatre opens at the Old Vic (22); BBC television broadcasts Ken Russell's *Elgar* (11 November); Antal Doráti appointed Chief Conductor of the BBCSO (until 1966); assassination of President Kennedy (22 November); Profumo scandal; John Robinson, *Honest to God* and E.P. Thompson, *Making of the English Working Class* published.

1964

Top of the Pops begins (1 January); Radio Caroline begins broadcasting (28 March); *Children's Hour* ends; BBC2 television begins broadcasting for London (21 April); BBC reaches agreement with the Musicians' Union and Music Programme begins broadcasting on Sundays from 8 am to 5 pm (30 August); Lou Reed founds The Primitives, later to become the Velvet Underground; Harold Wilson narrowly wins General Election (15 October); Third Programme starts earlier at 7.30 pm, Music Programme extends (12 December).

1965

Steve Reich stumbles upon the tape-recorder phenomenon which produces *It's Gonna Rain* (January); Music Programme on full hours (20 March); Peter Maxwell-Davies's *Revelation and Fall*; Race Relations Act;

Vietnam War escalates; 'Swinging London' coined; Early Bird communications satellite launched (6 April).

1966
BBC introduces permanent stereo broadcasts for some programmes; introduction of colour television (3 March); Labour wins working majority at General Election (31 March); Open University proposed; England wins the World Cup (30 July); Aberfan disaster (21 October); *Cathy Come Home* screened (16 November).

1967
Beatles' *Sergeant Pepper* links with the Darmstadt experiments (1 June); BBC2 starts broadcasting in colour (1 July); Marine &c., Broadcasting (Offences) Act (August); *Face the Music* first televised (3 August); Third Programme and its associated services grouped under the label of 'Radio 3'; Home becomes Radio 4; Light Programme becomes Radio 2; Radio 1 launches (30 September); Colin Davis becomes Chief Conductor of the BBCSO (until 1971); Pierre Boulez conducts Stockhausen's *Gruppen* at the Proms; Malcolm Sargent appears at the *Last Night of the Proms* (16 September), dying 17 days later (3 October); Frank Gillard establishes a Second Working Party under Marriott (December).

1968
Charles Hill invites McKinsey to examine BBC Radio (April), producing an interim report in September and a final report in February 1969; Martin Luther King assassinated (4 April); Marriott group replaced by Policy Study Group chaired by Gerard Mansell; Kubrick's film *2001, a Space Odyssey* released (10 May); USSR invades Czechoslovakia on the same day as the USSR State Orchestra plays at the Proms (20 August); *Die Meistersinger* broadcast from the Coliseum in a collaboration between the Third and the Music Programme (recorded 18 September, broadcast 2 February 1969); abolition of theatre censorship (September).

1969
Civil rights protests start the Northern Ireland 'troubles' (January); *Broadcasting in the Seventies* published (10 July); moon landing (20 July); Charles Curran becomes Director General; *Campaign for Better Broadcasting* launched (September); BBC1 and ITV broadcasting in colour (15 November); Peter Maxwell, Davies *Eight Songs for a Mad King* and Harrison Birtwistle, *Punch and Judy* first performed; Phillip

Glass completes a series of minimalist compositions including *Music in Fifths* and *Music in Contrary Motion*; *Monty Python* and *Civilisation* both begin; Rupert Murdoch buys *The Sun*.

1970
New radio schedules come into operation, with Radio 3 fully operational in its new form (4 April) and Radio 4 shedding all regular music programmes (for the time being); Ian Trethowan becomes Managing Director Radio (until 1975); first late-night Prom; all Proms' broadcasts on Radio 3; *Concert Hall* series on Radio 3; voting age reduced to 18; Edward Heath wins General Election (18 June); Ken Russell, *The Music Lovers* released (December).

1971
First Open University broadcast (3 January); Brian Eno attends the London concert of the Philip Glass ensemble playing *Music with Changing Parts* (26 January); radio-only licence abolished (1 February); *An Alternative Service of Radio Broadcasting* White Paper published (29 March); premiere of Morton Feldman's Rothko Chapel (April); David Munrow's *Pied Piper* series piloted (May); death of John Reith (16 June); Pierre Boulez becomes Chief Conductor of the BBCSO (until 1975); Richard Hoggart delivers the *Reith Lectures*; BBC adds full stereo capability to Radio 3; premiere of Morton Feldman's *Rothko Chapel*; Brian Eno attends the London concert of the Philip Glass ensemble playing *Music with Changing Parts*; internment introduced in Northern Ireland (9 August); Richard Hoggart delivers the Reith Lectures (November/December).

1972
Stanley Kubrick's *A Clockwork Orange* released (13 January); 'Bloody Sunday' (30 January); Sound Broadcasting Act (12 July); Independent Television Authority becomes Independent Broadcasting Authority; Stephen Hearst becomes Controller of the Third Programme (until 1978); Robert Ponsonby becomes Controller of Music (until 1986); BBC's 50th anniversary is the first concert simulcast by BBC2 and Radio 3 (11 November); *Jesus Christ Superstar* opens; home video-recorders on sale.

1973
UK joins the European Economic Community (Common Market); first ILR stations begin broadcasting with LBC (8 October), Capital

Radio (13 October), Radio Clyde (31 December); Radio 4 launches *Kaleidoscope*; schools programming restricted to Radio 4 VHF; UK school leaving age raised to 16; Arab-Israeli war and ensuing oil crisis (October).

1974
Three-Day Week (1 January-7 March); two General Elections: Harold Wilson forms a minority Government (28 February), then wins overall majority (10 October); Annan Committee established (10 April); BBC starts occasional quadraphonic broadcasts; Robert Ponsonbysucceeds Glockas Proms' Director; President Nixon resigns (9 August); Birmingham pub bombings (21 November).

1975
Rudolph Kempe becomes Chief Conductor of the BBCSO (until 1976); Parliamentary Broadcasting experiment; Capital Radio launches *Collection*; Radio Clyde relays the Cleveland Quartet and the Scottish Proms; *lieder* recitals on Radio City; Radio 3 and Radio 4 share programming.

1976
Howard Newby becomes Managing Director Radio (until 1978); Ian McIntyre becomes Controller Radio 4 (until 1978); ILR secondary rental £25,000 funding for 11 programmes of classical music on Radio Clyde; Apple Corporation founded; first portable computers; Rudolph Kempe dies (May); David Munrow commits suicide (May); Wren Orchestra first performance (8 August); 30th anniversary of Third Programme celebrated on air and in *Radio Times* (September/October).

1977
Ian Trethowan becomes Director General; Annan Report published (23 March); Queen Elizabeth's Silver Jubilee; *Abigail's Party* broadcast (April); Sex Pistols release *God Save the Queen* (27 May).

1978
Aubrey Singer becomes Managing Director Radio (until 1982); Ian McIntyre becomes Controller Third Programme (until 1987); Gennady Rozhdestvensky becomes Chief Conductor of the BBCSO (until 1981); ILR secondary rental of £1 million funding *inter alia* Capital Radio concert series *Great Orchestras of the World*; first AIRC Copyright Tribunal

reference (October); Radio 3 moves to Radio 1's old AM frequency (23 November); regular broadcasting from Parliament begins.

1979
First BBC radio programmes recorded digitally; Margaret Thatcher wins General Election (3 May); Ian McIntyre announces new schedules for Radio 3 (July); ILR secondary rental of £1.9 million; Independent Television strike (August–October); *Monty Python's Life of Brian* released in the UK (November); Seamus Heaney's *Fieldwork* published; commercialisation of the Internet begins; scandal over the alleged 'forgery' of Shostakovich's memoirs (November).

1980
BBC cancels all live opera relays as economy measure; *Mainly for Pleasure* replaces *Homeward Bound* as 'continuous stream' programming in the early evenings (2 January); Musicians' Union strike (May–August); Proms concerts cancelled (July and August); orchestras including the BBCSO play in alternative Wembley Conference Centre Proms; Arnold Goodman brokers a settlement to the strike (7 August); ILR secondary rental of £2.7 million funding classical music concerts in London, at the Snape Maltings and in Aberdeen, Sheffield and Belfast.

1981
ILR secondary rental of £1.3 million; Greenham Common peace camp established (January); Deptford fire, Toxteth and Moss Side riots (July); launch of MTV (1 August); Salman Rushdie's *Midnight's Children* published; Rupert Murdoch acquires *The Times*.

1982
'Bloody Sunday' in Derry (30 January); Falklands War (April–June); Alasdair Milne becomes Director General; Gramophone Department and Music Division combined into Radio 3 Music Department (Autumn); Richard Francis appointed Managing Director Radio (until 1986); *3: The Radio 3 Magazine* appears (October); John Pritchard becomes Chief Conductor of the BBCSO (until 1989); ILR secondary rental of £794,000.

1983
Voice of the Listener pressure group formed; Brodsky Quartet wins the EBU International String Quartet Days in Cambridge; Messiaen completes his opera, *St Francis of Assisi*; Harrods' car bomb (December); major growth in CD sales commences.

1984
IBA first moots national commercial radio; miners' strike; Orgreave Colliery confrontations (May, June); ILR Heathrow Conference (23 June); IRA Brighton hotel bombing (12 October); start of privatisation with flotation of British Telecom.

1985
Further BBC radio economies, and the scaling-back of the VHF transmitter programme; ILR secondary rental down to £168,000; Peacock Committee established (March); Brixton, Handsworth and Broadwater Farm riots; Heysel stadium disaster (29 May); first Live Aid concert (13 July).

1986
Brian Wenham becomes Managing Director Radio (until 1987); Michael Parkinson presents *Desert Island Discs* following the death in 1985 of Roy Plomley; Chernobyl nuclear disaster (April); Peacock Committee reports (July); revised ruling from the first Copyright Tribunal (23 October); 'Big Bang' deregulates City of London financial sector.

1987
BBC Governors sack Alasdair Milne; Michael Checkland becomes Director General (until 2002); David Hatch becomes Managing Director Radio (until 1993); Green Paper on Broadcasting (25 February); BBC Music Division disbanded, replaced by a Radio 3 Music Department (autumn); John Drummond takes over from Ian McIntyre and is Controller of Music, Proms Director and Controller Radio 3 (1 June); Richard Park at Capital Radio launches UK contemporary hits radio (28 September); John Adams' *Nixon in China* first performance at the Houston Grand Opera (22 October); Wapping strikes.

1988
Sue Lawley takes over *Desert Island Discs* from Michael Parkinson, and the programme transfers from the Gramophone Department to Magazine Programmes; ITV broadcasts *Death on the Rock* (28 April); secondary rental effectively abolished (September); Copyright Act 1988 (November); Brunel Radio in Bristol/Bath/Swindon splits frequencies to carry a 2½-hour early-evening show of classical music every weekday;

IBA advertises 'incremental' ILR licences (13 November); Monopolies and Mergers Commission Report into music licensing (7 December).

1989
Hillsborough disaster (15 April); first transatlantic fibre optic cable; Tiananmen Square massacre (4 June); Andrew Davis becomes Chief Conductor of the BBCSO (until 2000); Berlin Wall breached (9 November); Daniel Barenboim conducts performances of Beethoven's Seventh Symphony in the Potsdamer Platz (12 November); end of needletime limits indicated by Government response to MMC report (20 December); Leonard Bernstein conducts Beethoven's *Choral Symphony* in Berlin (25 December).

1990
German reunification; First Digital Audio Broadcasting (DAB) trials from Crystal Palace transmitter (January); David Mellor appointed Arts Minister; *Nessun Dorma* theme for Football World Cup (June/July); controversy over Gulf War leads to Mark Elder being replaced as conductor of Last Night of the Proms; Broadcasting Act passed (November); Shadow Radio Authority established; BSkyB formed by the merger of BSB and Sky; Major succeeds Thatcher as Prime Minister (November).

1991
Radio Authority comes into existence (1 January); 'Desert Storm' in Kuwait (January); John Birt becomes BBC Director General designate; first national commercial radio licence advertised to be non-pop music on FM (11 January); Showtime group is highest bidder (22 May) but fails to raise its capital finance and is replaced by Classic FM (30 September); BBC Radio Orchestra disbanded (spring); end of the USSR; Maastricht treaty signed.

1992
Drummond leaves Radio 3 to be replaced by Nicholas Kenyon (28 February); Radio 3's AM transmissions cease (29 February) with the frequency being transferred for eventual use by Virgin Radio; David Mellor becomes Secretary of State for National Heritage (10 April); second AIRC Copyright Tribunal reference (2 June); John Birt becomes Director General; Radio 3 launches *On Air*, *In Tune* and *Brian Kay's Sunday Morning* (July); Classic FM begins broadcasting (7 September); David Mellor resigns (24 September); Peter Ackroyd, *English Music* published.

1993
Future of BBC orchestras once again an issue (spring); Liz Forgan becomes Managing Director of Radio (until 1996); judgement of the second AIRC Copyright Tribunal (26 February); UK leaves European Exchange Rate Mechanism (May); Rachel Whiteread's *House* completed.

1994
Gardeners Question Time team 'defect' to Classic FM (February); Tony Blair becomes Labour Party leader (21 July); IRA ceasefire (August); Netscape founded; *Three Tenors* USA concert and CD release.

1995
Fairest Isle, BBC Radio 3's *Year of British Music and Culture*; *Morning Collection* presented by Paul Gambaccini (August); Proms' centenary; on Drummond's retirement, Kenyon takes over in addition as Proms' Director; BBC DAB multiplex launches (September); schools broadcasting moves out of daytime hours (November); merger of CNN and Time Warner.

1996
BBC Radio staff split into Broadcast and Production divisions (7 June); Matthew Bannister becomes Managing Director Radio (until 1998); Broadcasting Act introduces UK digital radio (24 July); GWR takes full control of Classic FM; Ralph Bernard becomes GWR executive chairman; first *Prom in the Park* (15 September).

Appendix D: Senior Personnel in Classical Music Radio 1945–1995[4]

BBC

Chairman
1939–1946 Allan Powell
1947   Philip Inman
1947–1952 Ernest Simon
1952–1957 Alexander Cadogan
1957–1964 Arthur fforde
1964   James Duff
1964–1967 Norman Brook
1967–1973 Charles Hill
1973–1980 Michael Swann
1980–1983 George Howard
1983–1986 Stuart Young
1986–1996 Marmaduke Hussey
1996–2001 Christopher Bland

---

[4]Titles and honorifics are omitted, as they often apply to only part of the period in question.

BBC Radio Senior Management

Director General
1944–1952   William Haley
1952–1959   Ian Jacob
1960–1969   Hugh Greene
1969–1977   Charles Curran
1977–1982   Ian Trethowan
1982–1987   Alasdair Milne
1987–1992   Michael Checkland
1992–2000   John Birt

Controller (Programmes)
1938–1944   Basil Nicholls
1944–1955   Lindsay Wellington

Senior Controller
1944–1948   Basil Nicholls
1952–1963   Lindsay Wellington
1963–1968   Frank Gillard

Managing Director Radio
1969–1970   Frank Gillard
1970–1975   Ian Trethowan
1976–1978   Howard Newby
1978–1982   Aubrey Singer
1982–1986   Richard Francis
1986–1987   Brian Wenham
1987–1993   David Hatch
1993–1996   Liz Forgan

Director of Programmes, Radio (Deputy Managing Director Radio)
1959–1970   Richard Marriott
1970–1971   Gerard Mansell
1971–1975   Howard Newby
1975–1980   Douglas Muggeridge
1980–1983   Charles McLelland
1983–1986   Monica Sims
1986–1987   David Hatch
1993–1996   Michael Green

APPENDIX D: SENIOR PERSONNEL IN CLASSICAL MUSIC RADIO 1945–1995   277

Controller of the Third Programme/Controller, Radio 3
1946–1948   George Barnes
1948–1952   Harman Grisewood
1953–1958   John Morris
1958–1971   Howard Newby (Radio 3 from 1970)
1972–1978   Stephen Hearst
1978–1987   Ian McIntyre
1987–1992   John Drummond (merged post with Controller of Music)
1992–1998   Nicholas Kenyon
1998–2014   Roger Wright

Controller of the Home Service
1942–1952   Lindsay Wellington
1953–1957   Andrew Stewart
1960–1965   Ronald Lewin
1965–1969   Gerard Mansell
1969–1975   Anthony Whitby
1975–1976   Clare Lawson Dick
1976–1978   Monica Sims

Music Department[5]

Director of Music
1930–1942   Adrian Boult
1942–1944   Arthur Bliss
1944–1946   Victor Hely-Hutchinson
1946–1948   Kenneth Wright (acting)

Head of Music
1948–1950   Steuart Wilson
1950–1952   Herbert Murrill

Controller of Music
1952–1959   Richard Howgill
1959–1972   William Glock
1972–1986   Robert Ponsonby (final year in tandemwith Drummond)

---

[5]Further details of other than senior posts in the Music Department/Division are listed in Kenyon (1980: 440–441), including Chief Assistant posts, some of which are mentioned in the narrative of this book.

1985–1992   John Drummond
1992–1998   Nicholas Kenyon

Gramophone Department

Head of Gramophone Department
1945–1948   Gerald Abraham
1948–1972   Anna Instone
1972–1975   John Lade
1976–1977   Anna Instone
1977–1989   Christine Hardwick (from 1982 as Head of Radio 3 Music Department)

BBCSO

Chief Conductor
1931–1950   Adrian Boult
1950–1957   Malcolm Sargent
1957–1962   Rudolf Schwartz
1963–1966   Antal Dorati
1967–1971   Colin Davis
1971–1975   Pierre Boulez
1975–1976   Rudolf Kempe
1978–1981   Gennady Rozhdestvensky
1989–2000   Colin Davis

Classic FM

Chairman
1992–1996   Peter Michael

Chief Executive
1991–1992   Ralph Bernard (Executive Chairman from 1996 until 2008)

Managing Director
1992–1996   John Spearman

Programme Controller
1992–1997   Michael Bukht

IBA

Director General
1954–1970   Robert Fraser
1970–1981   Brian Young
1981–1987   John Whitney
1987–1990   Shirley Littler

Director of Radio
1972–1987   John Thompson
1987–1990   Peter Baldwin

Radio Authority

Chief Executive
1991–1995   Peter Baldwin (of Shadow Radio Authority from 1990)
1995–2003   Tony Stoller

Appendix E: Glossary of Terms, Acronyms and Abbreviations

AIs	Audience Appreciation Indices, one of the measures gathered by BBC audience research
AM	Amplitude modulated transmission, also known as Medium Wave
BBC	British Broadcasting Corporation (from 1927) British Broadcasting Company (1922–1926)
BBCSO	BBC Symphony Orchestra
BBC WAC	BBC Written Archive Centre
CD	Compact disc
CEMA	Council for the Encouragement of Music and the Arts
DAB	Digital Audio Broadcasting, currently the UK's preferred digital radio transmission system
Drivetime	Usually weekdays between 4 pm and 7 pm
DG	Director General, often shortened in BBC parlance
EBU	European Broadcasting Union
ENSA	Entertainments National Service Association
FM	Frequency modulated transmission, in earlier parlance known as VHF
IBA	Independent Broadcasting Authority
ILR	Independent Local Radio

ITV	Independent Television
JICRAR	Joint Industry Committee for Radio Audience Research, audience numbers research conducted for the Independent Radio companies, advertisers and advertising agencies between 1974 and 1991
MP3	Audio coding format for digital audio material
MU	Musicians' Union
Needletime	Amount of commercially recorded music (records) licensed to be played by a radio station each day/week
Ofcom	Office of Communications, the communications regulator since December 2003
PPL	Phonographic Performance Limited, the record companies' association
PRS	Performing Rights Society, representing composers, arrangers and performers
RAJAR	Radio Joint Audience Research, audience numbers research conducted for the BBC and commercial radio from 1992
Reach	The number of people measured by audience research to be listening to a radio service over a specified time period (usually Weekly Reach)

Sequence programmes:

Specified	Programmes featuring as a series of works, or parts of works, without any conscious link between them and not within a concert setting, where the items are specified in listings
Unspecified	Programmes featuring as a series of works, or parts of works, without any conscious link between them and not within a concert setting, where the items are not specified in listings
Simulcast	A programme broadcast on two or more different stations, either two radio channels or a radio and television channel
VHF	Very High Frequency transmission, now usually expressed as FM

Bibliography

Ackroyd, P. 1992. *English music*. London: Hamish Hamilton.
Addison, P. 1985. *Now the war is over: A social history of Britain 1945–51*. London: British Broadcasting Corporation.
Adorno, T.W. 2007. *Philosophy of modern music*, 3rd ed. London: Continuum.
Adorno, T.W., and R. Leppert. 1933/2002. *Essays on music: Theodor W. Adorno*. London: University of California Press.
Adorno, T.W., and B. O'Connor. 1928/2000. *The Adorno reader*. Oxford: Blackwell.
Adorno, T.W., R. Tiedemann, and W. Hoban. 2009. *Night music: Essays on music 1928–1962*. London: Seagull Books.
Arnold, M. 1875. *Culture and anarchy*. 2009 ed. Oxford: Oxford University Press.
Baade, C.L. 2006. 'The dancing front': Dance music, dancing, and the BBC in World War II. *Popular Music* 25 (3): 347–368.
Baade, C.L. 2012. *Victory through harmony: The BBC and popular music in World War II*. Oxford: Oxford University Press.
Babbitt, M., S. Bradshaw, W. Glock, A. Goehr, M. Graubart, J. Harvey, et al. 1986. Hans Keller Memorial Symposium. *Music Analysis* 5 (2/3): 374–405.
Beckett, A. 2009. *When the lights went out: Britain in the Seventies*. London: Faber.
Benjamin, W., and J.A. Underwood. 1936/2008. *The work of art in the age of mechanical reproduction*. London: Penguin.
Betts, G. 2005. *Complete UK hit singles 1952–2005*. London: Collins.
Birt, J. 2002. *The harder path: The autobiography*. London: Time Warner.

Black, L., C. Wintle, and K. Hopkins. 2010. *BBC music in the Glock era and after: A memoir*. London: Cosman Keller Art and Music Trust in association with Plumbago Books.

Blake, A. 1997. *The land without music: music, culture and society in 20th-century Britain*. Manchester University Press.

Born, G. 2005. *Uncertain vision: Birt, Dyke and the reinvention of the BBC*. London: Vintage.

Bourdieu, P. 1984. *Distinction: A social critique of the judgement of taste*. London: Routledge.

Bowman, P. 2012. *Culture and the media*. London: Palgrave Macmillan.

Briggs, A. 1961. *The history of broadcasting in the United Kingdom*, vol. 1. The birth of broadcasting: Oxford University Press.

Briggs, A. 1965. *The history of broadcasting in the United Kingdom*, vol. 2. The Golden Age of Wireless: Oxford University Press.

Briggs, A. 1970. *The history of broadcasting in the United Kingdom*, vol. 3. The War of Words: Oxford University Press.

Briggs, A. 1979. *The history of broadcasting in the United Kingdom*, vol. 4. Sound and Vision: Oxford University Press.

Briggs, A. 1980. Problems and possibilities in the writing of broadcasting history. *Media, Culture and Society* 2 (5).

Briggs, A. 1985. *The BBC: The first fifty years*. Oxford: Oxford University Press.

Briggs, A. 1995. *The history of broadcasting in the United Kingdom, vol. 5, competition*. Oxford: Oxford University Press.

British Broadcasting Corporation, 1947. *The Third Programme. A symposium of opinions and plans*. London: British Broadcasting Corporation.

British Broadcasting Corporation. 1969. *Broadcasting in the Seventies: The BBC's plan for network radio and non-metropolitan broadcasting*. London: British Broadcasting Corporation.

British Broadcasting Corporation, 1974. *Annual review of BBC audience research findings. No. 1, 1973–74*. London: British Broadcasting Corporation.

British Broadcasting Corporation, Audience Research Department, 1959. *The public and the programmes. An audience research report on listeners and viewers, etc*. London: British Broadcasting Corporation.

Britten, B. 1964. *On receiving the first Aspen award: A speech*. London: Faber & Faber.

Brown, M. 2007. *A licence to be different: The story of Channel 4*. London: British Film Institute.

Calder, A. 1992. *People's War: Britain, 1939–45*. Revised ed. London: Pimlico.

Cannadine, D. 2004. *History and the media*. Houndmills: Palgrave Macmillan.

Carey, J. 1992. *The intellectuals and the masses: Pride and prejudice among the literary intelligentsia 1880–1939*. London: Faber.

Carpenter, H., and J.R. Doctor. 1996. *The envy of the world: Fifty years of the BBC Third Programme and Radio 3, 1946–1996*. London: Weidenfeld & Nicolson.

Carr, E.H. 1964. *What Is history? The George Macaulay Trevelyan lectures delivered in the University of Cambridge January–March 1961*. Harmondsworth: Penguin.

Chignell, H. 2006. The birth of Radio 4's analysis. *Journal of Radio Studies* 13 (1): 89–101.

Chignell, H. 2011. *Public issue radio: talks, news and current affairs in the 20th century*. Basingstoke: Palgrave Macmillan.

Cook, N., and A. Pople. 2004. *The Cambridge history of 20th-century music, The Cambridge history of music*. Cambridge: Cambridge University Press.

Crisell, A. 2009. *Radio*. London: Routledge.

Crisell, A. 2012. *Liveness and recording in the media*. New York: Palgrave Macmillan.

Curran, J. 2002. *Media and power*. London: Routledge.

Curran, J. 2002. Media and the making of British society, c. 1700–2000. *Media History* 8 (2): 135–154.

Dartington, 1949. *Music: A report on musical life in England sponsored by the Dartington Hall Trustees*. London: Political and Economic Planning.

De Groot, G.J. 2013. *The Sixties unplugged: A kaleidoscopic look at a disorderly decade*. London: Pan.

De Groot, G.J. 2011. *The Seventies unplugged: A kaleidoscopic look at a violent decade*. London: Pan.

Doctor, J.R. 1995. *The BBC and the ultra-modern problem: A documentary study of the British Broadcasting Corporation's dissemination of Second Viennese School repertory, 1922–36*. Ann Arbor, MI: UMI.

Doctor, J.R. 1999. *The BBC and ultra-modern music, 1922–1936: Shaping a nation's tastes*. Cambridge: Cambridge University Press.

Doctor, J.R., A. Garnham, D.A. Wright, and N. Kenyon. 2007. *The Proms: A new history*. London: Thames & Hudson.

Dolan, J. 2003. The voice that cannot be heard. *Radio Journal: International Studies in Broadcast & Audio Media* 1 (1): 63.

Drummond, J. 2000. *Tainted by experience: A life in the arts*. London: Faber.

Dubber, A. 2013. *Radio in the digital age*. Cambridge: Polity.

Edmunds, N. 2006. William Glock and the British Broadcasting Corporation's music policy, 1959–73. *Contemporary British History* 20 (2): 233–261.

Eisenberg, E. 2005. *The recording angel: Music, records and culture from Aristotle to Zappa*. Yale University Press.

Eliot, T.S. 1962. *Notes towards the definition of culture*. London: Faber.

Fisher, T. 1947. Third Programme: First Birthday. *Tempo* 5: 25.

Fox, C. 2007. Darmstadt and the institutionalisation of modernism. *Contemporary Music Review* 26 (1): 115–123.
Fox, C. 2007. Music after Zero Hour. *Contemporary Music Review* 26 (1): 5–24.
Gaddis, J.L. 2002. *The landscape of history: how historians map the past*. Oxford: Oxford University Press.
Garnham, A.M. 2003. *Hans Keller and the BBC: The musical conscience of British broadcasting, 1959–79*. Aldershot: Ashgate.
Garnham, A.M., and C. Wintle. 2011. *Hans Keller and internment: The development of an emigre musician, 1938–48*. London: Plumbago.
Gillard, F. 1964. *Sound Radio in the Television age*. Frank Gillard BBC Lunchtime Lecture 11 March 1964.
Glock, W. 1963. *The BBC's music policy*. London: British Broadcasting Corporation.
Glock, W., 1991. *Notes in advance*. Oxford: Oxford University Press.
Goggin, C. 2006. Radio 3 or Classic FM. Thesis (BMus) University of Wales, Bangor.
Goodman, D. 2011. *Radio's civic ambition: American broadcasting and democracy in the 1930s*. Oxford: Oxford University Press.
Grimley, M., and M. Wiegold. 1977. *Catalogue of music broadcast on Radio 3 and Radio 4 in 1974*. London: British Broadcasting Corporation.
Grove, G., and S. Sadie. 1980. *The New Grove dictionary of music and musicians*. London: Macmillan.
Habermas, J. 1987. *The philosophical discourse of modernity: Twelve lectures*. Cambridge: Polity in association with Basil Blackwell.
Habermas, J. 1989. *The structural transformation of the public sphere: An inquiry into a category of bourgeois society*. Cambridge, MA: MIT Press.
Hall, B. 1981. *The proms: And the men who made them*. London: Allen & Unwin.
Hall, S. 1980. *Culture, media, language: Working papers in cultural studies, 1972–79*. London: Hutchinson in association with the Centre for Contemporary Cultural Studies, University of Birmingham.
Harris, K., and J. Chociowski. 1992. *Margaret Thatcher*. London: Fontana.
Heartz, D. 1980. Classical. In *The new Grove dictionary of music and musicians*, ed. S. Sadie. London: Macmillan.
Hendy, D. 2000. *Radio in the global age*. Cambridge: Polity.
Hendy, D. 2007. *Life on air: A history of Radio Four*. Oxford: Oxford University Press.
Hendy, D. 2010. Listening in the dark. *Media History* 16 (2): 215–232.
Hendy, D. 2012. Biography and the emotions as a missing 'narrative' in media history. *Media History* 18 (3/4): 361–378.
Hendy, D. 2013. *Public service broadcasting*. London: Palgrave Macmillan.
Hennessy, P. 1992. *Never again: Britain, 1945-51*. London: Cape.
Hennessy, P. 2006. *Having it so good: Britain in the fifties*. London: Allen Lane.

Hobsbawm, E.J. 1995. *The age of extremes: The short 20th century, 1914–1991.* London: Abacus.
Hobsbawm, E.J., and T.O. Ranger. 1983. *The Invention of tradition, past and present publications.* Cambridge: Cambridge University Press.
Hoggart, R. 1972. *Only connect: On culture and communication: the B.B.C. Reith lectures 1971.* London: Chatto & Windus.
Hoggart, R. 2004. *Mass media in a mass society: Myth and reality.* London: Continuum.
Horsman, M. 1997. *Sky high: The inside story of BSkyB.* London: Orion Business.
Hughes, R. 1980. *Shock of the new: Art and the century of change.* London: British Broadcasting Corporation.
Keller, H., C. Wintle, B. Northcott, and I. Samuel (eds.). 1994. *Essays on music.* Cambridge: Cambridge University Press.
Kennedy, M. 1991. *Britten.* London: J.M. Dent.
Kenyon, N. 1981. *The BBC symphony orchestra: The first fifty years 1930–1989.* London: British Broadcasting Corporation.
Kyle, K. 2011. *Suez: Britain's end of Empire in the Middle East.* Revised ed. London: I.B. Tauris.
Kynaston, D. 2008. *Austerity Britain, 1945–1951.* London: Bloomsbury.
Kynaston, D. 2009. *Family Britain, 1951–1957.* New York: Walker & Co.
Lacey, K. 2011. Listening overlooked. *Javnost - the public?* 18 (4): 5–20.
Lacey, K. 2013. *Listening publics: The politics and experience of listening in the media age.* Cambridge: Polity.
Langham, J. 1986. *Radio research: A comprehensive guide, 1975–85: An annotated bibliography of radio research resources.* London: BBC Data.
Langham, J., and J. Chrichley. 1989. *Radio research: An annotated bibliography 1975–1988.* 2nd ed. *Radio Academy and Independent Broadcasting Authority.* Avebury: Radio Academy and Independent Broadcasting Authority. Aldershot.
Laslett, P. 1958. Crisis in British broadcasting. In *Granta*, 18 October 1958.
Lawson, C., and R. Stowell (eds.). 2012. *The Cambridge history of musical performance.* Cambridge: Cambridge University Press.
Leavis, F.R. 1965. *The common pursuit.* London: Chatto & Windus.
Leavis, Q.D. 1932. *Fiction and the reading public.* London: Chatto & Windus.
Lebrecht, N. 1997. *When the music stops: Managers, maestros and the corporate murder of classical music.* London: Pocket.
LeMahieu, D.L. 1988. *A culture for democracy: Mass communication and the cultivated mind in Britain between the wars.* Oxford: Clarendon.
Lüthje, C. 2008. *Das Medium als symbolische Macht: Untersuchung zur soziokulturellen Wirkung von Medien am Beispiel von Klassik Radio.* Norderstedt: Books on Demand.
MacKay, R. 2000. Being Beastly to the Germans: Music, censorship and the BBC in World War II. *Historical Journal of Film, Radio and Television* 20 (4): 513–525.

Manduell, J. 2016. *No Bartok before breakfast*. Arc Publications.
Marshall, G. 1988. *Social class in modern Britain*. London: Hutchinson.
Marwick, A. 1980. *Class—Image and reality in Britain, France & the USA since 1930*. London: Collins.
Marwick, A. 1990. *British society since 1945*, 2nd ed. London: Penguin.
Marwick, A. 1991. *Culture in Britain since 1945: Making contemporary Britain*. Oxford: Basil Blackwell.
Marwick, A. 1998. *The Sixties: cultural revolution in Britain, France, Italy, and the United States*. Oxford : Oxford University Press.
McKibbin, R. 2000. *Classes and cultures: England, 1918–1951*. Oxford: Oxford University Press.
McSmith, A. 2011. *No such thing as society*. London: Constable.
Ministry of Posts and Telecommunications (UK), 1971. *An alternative service of radio broadcasting*. Cmnd 4636. London: HMSO.
Mollgard, M. (ed.). 2012. *Radio and Society; New thinking for an old medium*. Newcastle upon Tyne: Cambridge Scholars.
Monod, D. 2005. *Settling scores: German music, denazification, and the Americans, 1945–1953*. Chapel Hill: University of North Carolina Press.
Morgan, K.O. 1999. *The people's peace: British history since 1945*. 2nd ed. Oxford: Oxford University Press.
Murphy, C. 2011. *On an equal footing with men? Women and work at the BBC, 1923–1939*. Ph.D. thesis, University of London.
Nicholas, S. 1996. *The echo of war: Home Front propaganda and the wartime BBC, 1939–45*. Manchester University Press.
Pieper, A. 2008. *Music and the making of middle-class culture: A comparative history of Nineteenth-century Leipzig and Birmingham*. Basingstoke: Palgrave Macmillan.
Pirie, P.J. 1979. *The English musical renaissance*. London: Gollancz.
Ponsonby, R. 2009. *Musical heroes: A personal view of music and the musical world over sixty years*. London: DLM.
Rehding, A. 2005. *Ode to Freedom: Bernstein's Ninth at the Berlin Wall*. Beethoven Forum: University of Illinois.
Ridley, A. 1993. Bleeding chunks: Some remarks about musical understanding. *The Journal of Aesthetics and Art Criticism* 51 (4): 589–596.
Rose, J. 2010. *The intellectual life of the British working classes*. New Haven, CT: Yale University Press.
Rose, P.L. 1992. *Wagner: Race and revolution*. New Haven, CT: Yale University Press.
Ross, A. 2008. *The rest is noise: Listening to the 20th century*. London: Harper Perennial.
Ross, A. 2010. *Listen to this*, Kindle ed. New York: Farrar, Straus & Giroux.
Sachs, H. 2010. *The Ninth: Beethoven and the world in 1824*. London: Faber.

Said, E.W. 1991. *Musical elaborations.* London: Vintage.
Said, E.W. 1994. *Culture & imperialism.* London: Vintage.
Said, E.W. 2006. *On late style: Music and literature against the grain.* New York: Pantheon Books.
Said, E.W. 2008. *Music at the limits: Three decades of essays and articles on music.* London: Bloomsbury.
Said, E.W., and D. Barsamian. 2003. *Culture and resistance: Conversations with Edward W.* Pluto: Said. London.
Said, E.W., and G. Viswanathan. 2002. *Power politics and culture: Interviews with Edward W. Said.* New York: Vintage Books.
Sandbrook, D. 2006. *Never had it so good: A history of Britain from Suez to the Beatles.* London: Abacus.
Sandbrook, D. 2006. *White heat: A history of Britain in the swinging Sixties.* London: Little, Brown.
Sandbrook, D. 2010. *State of emergency: The way we were: Britain, 1970–1974.* London: Allen Lane.
Sandbrook, D. 2012. *Seasons in the sun: The battle for Britain 1974–1979.* London: Allen Lane.
Scannell, P. 1981. Music for the multitudes? The dilemmas of BBC music policy 1923–1946. *Media Culture and Society* 3 (3): 243–260.
Scannell, P. 1992. *Culture and power: Media, culture and society reader.* London: Sage Publications.
Scannell, P. 2007. *Media and communication.* London: Sage Publications.
Scholes, P.A. (ed.). 1965. *The Oxford companion to music.* 9th ed. Oxford: Oxford University Press.
Scott, D. 2001. *Manduell, Sir John (born 1928), music educationist, composer, administrator. Oxford History of Music.* Oxford: Oxford University Press.
Seaton, J. 1987. The BBC and the Holocaust. *European Journal of Communication* 2 (1): 53–80.
Seaton, J. 1997. *Power without responsibility: The press and broadcasting in Britain,* 5th ed. London: Routledge.
Seaton, J. 2015. *Pinkoes and Traitors. The BBC and the nation 1974–1987.* London: Profile Books.
Selwood, S. 1998. Born again or 'dumbing down'? Cultural trends in the 1990s. *Journal of Art & Design Education* 17 (1): 7–16.
Sendall, B. 1982. *Independent television in Britain, vol. 1, Origin and foundation 1946–62.* London: Macmillan.
Silvey, R. 1963. *Reflections on the impact of broadcasting.* London: British Broadcasting Corporation.
Silvey, R. 1966. *The measurement of audiences.* London: British Broadcasting Corporation.

Silvey, R. 1974. *Who's listening? The story of BBC Audience Research*. London: Allen & Unwin.
Silvey, R., and R. Lee. 1966. *The measurement of audiences: A lecture. BBC lunchtime lectures. Fourth series*. London: British Broadcasting Corporation.
Simpson, R. 1981. *The Proms and natural justice: A plan for renewal*. London: Toccata.
Sissons, M., and P. French. 1963. *Age of austerity*. Oxford: Oxford University Press.
Small, C. 1977. *Music, society, education*. London: Calder.
Starkey, G. 2002. Radio audience research: Challenging the 'gold standard'. *Cultural Trends* 12 (45): 43.
Starkey, G. 2004. Estimating audiences. *Cultural Trends* 13 (49): 3–25.
Starkey, G. 2011. *Local radio, going global*. Basingstoke: Palgrave Macmillan.
Steedman, C. 2002. *Dust; the archive and cultural history*. New Brunswick, NJ: Rutgers UR.
Stewart, G. 2013. *Bang! A history of Britain in the 1980s*. London: Atlantic Books.
Stoller, T. 2010. *Sounds of your life: The history of independent radio in the UK*. New Barnet: John Libbey.
Stoller, T., and E. Wray 2010. 1984 and all that. The impact of political change on independent radio in the UK. *Communication Journal of New Zealand* 11 (1).
Street, S. 2005. *A concise historical dictionary of British radio*, 2nd ed. Tiverton: Kelly Publications.
Street, S. 2006. *Crossing the ether: British public service radio and commercial competition 1922–1945*. Eastleigh: John Libbey Publications.
Taruskin, R. 2010a. *Music in the nineteenth century*. Oxford: Oxford University Press.
Taruskin, R. 2010b. *Music in the early 20th century*. Oxford: Oxford University Press.
Taruskin, R. 2010c. *Music in the late 20th century*. Oxford: Oxford University Press.
Taylor, A.J.P. 1965. *English History: 1914–1945*. Oxford: Oxford University Press.
Thacker, T. 2002. 'Liberating German Musical Life': The BBC German service and planning for music control in occupied Germany 1944–1949. *The Yearbook of the Research Centre for German and Austrian Exile Studies* 5 (1): 77–92.
Thacker, T. 2007. *Music after Hitler, 1945–1955*. Aldershot: Ashgate.
Towse, R. 1997. *Cultural economics: the arts, the heritage, and the media industries*. Cheltenham: E. Elgar.

Trethowan, I. 1970. *Radio in the Seventies, BBC lunch-time lectures. 8th series.* London: British Broadcasting Corporation.
Turner, A.W. 2008. *Crisis? What crisis? Britain in the 1970s.* London: Aurum.
Turner, A.W. 2010. *Rejoice, rejoice! Britain in the 1980s.* London: Aurum.
Turner, A.W. 2013. *A classless society: Britain in the 1990s.* London: Aurum.
Tyrrell, J., and S. Sadie. 2001. *The new Grove dictionary of music and musicians*, 2nd ed. London: Macmillan.
Upchurch, A.R. 2013. 'Missing from policy history': The Dartington Hall Arts Enquiry, 1941–1947. *International Journal of Cultural Studies* 19 (5): 610–622.
Wagner, R., and E. Evans. 1850 and 1869/1910. *Das Judenthum in der Musik (Judaism in Music).* London: William Reeves.
Wall, T., and A. Dubber. 2009. Specialist music, public and service and the BBC in the internet age. *Radio Journal: international studies in broadcast and audio media* 7 (1): 27–47.
Weber, W. 1984. The contemporaneity of eighteenth-century musical taste. *The musical quarterly.* Oxford: Oxford University Press.
Weber, W. 2004. *Music and the middle class: The social structure of concert life in London, Paris and Vienna between 1830 and 1848*, 2nd ed. Aldershot: Ashgate.
Weber, W. 2008. *The great transformation of musical taste: Concert programming from Haydn to Brahms.* Cambridge: Cambridge University Press.
Weber, W. 2012. Political process, social structure and musical performance in Europe since 1450. *Cambridge History of Musical Performance*, ed. C. Lawson, and R. Stowell. Cambridge. Cambridge University Press.
Whitehead, K. 1989. *The third programme: A literary history.* Oxford: Clarendon.
Wiegold, M., C. Wilkinson, and P. Plaistow. 1976. *British Broadcasting Corporation catalogue of music broadcast on Radio 3 in 1975.* London: British Broadcasting Corporation.
Williams, R. 1965. *The long revolution.* Harmondsworth: Penguin Books.
Williams, R. 1967. *Culture and society 1780–1950.* London: Chatto & Windus.
Witkin, R.W. 1998. *Adorno on music.* London: Routledge.
Wray, E. 2009. *Commercial radio in Britain before the 1990s: An investigation of the relationship between programming and regulation.* Ph.D. thesis, Bournemouth University.

INDEX

A
Adorno, Theodor, 4, 10, 20, 67, 68, 87, 204, 235, 238, 261
An Alternative Service of Radio Broadcasting, 5, 128, 135–137, 151, 269
Annan Committee, 128, 136, 147, 153, 270
Appleby, Kevin, 172, 179, 185
Arts Council, 35, 41, 49, 147, 160, 263

B
Barenboim, Daniel, 182, 273
Barnes, George, 50–52, 56, 59, 63, 263, 277
BBC
  Audience Research Department, 24, 91
  Charter, 73, 174, 196, 211, 263, 264, 267
  Daily Barometer, 258
  Gramophone Department, 15, 119, 146, 162, 234, 271, 272, 278
  iPlayer, 222, 223, 239

  Music Department, 15, 57, 71, 106, 121, 138, 157, 162, 177, 234, 264, 271, 272, 277, 278
  Music Programme launch, 105, 107, 117
  Music Programme origins, 19, 84, 95, 105
  Oral History project, 21, 64, 110
  Radio 3 launch, 273
  Radio 3 origins, 14, 121, 122, 129, 133
  Symphony Orchestra, 2, 33, 36, 38, 100, 142, 144, 148, 157, 159, 160, 163, 164, 174, 175, 180, 261, 262, 265
  Third Programme launch, 1, 47, 227
  Third Programme origins, 2, 49
  Variety Department, 15
Benjamin, Walter, 19, 68, 234, 235, 262
Bennett, Alan, 188, 202
Bernard, Ralph, 197, 199, 202, 203, 208, 242, 274, 278
Bernstein, Lenard, 147, 182, 183, 206, 273

Biography, 6, 9, 241
Birtwistle, Harrison, 97, 132, 149, 207, 217, 237, 268
Black, Leo, 100, 130, 133, 134
Bliss, Arthur, 33, 39, 42, 46, 48, 79, 80, 86, 262, 277
Boulez, Pierre, 101, 117, 132, 138, 140, 237, 268, 269, 278
Boult, Adrian, 32, 33, 39, 57–58, 71, 167, 261, 277, 278
Bourdieu, Pierre, 8, 10, 219, 236
Britten, Benjamin, 42, 47, 53, 87, 88, 102, 103, 107, 119, 157, 165, 195, 210, 237, 253, 254, 263, 266, 267
Broadcasting in the 90s: Choice and Quality, 176
Broadcasting in the Seventies, 5, 95, 105, 111, 117, 119–121, 123, 128, 129, 134, 152, 157, 162, 230, 268
Brodsky Quartet, 164, 171, 173, 271
Bukht, Michael, 199, 201, 203, 204, 206, 220, 224, 241, 242, 278

C
Campaign for Better Broadcasting, 121, 133, 196, 230, 268
Carr, E.H., viii
Checkland, Michael, 177, 188, 190, 191, 193, 210, 223, 224, 272, 276
Classical music
 canonic repertoire, 8, 10, 13–19, 47, 48, 60, 71, 74, 80, 86, 87, 112, 118, 119, 158, 174, 178, 180, 196, 203–205, 217, 233, 239
 definition, 4, 9, 18, 20, 242
 taxonomy, 4, 14, 15, 17, 18, 74

Classic FM application process, 197–199
Cooper, Joseph, 138, 139
Copyright, 136, 137, 147, 181, 190, 204, 270, 272, 273, 274
Council for the Encouragement of Music and the Arts (CEMA), 35, 41, 43
Cultural renaissance, 35, 42, 45, 47, 53, 54, 56, 229
Curran, Charles, 130, 132, 152, 268, 276

D
Darmstadt *Ferienkurse*, 40
Death on the Rock, 166, 177, 180, 272
Digital Audio Broadcasting (DAB), 218, 221, 222, 238, 273, 274
Drummond, John, 156, 175, 177–179, 183, 187, 189, 190, 192, 198, 223, 241, 272–274, 277, 278

E
Entertainments National Service Association (ENSA), 35, 43

F
Francis, Richard, 162, 271, 276

G
Gambaccini, Paul, 201, 205, 211–213, 215, 224, 225, 226, 240, 274
Gillard, Frank, 26, 27, 64, 90, 104, 105, 107, 109, 115, 121, 124, 125, 130, 134, 267, 268, 276
Glock, William, 5, 14, 56, 57, 76, 89, 98, 100–108, 116, 117, 124,

125, 129, 132, 133, 138, 156, 175, 198, 241, 266, 267, 270, 277
Grisewood, Harman, 59, 90, 264, 277

H
Haley, William, 7, 18, 27, 31, 45, 47, 50–52, 54, 60, 63, 64, 70, 73, 75, 77, 80–82, 90, 109, 139, 228, 229, 241, 242, 262, 264, 276
Hardwick, Christine, 162, 234, 278
Hearst, Stephen, 134, 141, 153, 162, 191, 269, 277
Heathrow Conference, 5, 172, 173, 272
Hess, Myra, 35, 37
Hill, Charles, 119, 120, 268, 275
Howgill, Richard, 57, 73, 75, 87, 124, 264, 277

I
Independent Local Radio, 2, 123, 128, 196, 217, 229
 programme sharing, 5, 170–172
 secondary rental, 5, 136, 145, 147, 166, 168, 170, 172, 175, 270–272
 statutory obligations, 147
Instone, Anna, 146, 278
Internet radio, 218
Internment, 38, 39, 269

J
Jacob, Ian, 73, 75, 76, 81, 90, 264, 276
Jenkins, Lyndon, 167

Joint Industry Committee for Radio Audience Research (JICRAR), 24, 153, 255, 258, 259

K
Kaufman, Gerald, 194, 211, 224
Kenyon, Nicholas, 2, 33, 35, 36, 38, 39, 43, 46, 56, 58, 71, 98, 100, 111, 132, 146, 157, 160, 180, 187, 190—194, 196, 203, 208–212, 216, 219, 223, 225, 234, 240–242, 273, 274, 277, 278

L
LeMahieu, D.L., 8, 219
Lyric FM, 15, 16

M
Manduell, John, 26, 110, 111, 114–116, 119, 125, 242
Mansell, Gerard, 130, 134, 268, 276, 277
Marriott, Richard, 80–84, 87, 89, 105–109, 114, 117, 120, 121, 241, 265, 266, 268, 276
McIntyre, Ian, 145, 146, 149, 150, 162, 177, 208, 225, 270–272, 277
Menuhin, Yehudi, 70, 171, 189, 190, 217, 223
Milne, Alasdair, 162, 177, 271, 272, 276
Minerva programme, 50, 261
Morris, John, 75, 78, 80, 91, 265, 277
Munrow, David, 17, 133, 140, 269, 270
'Musical wallpaper', 107, 116, 207

Musicians' Union (MU), 108, 136, 184, 231, 267, 271
strike, 159, 163, 271

N
Needletime. *See* Copyright
Nessun Dorma, 183, 187, 273
Newby, Howard, 14, 107, 121, 134, 150, 152, 266, 270, 276, 277
Newman, Ernest, 68
Nicholls, Basil, 46, 63, 73, 90, 262, 276
Nicholson, Harold, 104

O
Owen Norris, David, 10, 11, 16, 17, 26, 27, 180

P
Peacock Committee, 166, 174, 175, 272
Pelletier, Rooney, 83, 91, 102, 108, 124
Pilkington Committee, 103, 107, 266, 267
Pirate radio, 95, 97, 117, 120, 132, 135
Ponsonby, Robert, 133, 138, 146, 149, 152, 153, 156, 159–163, 184, 189, 266, 269, 270, 277
Promenade concerts (Proms), 8, 13, 26, 33, 35–37, 56, 57, 61, 87, 92, 100, 101, 103, 104, 117, 133, 138, 140, 142, 143, 149, 152, 160, 161, 167, 169, 175, 177, 184, 191, 262, 265, 267–271, 273, 274
Public service (radio) broadcasting, 6, 9, 129, 135, 166, 169, 180, 191, 228, 241

Q
Queen's Hall, 33, 35, 37, 45, 262

R
Radio Joint Audience Research (RAJAR), 24, 184, 215, 224, 226, 255, 256, 259, 260
Ray, Robin, 15, 23, 27, 131, 139–142, 203, 204, 242
Reynolds, Gillian, 139, 153, 185, 223, 226
Ritualisation. *See* Sacralisation
Royal Manchester College of Music, 87, 97

S
Sacralisation, 11, 12, 161, 231, 239, 240
Said, Edward, 11, 237
Sargent, Malcolm, 36, 58, 69, 71, 72, 75, 80, 117–118, 264, 268, 278
Silvey, Robert, 77, 79, 91, 119, 192
Simons, Susannah, 201, 205, 212, 224, 225
Simpson, Robert, 161, 184
Singer, Aubrey, 64, 108, 146, 150, 151, 156–160, 162, 241, 270, 276
Strauss, Richard, 38, 44–45, 61, 63, 71, 72, 74, 83, 103, 141, 143, 171, 200, 204

T
Talkington, Fiona, 143, 153, 180, 181, 185, 235, 244
Thompson, John, 137, 152, 180, 224, 241, 279
Tippett, Michael, 42, 53, 82, 98, 112, 113, 133, 174, 175, 188, 210, 252

Trethowan, Ian, 130, 133, 138, 139, 146, 150, 152, 158, 159, 269, 270, 276

W

Wagner, Richard, 35, 38, 44, 49, 55, 71, 74, 80, 83, 88, 119, 131, 165, 174

Wellington, Lindsay, 73, 81, 82, 84, 85, 87, 89, 105–107, 264, 276, 277

Whitney, John, 142, 180, 279

Wilson, Steuart, 57–58, 61, 64, 69, 71, 264, 277

Wren Orchestra, 142, 167, 169, 171, 172, 179, 185, 270

Wright, Roger, 27, 210, 219, 222, 234, 235, 239, 244, 277

The manufacturer's authorised representative in the EU is Springer Nature Customer Service Centre GmbH, Europaplatz 3, 69115 Heidelberg, Germany. If you have any concerns regarding our products, please contact ProductSafety@springernature.com

Printed and bound by CPI Group (UK) Ltd, Croydon, CR0 4YY

23/03/2026

02076735-0015